Gail Duff's Vegetarian Cookbook

Gail Duff lives in Kent with her husband, Mick Duff,
the photographer. She is well known for her original and lively
broadcasts on Radio Medway and for her contributions to *Kent Life*
and other local magazines and papers, taking her topics from all her
main interests – cookery, wine-making, country life and local
customs. The strikingly original quality of her personality and
approach makes Gail Duff the most exciting new voice to emerge
in the field of cooking and food writing. She is the winner of
the 1978 Glenfiddich Award, Cookery Journalist of the Year.

Other cookery books available in Pan

Gail Duff's Vegetarian Cookbook

Pan Books
in association with
Macmillan London

First published 1978 by Macmillan London Limited
This edition published 1979 by Pan Books Ltd,
Cavaye Place, London, SW10 9PG
in association with Macmillan London Limited
19 18 17 16
© Gail Duff 1978
ISBN 0 330 25643 2
Printed and bound in Great Britain by
Richard Clay (The Chaucer Press) Ltd, Bungay, Suffolk

Contents

Contents

for my parents
and
for Carol and Bernard
for having such
voracious appetites

Introduction

I have always loved vegetables, enjoyed using them in season and cooking them in as many varied and appetising ways as possible, both as accompaniments and as a part of a more complicated main dish. I have crunched my way through a salad a day for years and have often served a completely vegetable soup or first course before a meat meal, for both every day and grander occasions. The vegetables I buy are always fresh and locally grown (organically whenever possible) and there has never been a place in my kitchen for tinned and convenience foods. White flour, pasta and rice literally went into the dustbin in one big clear-out several years ago, to be replaced by their more wholesome brown counterparts. The smell of baking pervades the house several times a week and I am often to be seen driving miles across Kent for locally-made cheese and butter or unadulterated cider.

Even so, when a vegetarian book was first suggested, I was surprised. As a member of the Soil Association I believe that animals play a part in the natural cycle of life – soil, plant, animal, man – and also that a certain amount of meat is essential to provide all the necessary ingredients for good health. Besides, I enjoy eating meat, so long as it has not been processed or frozen and then sliced to make it look like a section of a wooden plank, and I know more or less where it comes from. Like my vegetables, I have always chosen it carefully from small, family butchers who know their trade.

However, variety is the spice of life; we don't have to eat meat every day, and there have been some suspicious tales lately about hormone injections, chemical foodstuffs and the like. So why shouldn't I change my habits a little and experiment with ingredients and types of meals that I had not previously considered at all? After all, with my whole-food ways I was half-way there already. I just had to turn around and look at food from a slightly different angle.

The whole project proved to be an exciting challenge. First of all, there was a new set of ingredients to be bought in and a minor research to be done into other types of protein: beans and lentils, nuts and seeds, and various soya products. Apart from these, everything else seemed quite familiar. I had a cupboard full of spices, a garden full of herbs and a regular supply of free-range eggs; and what a lovely excuse it was to buy a few more exotic vegetables and different kinds of cheese! Money that might have been spent on meat went instead on things like pineapples, avocado pears and green peppers out of season. As a result, although I had thought that the weekly expenses would be less, they worked out about the same. It was worth it, though, for the end results.

Ingredients assembled, my first aim was to destroy that awful biased attitude to vegetarian food: that it is either 'a lettuce leaf and a few soya beans' or 'something sloppy poured over brown rice'. Food had to be made to look attractive and taste even better, with each dish as different as possible in flavour, texture and basic ingredients.

Perhaps when it comes to taking a completely fresh look at any type of cooking someone used to other methods has a certain advantage. Using vegetarian ingredients I tried out the different ways in which meat can be cooked and presented and found this worked particularly well with the pulses, often producing superb combinations and final results.

Something else that I enjoyed tremendously was altering the whole structure of meals. On some days I served the first course, and then the main dish and its accompaniments, as I had been used to do with meat cookery; but on others there was no real division. Sometimes a thick soup (which I called a pottage), a salad and a savoury bread appeared on the table together; or there could be just bread and a substantial main-course salad; or perhaps a whole selection of Chinese or Indian dishes that could be sampled together or separately. I discovered a whole new freedom both in types of dishes and in presentation which can apply to meat as well as vegetable cookery, but which I would probably never have thought feasible if I had not tried them out in vegetarian ways first.

To test my new style of vegetarian cookery unsuspecting visitors were seized upon and sat down at the table. Family, friends and colleagues were entertained far more than usual. The kitchen had never been so busy.

There were a few peculiar results or tasteless disasters but not very many, and their recipes were either altered completely or scrapped. All those that found a place in the book have pleased and satisfied and, to a certain extent, changed the opinions of non-vegetarians. I have gained a wealth of experience with new ingredients and cooking methods that will never be forgotten and that I hope will interest and inspire other cooks, vegetarian and non-vegetarian alike. Although I haven't convinced myself that I should give up meat (I did start with an open mind and wonder if I should) there will be many more vegetarian dishes on my menus in the future.

Here, then, is a vegetarian book, written by a confessed non-vegetarian. As its title implies, it describes the ways in which I like to cook vegetarian ingredients. I hope that both vegetarians and non-vegetarians alike may discover in it aspects of the other group's cooking methods that can be used without prejudice. Everyone enjoys good food, so let's enjoy as much of it as we can together.

A Few Words About Ingredients

Most of the ingredients used in this book will be familiar to all lovers of good and natural foods who like to search for the different flavourings and small delicacies which help to make the most ordinary and basic ingredients into exciting meals.

Always buy good quality fresh ingredients and, when it comes to the extras, buy those made by the smaller firms with no chemical additives, or at any rate with the absolute minimum. I personally believe that whole food is best for everyone, vegetarian or not. But vegetarians give up what many people consider an essential part of a balanced diet, so it becomes even more important that everything used to replace it is fresh and wholesome and in peak condition to give as much goodness as possible. That way you can be a vegetarian and stay healthy.

In some cases, pure, natural ingredients can be more expensive than those which, for example, contain artificial colourings and flavourings, but I think we should try to get our priorities right. The saying 'you are what you eat' is very true, and the more naturally we eat the healthier we will be. Very often you will find that you need less of a whole food anyway, but if it does cost a little more, perhaps something unnecessary may be cut from the budget.

Discover the best sources of supply for all your ingredients. I prefer the smaller, specialist shops to supermarkets. Perhaps I'm lucky, but within easy reach I have a delicatessen, an Indian shop and various whole-food shops, each packed from floor to ceiling with different kinds of goodies, and with friendly people running them who are always ready for an enthusiastic chat about their wares, and (even more invaluable) always willing to provide information and advice. Each shop has its advantages and specialities and, although some may stock the same ingredients, they differ in quality and also in price.

In the past some health shops have been expensive and have seemed more like specialist stockists for 'bio-pills' and potions than sellers of real foods. (If your diet is adequate, you shouldn't need them anyway!) Lately, however, a new breed of shops has emerged that sell 'whole' rather than 'health' food. They are often run by groups of people dedicated to the natural food idea, and they sell things in bulk – rice, pulses, flour, wheat and nuts. They are usually cheaper than the shops owned by large companies, their range is often wider, and there are no flashy packets or 'pseudo-foods'.

However, if you haven't time to shop around quite so much and like to get your supplies all in one go, or if in your area there are no such shops, there is good news for you too. Many once unusual ingredients are now being stocked quite regularly by the larger supermarkets. A few years ago, for example, sea salt was almost unheard-of, but now it seems to be as common on the supermarket shelf as any other variety. The Mediterranean type is the most readily available, but there are also English ones such as that produced in Maldon in Essex. I personally use little salt, but this is very much a matter of taste. Tomato purée is now as much of a staple in people's store-cupboards as tomato ketchup; and pickles, capers and olives can be bought quite readily all the year round.

Foreign spices are becoming more familiar and the ones like cinnamon, mace and nutmeg, that have been used in this country for centuries, are being rediscovered. These vary tremendously in price and the best advice is don't buy for the packet or the pretty jar. The own-brand ones sold in supermarkets and large chemists in cardboard tubs and cellophane packs are just the same, and the best of all come from Indian and Middle Eastern shops, where they are sold from large, spilling sacks by the ounce.

Grow your own herbs if you can, in a window-box, flower pots, or a small plot in the garden. If you would rather use dried ones, don't keep them for too long and remember to halve the amounts when putting them into a recipe.

Used in small quantities, mustard makes an excellent flavouring, and there are some really good English ones about now, as well as the French and German varieties. Gordon's English Vineyard Mustard comes from Surrey, and the range of Urchfont mustards with their attractive, hand-written labels, from Wiltshire. There is a black mustard, a full-strength, a milder one made with honey and one flavoured with tarragon. New mustards are appearing on the market all the time and it's good to buy several and do some experimenting, particularly with salad dressings.

Wine vinegars are no longer unusual, and most supermarkets stock at least one variety. I have developed a great liking for cider vinegar lately and am lucky enough to be able to get my supplies from a cider farm by the gallon. This isn't possible,

I know, for most people, but all health shops and large chemists have it on their shelves.

The cider I use comes from the same source as the vinegar. It is still and dry and made entirely without sugar. If you live in a cider county, you should have no problem finding something similar. If not, have a look round in your smaller off-licences and see what you can find. As for wines – use the cheapest red and white plonks for cooking. They will probably taste so bad as to put you off having even one crafty swig whilst preparing the meal, but once they are in the pot you will notice little or no difference.

Regrettably, olive oil is becoming increasingly expensive. I still prefer it in flavour to any of the others, both for salads and for cooked dishes (and there is nothing to beat its smell as you gently sauté onions and garlic!), so this is one of my main culinary extravagances. Next best are groundnut and sunflower oils. They taste good and are nutritionally excellent. For chips and deep-frying use peanut or corn oil.

I never use white flour, and at one time had to take a trip to the nearest big town to find wholemeal or the 81% or 85% varieties. Now I just have to run up the road to the local shop to find both plain and self-raising. I think you can do this in most places now. From flour to bread. There is nothing like making your own, be it granary or wholemeal. If you buy it, make sure it really is wholemeal and not just coloured white bread. Search out your nearest master-baker, buy it from health shops, or try the stone-ground and bran-supplemented varieties that are sold now in well-known supermarkets and chain stores.

Say bread and, unless you are a vegan (someone who does not eat any dairy products or eggs), the next thing you will probably say is butter. There has been a lot of discussion lately about cholesterol and heart disease, and a swing towards buying vegetable margarines. You can use these in nearly all the recipes where butter is suggested (even where no alternative is actually given). The best margarines are those that contain only natural ingredients from health shops. Some of the more widely sold brands seem, when you read the labels, to be a little too chemical. I am very concerned about health and nutrition and have thought a great deal about the cholesterol question. We have been eating butter and naturally reared fat meat for centuries, yet the increase in heart disease is fairly recent. Our consumption of refined carbohydrates, however (white flour and sugar in particular), has rocketed and until fairly recently fresh, and particularly raw, vegetables and fruit were very neglected commodities. Far more chemicals and additives are used now than ever before, not only in food intended for human consumption but also in that given to animals. One preservative, potassium nitrate, or saltpetre, has been used to preserve and colour salt meat and fish since Medieval times. I was researching recently into the history of salt and preserving, and in all the old recipes and in many of the more up-to-date pieces of information, I read words of warning that unless saltpetre was used sparingly (one suggested only $\frac{1}{2}$ oz to 100 lbs of meat, but that was the most extreme) the flesh would harden and the pickle turn green and rancid. Then, in a book originally written in 1967, *The Gentle Art of Flavouring*, by Robert Landry, I discovered that as well as the salt that is put into most of our butter today, $\frac{1}{4}$ ounce of saltpetre is added per pound. To me, this was a quite startling discovery. Could this be the culprit? If it hardens animal flesh, does it have the same effect when it is consumed? I am not a qualified nutritionist or scientist but now when I buy commercially made butter I always make sure it is the saltless variety.

I tend to believe that animal fats are not the sole cause of the cholesterol problem and that its roots probably lie in a combination of all our bad habits. Perhaps if we ate whole food with more raw vegetables, gave up smoking and sugar and exercised more, natural unadulterated animal fats would do us no harm. Everyone has their own attitude to this, and I leave it to the individual to decide.

Yoghurt is another dairy product used frequently in the book. If you can, buy natural yoghurt from health-food shops or make your own. You can find locally made ones all over the country, and their flavour and texture is far better than those of commercial yoghurts. I prefer goat's milk yoghurt to any other, but it is very much a matter of taste.

Two things that I would always prefer to buy in whole-food shops rather than in supermarkets are nuts and dried fruits. They seem to be larger, moister and fresher, and there is no significant difference in the price, especially if you go to one of the shops mentioned earlier. In fact, you can very often buy broken nuts far more cheaply, which is a good idea, especially if you are going to chop them up anyway. Excellent almonds can be found in Indian shops. They are big and fat and, like the spices, sold from sacks.

If you are a supermarket shopper, all ingredients I have mentioned above can be bought in some form from that source, but a few of those used in the book can only be obtained from specialist shops.

If you like nuts, then you will like sunflower and sesame seeds. They are crunchy and full of goodness and make superb additions to all kinds of salads. Sesame seeds can be put into bread, made into toppings for vegetable pies and crumbles and used like breadcrumbs to coat vegetables or croquettes before cooking.

Tahini is a paste made from crushed sesame seeds. It is rather like peanut butter, only slightly duller in colour and a little more runny, with a slightly bitter quality in its flavour. It can be put into spreads, sauces, lentil pâtés and salad dressings. Its texture in dressings in particular takes a little getting used to. The first time I used it, I mixed a fairly large amount with wine vinegar, thinking it would thin down. Instead, it went all thick and lumpy! It tasted delicious so I still used it (I practically had to mash it into the salad!) but the next time I took care to use less and blend it carefully with the other ingredients.

Products made from soya beans are very important in meatless diets as they are rich sources of many B group vitamins. I have always used soy sauce, but hadn't realised until I came to write this book that many of the commercially made ones contain sugar, caramel and only soya bean extract or defatted soya beans. Tamari is the genuine traditional Japanese soy sauce made only by natural methods from a mixture of wheat and whole soya beans. It also tastes far better than the other kinds and I would recommend it to anyone, vegetarian or not. It will certainly be an essential item in my storecupboard from now on.

Another soya product which is being used increasingly by vegetarian (and vegans in particular) is miso, a rich, salty paste made from fermented soya beans. You can get three kinds: hacho, a really dark, thick one that is recommended for use during the winter months but is at the time of writing the most easily obtainable; mugi, the most neutral and universal that can be used at any time; and kome which is light and delicate but very salty. Hacho miso is made only from soya beans, mugi from a mixture of barley and soya beans and kome, from rice and soya beans. You need a very little miso to make a rich, thick sauce or soup very similar in flavour to those made with beef extract.

TVP (textured vegetable protein) does not feature in the book at all. I have tried cooking it in a number of ways and have disliked it intensely. I became very fond of soya beans, served as they are with sauces and spices and fresh vegetables, but TVP seems like a processed substitute. I really see no reason for using so much energy and so many resources in making a good, basic ingredient look like something it isn't. With a little ingenuity and cooking skill the real thing can be so much better.

The last soya product is soya flour, which is coarser than wheat flour and biscuit coloured. You can make it into bechamel-type sauces and add it very sparingly to breads; and, if you don't eat eggs, it makes a good substitute mayonnaise.

Fresh Vegetables – The Basic Ingredients

You don't have to be a vegetarian to cook vegetables. They are an essential part of everyone's diet both for enjoyment and from the nutritional point of view. Very often even non-vegetarians cook three separate vegetables for the main meal, but for them it is too easy to lavish attention on the meat dish and forget the rest. Vegetarians are more aware of their importance and really want to cook them to bring out all their qualities: a mouth-watering appearance, a tantalising smell, and a taste that makes you ask for more, while preserving all their natural vitamins and minerals. Whatever our beliefs and eating habits, we should all strive to attain this, treating vegetables as an essential part of a truly balanced diet even if they do not make up the whole meal.

When you are buying vegetables, for whatever purpose, always make sure they look firm and fresh and alive. Old, limp, tired ones may be a little cheaper in some places but you are not really getting a bargain as far as flavour and goodness are concerned. For better value buy as many as possible that are locally grown and in season, combining these with just a few expensive luxuries, such as green peppers (during the winter) and Florence fennel.

If I could, I would always buy organically grown vegetables, but although there are some co-operatives of organic farmers and growers, at the moment their produce is still hard to come by. Growing your own is the best way of ensuring good supplies, but if you are unable to do so shop around in farm shops and at market stalls. Well-known supermarkets, I must admit, do sell top-quality produce (not organically grown, though). They inspect it strictly and sell it, beautifully scrubbed and clean, in plastic bags or stretch-wrapping. I have my doubts as to the advantages of these. I was present once at an asparagus-tasting session. Two bundles of asparagus were cooked in exactly the same way. One had come in from the fields with no wrapping but an elastic band to hold the stems together. The other had been picked at the same time (about three hours previously) and immediately stretch-wrapped in polythene. Two plates were carried into the room by a slightly worried-looking quality controller. The asparagus on each looked exactly the same so we eagerly sampled. One bundle tasted sweet and rather like the freshest of green peas, just as asparagus is supposed to; but the other, well, it didn't taste of anything. Need I say which was which? Asparagus has such a delicate, subtle flavour that the least unnatural treatment will have a marked effect, but the same thing must happen with other, more robust produce without our noticing it. What vitamins, I wonder, also disappear with the flavour? The moral of the story is – stay away from stretch-wrapping if you possibly can, or at least take the beastly stuff off as soon as you get home.

Part of the joy of cooking is choosing and buying the ingredients, looking round the greengrocers, finding what you need and chatting about the best vegetables of the day. I get great pleasure from picking out the size of leeks I want, for example, the whitest head of celery that almost gleams through its black mud, the potatoes that are just the right size for baking or the lettuce with the firmest heart. There is also a great sense of satisfaction in taking everything home, sorting it all out (very often all kinds of vegetables are mixed up loose in the same bag) and storing it away in the right places. Things like celery and leeks are best washed as soon as possible, but keep the mud on root vegetables until you need them.

All this takes more time than just whipping round with a trolley and grabbing a few bags, but the natural cook comes into her own later when she actually prepares the meal. The more you handle vegetables and the more you take away from them in the way of peelings, the more goodness (and, just as important, flavour) you destroy. This applies particularly to potatoes and most of the root vegetables. The only one that definitely needs to be peeled before cooking is celeriac because its skin is so rough and coarse. Parsnips, swedes, carrots and turnips can nearly always be left unpeeled and unscraped however you are going to cook them. It is usually unnecessary to scrape celery; never peel mushrooms (all the goodness lies just beneath the surface); and don't waste time making neat little crosses in the base of Brussels sprouts for all the flavour to escape. Take out the stalks of leafy vegetables, such as spring greens or curly kale, as they are very tough; but spinach stalks need only be nicked off at the base of the leaf. The outer leaves of green cabbages can be tough, too. Break them off and put them into the stock bag.

Most vegetables need washing to rid them of gritty dirt and any chemical fertilisers that may have been used on them. Root vegetables and celery can be scrubbed, and leeks must be held under running water, but take care with everything else. Very often only the outer parts of cabbages are dirty, especially if they are tightly packed, and if you trim sprouts well they need no washing at all. Wash vegetables as quickly as you can and don't leave them soaking as some of their vitamins are water soluble.

All the recipes are for four people unless otherwise stated.

First courses

Vegetable first courses can be enjoyed by vegetarians and non-vegetarians alike. They can be fairly cheap, and they both look and taste good. They are light, and not too filling, but delicious enough to wake up the taste buds and lead the way to appreciating the main course.

Try, if you can, to make the first course a complete contrast to what is to follow in ingredients, appearance and cooking methods, to make the meal as interesting and varied as possible. Don't, for example, serve cheese before cheese, or a salad before another salad, or choose two courses with a similar savoury sauce. Even when a meat or fish main dish provides a definite contrast of ingredients a certain amount of thought must still be given. Use different flavourings and a contrasting texture and degree of richness.

When you rely solely on vegetables to make the first course it is good sometimes to buy expensive and unusual ones.

Globe artichokes always seem to be a luxury. Fill the middles with delicate, young seasonal vegetables and lemony butter and you have a dish delightful to look at, seemingly deliciously extravagant and yet not altogether bank-breaking.

Globe artichokes filled with mushrooms

4 small globe artichokes
8 oz (225 g) mushrooms
1 oz (25 g) butter
juice 2 small or 1 really large lemon
freshly ground black pepper
4 teaspoons (20 ml) grated Parmesan cheese

Trim the stalks and tops from the artichokes and boil them in salted water for 45 minutes. Prepare the mushrooms while they are cooking so they will both be ready and hot together. Thinly slice the mushrooms and put them into a saucepan with the butter, lemon juice and pepper. Cover, set on a low heat and cook gently for 10 minutes. Drain the artichokes well and remove the chokes. Sprinkle the middles of each with 1 teaspoon (5 ml) of the cheese. Spoon in the mushrooms, together with all their lemony, buttery juices.

Globe artichokes filled with peas

4 fairly small globe artichokes
1½ lb (675 g) peas, weighed before shelling
1½ oz (40 g) butter
2 tablespoons (30 ml) chopped parsley
4 tablespoons (60 ml) double cream
juice 1 lemon

Trim the stalks and tips of the leaves from the artichokes and cook them in boiling salted water for 45 minutes. Prepare the peas while they are cooking so both will be ready together. Shell the peas. Melt the butter in a saucepan on a low heat and mix in the peas and parsley. Cover, and simmer gently for 15 minutes. Stir in the cream and let it bubble. Stir in the lemon juice, let it come to simmering point and take the pan from the heat. Drain the artichokes well and remove the choke. Fill the middles with the peas in their creamy lemony sauce.

℈   ℈   ℈

Plain, simply boiled asparagus is too good to accompany anything in the main course, so even if you only have a little, make a feature of it at the beginning of the meal. It is one of the few vegetables that is best boiled. When it is done serve it with melted butter and grated Parmesan cheese or with egg and lemon sauce (*see under* sauces).

Simply boiled asparagus

1 lb (450 g) asparagus

for serving:
either 2 oz (50 g) melted butter and 2 tablespoons (30 ml) grated
 Parmesan cheese
or egg and lemon sauce served separately

To cook asparagus to absolute perfection, with the bottom parts
of the stalks tender and the tips firm and juicy and not disintegrat-
ing before your eyes, use a tall, narrow saucepan. (Asparagus
boilers are of course the best of all, but it is probably not worth
buying one for such an expensive vegetable with so short a
season.) Trim the tough bases of the asparagus stalks and scrape
any stringy pieces that may be left on the lower parts. Tie the
stems into separate bundles, one for each person. Put enough
water in the saucepan to come about 2½ in (8 cm) from the tips,
and salt it lightly. Bring it to the boil and stand your bundles in
upright. If you can cover them easily with the saucepan lid, then
do so, but if it looks as though it is going to bend or squash them,
cover the saucepan with a piece of foil raised up in a dome-shape.
Simmer the asparagus for 15 minutes. Lift it out with tongs and
let it steam dry for a few seconds.

Kohlrabi isn't so much expensive as hard to find unless you grow
it yourself. It isn't particularly special or attractive in itself but
if you have something only once in a while it is good to make
the most of it by serving it alone. So here is just a plain and
simple recipe with vinaigrette. N.B. I find I have made a note at
the end 'Don't use woody old kohlrabi'. A tough one once got
mixed up with a selection of young tender ones and its fibres
seemed to be everywhere – so watch out!

Kohlrabi in vinaigrette

4 medium sized kohlrabi
4 tablespoons (60 ml) olive oil
juice 1 lemon
2 teaspoons (10 ml) Dijon mustard

2 tablespoons (30 ml) chopped parsley
1 tablespoon (15 ml) grated Parmesan cheese (optional)

Trim the kohlrabi, cut them in half and slice them thinly. Put them into a saucepan with the oil, cover, and set them on a low heat. Cook them for 20 minutes, stirring them around fairly frequently. By the end they should be translucent and still slightly crunchy. Stir in the lemon juice, mustard and parsley and bring them to the boil. Serve immediately, scattered, if you are using it, with the cheese.

❧ ❧ ❧

Florence fennel is another fairly expensive vegetable and in some provincial areas it can be quite hard to find although it should be available from November to February. Whether you only buy it once or buy it every week it is certainly worth making the most of its delicate, aniseedy flavour by serving it as a first course.

Fennel with green grapes

2 small or 1 large bulb fennel, weighing around 1 lb (450 g)
4 oz (125 g) green grapes
2 tablespoons (30 ml) olive oil
1 clove garlic, finely chopped
⅛ pint (75 ml) dry white wine
2 tablespoons (30 ml) grated Parmesan cheese (optional)

Cut off, chop and reserve any of the feathery fennel leaves, then cut the smaller fennel bulbs into halves lengthways or the large into quarters. Chop them into ¼ in (0.75 cm) slices. Halve and de-seed the grapes. Heat the oil in a frying pan on a moderate heat. Put in the fennel and stir it around for 5 minutes. Pour in the wine and bring it to the boil. Cover the pan and set it on a very low heat for 10 minutes. Add the grapes and half the cheese to the pan. Put in small bowls with the remaining cheese scattered over the top. Preheat the grill to high and put the bowls underneath for the cheese to just brown. If you are not using the cheese, add the grapes and serve. Probably the best implement with which to eat a dish such as this is a dessert spoon.

꙳   ꙳   ꙳

Aubergines, green peppers and courgettes are now familiar vegetables in most households, but even so during the winter months they are still expensive. Served in small amounts at the beginning of the meal you can savour them to the full. Since aubergines are often used in Italian dishes here are two recipes with different Italian cheeses, the blue Dolcelatte and Taleggio, a creamy white cheese.

Aubergines with Dolcelatte

2 small to medium aubergines
a little olive oil for greasing
4 small firm tomatoes
6 oz (175 g) Dolcelatte cheese

Preheat the oven to Reg 6/400°F/200°C. Wrap the aubergines in lightly oiled kitchen foil and bake them for ½ hour. Slice each tomato into 4 rounds and thinly slice the cheese. When the aubergines are done, cut each one into 4 lengthways slices. Arrange these on a heatproof serving dish that will fit under the grill. Preheat the grill to high and grill the aubergines for 2 minutes on one side. Turn them over and lay on the cheese. Put two tomato slices on top of each aubergine slice. Return to the grill and cook until the cheese is soft and melty.

Aubergines with Taleggio

2 small to medium aubergines
little oil for greasing
4 medium-sized, firm tomatoes
4 oz (125 g) Taleggio cheese
1 clove garlic, crushed with a pinch sea salt
2 tablespoons (30 ml) chopped parsley

Preheat the oven to Reg 6/400°F/200°C. Wrap the aubergines in lightly oiled kitchen foil and bake them for ½ hour. While they are cooking, scald, skin, de-seed and roughly chop the tomatoes. Remove the rind from the cheese and chop the rest into small pieces. Combine it with the tomatoes. When the aubergines are done, cut them in half lengthways and scoop out the flesh. Discard the larger seeds and chop the rest finely. Mix it into the tomatoes and cheese and add the garlic and parsley. Pile the mixture back into the shells and put them on a heat-proof serving dish. Put the dish into the oven for 15 minutes so all the ingredients in the filling melt deliciously together.

If you don't eat cheese, brush aubergine slices with oil and cinnamon, and top them with pine-nuts.

Grilled cinnamon aubergine slices

2 aubergines each weighing 5–6 oz (150–175 g)
2 teaspoons (10 ml) fine sea salt
4 tablespoons (60 ml) olive oil
1 clove garlic, crushed with a pinch sea salt
½ teaspoon (2.5 ml) ground cinnamon
4 pine-nuts for each slice aubergine

Cut the aubergines into ¼ in (0.75 cm) slices. Put them in a colander, sprinkle them with the salt and leave them to drain for 30 minutes. Wash them and pat them dry with kitchen paper. Mix the oil, garlic and cinnamon together. Lay the aubergine slices on a flat, ovenproof plate or dish so they are not over-lapping and brush the upper sides with half the oil mixture. Preheat the grill to high. Put the aubergines underneath, fairly close to the heat, and grill them for 2 minutes. Turn the slices over, brush them with the remaining oil and lay the pine nuts on top in a star pattern. Grill them for 2 minutes more so the aubergines are a soft, dusky colour and the pine-nuts slightly browned.

Halved green peppers make excellent containers for all sorts of things. Here are two completely different methods.

Green peppers stuffed with cheese and tomato

2 medium-sized green peppers
8 medium-sized, firm tomatoes
2 tablespoons (30 ml) olive oil
1 medium onion, thinly sliced
1 clove garlic, finely chopped
4 oz (125 g) curd cheese
1 tablespoon (15 ml) chopped marjoram
1 tablespoon (15 ml) chopped parsley

Cook the peppers whole in gently simmering water for 10 minutes. Drain them well, cut them in half and remove the core and seeds. If you can, prepare the rest while the peppers are cooking so everything is more or less ready at the same time. Scald, skin, de-seed and roughly chop the tomatoes. Heat the oil in a frying pan on a moderate heat. Stir in the onion and garlic and cook them until they are golden. Stir in the cheese, tomatoes and herbs and let them all heat through without letting the cheese get too stringy or the tomatoes over-soft. Pile the mixture quickly into the pepper halves and serve.

Green pepper and mushroom ramekins

2 large green peppers
8 oz (225 g) mushrooms
3 tablespoons (45 ml) olive oil
1 large clove garlic, finely chopped
4 tablespoons (60 ml) dry white wine
2 tablespoons (30 ml) tomato purée
2 tablespoons (30 ml) browned breadcrumbs

Preheat the oven to Reg 6/400°F/200°C. Char the peppers under a high grill and skin them. Cut out the cores and then cut each pepper in half lengthways. Scoop out any remaining seeds. Use each pepper-half to line a small ramekin or individual soufflé dish. Finely chop the mushrooms. Heat the oil in a frying pan on a moderate heat. Stir in the mushrooms, and garlic and cook them for 2 minutes. Pour in the wine and stir in the tomato purée. Bring them to the boil and cook until the liquid is reduced by half. Spoon the mushroom mixture into the pepper-lined pots and scatter the breadcrumbs over the top. Put the ramekins into the oven for 10 minutes.

This courgette recipe makes an excellent first course and also an accompaniment to egg dishes.

Courgettes stuffed with mushrooms

1 lb (450 g) courgettes of the size that gives around 6 to the pound
a little oil for greasing
3 tablespoons (45 ml) olive oil
1 medium onion, finely chopped
1 clove garlic, finely chopped
4 oz (125 g) mushrooms, finely chopped
4 tablespoons (60 ml) dry white wine
1 tablespoon (15 ml) chopped thyme
1 tablespoon (15 ml) chopped parsley

Preheat the oven to Reg 4/350°F/180°C. Wrap the courgettes together in oiled kitchen foil and bake them for 30 minutes. Cut them in half lengthways, leaving the stalks intact, and scoop out the middles. Lay the shells in a flat, oven-proof dish. Discard the largest seeds and chop the rest of the flesh. Drain it in a sieve if there is a lot of excess liquid. Heat the oil in a frying pan on a low heat. Put in the onion and garlic and cook gently until golden. Raise the heat to moderate, put in the mushrooms and cook them, stirring, for 1 minute. Pour in the wine and bring it to the boil. Let it reduce by half and add the herbs. Take the pan from the heat and mix in the chopped courgettes. Spoon the mixture into the shells. Cover the courgettes with foil and return them to the oven for 15 minutes.

Plainly-cooked vegetables coated with sesame seeds make a light, nutty-flavoured and attractive first course. You can serve just one vegetable or a selection of several. Garnish them if you like with parsley sprigs, watercress, mustard and cress or lemon slices.

Leave the centre part of marrow intact instead of scooping it out and you will have firm marrow rounds with a succulent middle and a tasty, crunchy topping.

Marrow baked with sesame seeds

1 small marrow, weighing about 1½–2 lb (675–900 g)
1 oz (25 g) butter or vegetable margarine
2 tablespoons (30 ml) tomato purée
2 tablespoons (30 ml) tamari sauce
2 tablespoons (30 ml) sesame seeds
2 tablespoons (30 ml) wheatgerm

Preheat the oven to Reg 6/400°F/200°C. Peel the marrow, leave in the seeds, and cut it into 8 slices about 1 in (3 cm) thick. Put the butter or margarine into a large, flat ovenproof dish and put into the oven to melt. Turn the marrow slices in the butter so they are well coated and bake them for 30 minutes. While they are in the oven, mix the purée, tamari, sesame seeds and wheatgerm together. Spread the mixture evenly over the marrow slices and return them to the oven for a further 15 minutes.

To make the sesame seeds stay put on the smooth surface of leeks, first coat the vegetables in a mustardy dressing.

Leeks in sesame seeds

1 lb (450 g) medium-sized leeks
2 tablespoons (30 ml) white wine vinegar
1 tablespoon (15 ml) olive oil
1 teaspoon (5 ml) Dijon mustard
4 tablespoons (60 ml) sesame seeds
4 firm tomatoes for garnish (optional)

Preheat the oven to Reg 6/400°F/200°C. Wash the leeks well and cut them into 2½ in (8 cm) pieces. Steam them for 15 minutes. Mix the vinegar, oil and mustard together and dip the leeks in this dressing while they are still warm, then roll them in the sesame seeds. Arrange them on a flat, ovenproof plate and spoon any remaining dressing over the top. Put them into the oven for 15 minutes. Serve them garnished with tomato slices.

For cauliflower use thick tahini as the 'glue' and lighten the flavour with lemon juice.

Sesame cauliflower

2 very small or 1 medium-sized cauliflower
2 bayleaves
2 tablespoons (30 ml) tahini
juice 1 lemon
approx 4 tablespoons (60 ml) sesame seeds
a little oil for greasing flat ovenproof dish

Cut the cauliflower into quarters and steam them with the bayleaves for 15 minutes. Preheat the oven to Reg 6/400°F/200°C. Carefully blend the tahini and lemon juice together and coat the cauliflower pieces with the mixture on one flat side and the rounded side. Stand them in the dish with the uncoated side down. Press the sesame seeds into the coated surfaces. Bake for 15 minutes.

Here's a quick way with tomatoes and sesame seeds. Simply grill them and serve them surrounded by a watercress salad. If you grill tomatoes with a thick topping, remember that the heat won't penetrate through to the bottom quite so easily as if they were just sprinkled with herbs. Keep the heat moderate and don't put the grill pan too close to give time for the heat to get right through.

The contrast to the tahini in this recipe is provided by the tomato purée and the juice of the tomatoes themselves.

Grilled sesame tomatoes

1 lb (450 g) firm medium-sized tomatoes
2 tablespoons (30 ml) tahini
2 tablespoons (30 ml) tomato purée
4 tablespoons (60 ml) sesame seeds
for serving:

2 bunches watercress, either broken up and tossed in an oil and vinegar dressing or simply broken into sprigs.

Cut the tomatoes in half. Carefully mix the tahini and tomato purée together and spread them over the cut surfaces. Press a thick layer of sesame seeds on top. Preheat the grill to moderate. Grill the tomatoes about 1 in (3 cm) away from the heat until the sesame seeds are golden brown. Put the cooked tomatoes in the centre of a serving dish and surround them with the watercress.

Grilled celery might seem a little strange but it can be very welcome on a cold day. Although hot, its texture is as crisp and fresh as the raw vegetable. This first recipe is rather like a hot celery, cheese and walnut salad.

Celery, cheese and walnut grill

8 medium-sized sticks celery
4 oz (125 g) grated farmhouse Cheddar cheese
3 oz (75 g) chopped walnuts
1 clove garlic, very finely chopped

Cut the celery into 3 in (10 cm) lengths and lay them in a heat-proof serving dish. Mix the cheese, walnuts and garlic together and press them into the hollows in the celery. Preheat the grill to high and grill the celery until the cheese is melted and bubbly and the nuts are dark brown. Serve hot, straight from the dish.
Alternative:
Pack the celery sticks with crumbled or grated Stilton cheese (use 6 oz (175 g) cheese) and omit the walnuts.

If you buy a large piece of Stilton at Christmas, you'll have enough to make another first course. Try it with grilled tomatoes.

Grilled tomatoes and Stilton

8 medium-sized firm tomatoes
6 oz (175 g) soft Stilton cheese

Thinly slice the tomatoes and lay half of them in a flat heatproof
serving dish. Crumble or grate the Stilton and scatter half over
the tomatoes in the dish. Preheat the grill to high and put the
dish under the grill until the Stilton has melted. Lay on the
remaining tomatoes and then the remaining cheese and return
the dish to the grill. Serve hot before the Stilton has time to set
again.

Tomatoes go with all kinds of cheese. Melt some Camembert
quickly over the top to make a smooth, creamy dressing.

Camembert melted over watercress and tomatoes

1 lb (450 g) tomatoes
1 bunch watercress
4 oz (125 g) soft Camembert

Chop the tomatoes and put them into the bottom of 4 heatproof
serving bowls. Preheat the grill to high and cook the tomatoes for
1 minute so they heat through but stay firm. Chop the watercress
and scatter it over the top. Slice the Camembert thinly and lay
it over the cress. Put the dishes back under the grill until the
cheese melts and sinks down into the tomatoes.

꙳   ꙳   ꙳

Vegetables coated with crumbs and deep-fried make an excellent
first-course, particularly if they are served with a savoury sauce.
They can also be served as accompanying vegetables. You can
again leave the centre seeds inside rings of marrow. Without any
pre-cooking, the outer part softens only slightly to make a firm
ring around a soft and melty centre.

Deep-fried marrow

1 small, young marrow weighing around 1½–2 lb (675–900 g)
1 egg, beaten
4 tablespoons (60 ml) seasoned flour
breadcrumbs
deep fat for frying
for serving:
Spicy tomato sauce; Quick tomato and tamari sauce *or* Parsley
  lemon and egg sauce (*see* under sauces)

Peel the marrow and leave the centre seeds in place. Cut it into
8 slices about 1 in (3 cm) thick. Coat the slices with flour, dip
them in the beaten egg and then coat them with crumbs. Deep
fry them in hot oil for 5 minutes. Drain them on absorbent
kitchen paper. Serve garnished with parsley sprigs and hand the
sauce separately.

Deep-fried mushrooms never fail to impress. They always look
as though you have spent ages preparing them, but in fact they
take relatively little time and are cheap as well.

Deep-fried button mushrooms

8 oz (225 g) button mushrooms
1 egg, beaten
approx 3 tablespoons (45 ml) seasoned wholemeal flour
deep fat for frying

suggested sauces:
Watercress and lemon or Quick tomato and tamari (*see* under
  sauces)
garnishes:
Watercress sprigs if serving the watercress sauce; tomato slices
  with the tomato sauce

Trim the stalks of the mushrooms leaving a piece no longer than
½ in (1.5 cm). Dip each mushroom into the beaten egg and then
coat with the flour. Deep fry in hot oil until they are golden
brown (about 3 minutes). Drain on absorbent kitchen paper.

Serve with the chosen garnish and hand the sauce separately.

❦   ❦   ❦

The next four recipes are all made with the versatile mushroom. Marinate them in yoghurt and lemon to make refreshing kebabs.

Marinated mushroom kebabs

1 lb (450 g) button mushrooms
1 carton natural yoghurt
2 tablespoons (30 ml) olive oil
grated rind and juice 1 lemon
1 tablespoon (15 ml) chopped savory
1 clove garlic, very finely chopped
freshly ground black pepper
for serving:
2 boxes mustard and cress

Trim the stalks from the mushrooms so each is about ½ in (1.5 cm) long. Put the yoghurt into a large bowl big enough to hold all the mushrooms, and beat in the oil and lemon rind and juice. Add the savory, garlic and pepper. Put the mushrooms into the bowl and turn them in the dressing. Leave them to stand at room temperature for at least 2 hours, turning them several times. Thread them onto 4 kebab skewers and reserve the marinade. Preheat the grill to high. Lay the kebabs on the hot rack and grill for 4 minutes, turning them once. Serve them on a bed of mustard and cress with the remaining marinade spooned over the top.

Mushrooms baked with clotted cream

8 oz (225 g) open mushrooms
4 oz (125 g) clotted cream
juice 1 lemon
2 tablespoons (30 ml) chopped parsley

Preheat the oven to Reg 6/400°F/200°C. Chop the mushrooms very finely. Divide half the cream between 4 individual ramekins or soufflé dishes, crumbling it over the base. Put in all the mushrooms and spoon a little lemon juice into each pot. Sprinkle them with the parsley and top with the remaining cream. Bake for 15 minutes. Simple but superb.

Cook them with spring onions and mix in some tangy curd cheese.

Mushrooms and spring onions with curd cheese

8 oz (225 g) flat mushrooms
12 small spring onions (white and green parts)
4 oz (100 g) curd cheese
juice 1 lemon
1 oz (25 g) butter
for serving and garnish:
one small lettuce and thin lemon slices

Slice the mushrooms and chop the spring onions. Melt the butter on a moderate heat and cook the mushrooms and onions for 2 minutes. Stir in the cheese, and when it is hot and blended in, stir in the lemon juice. Pile it onto lettuce leaves on 4 individual plates and garnish with the lemon slices.

If you like the idea of that recipe but don't eat cheese, use more mushrooms and flavour them with capers and mustard.

Mushrooms with capers and mustard

12 oz (350 g) flat mushrooms
1 oz (25 g) butter or vegetable margarine
1 tablespoon (15 ml) chopped capers
2 teaspoons (10 ml) Dijon mustard
for serving:
1 small lettuce, arranged on 4 individual plates
4 thin lemon slices
hot brown toast

Thinly slice the mushrooms. Melt the butter or margarine in a frying pan on a high heat. Stir in the mushrooms and cook them for 2 minutes, still stirring. Mix in the capers and mustard and remove the pan from the heat. Pile the mushrooms onto the lettuce leaves, garnish with the lemon slices and hand the toast separately.

℣   ℣   ℣

This next recipe is based very roughly on one I found in an old cookery book called 'Parsnips Fried to look Like Trout'. I don't think they actually do, but nevertheless they are extremely attractive – golden brown and slightly crisp on the outside and soft, melting and golden in the middle. The gherkins add just enough sharpness to make the dish a savoury rather than a sweet one.

Fried parsnips with gherkin butter

4 medium sized very even-shaped parsnips
2 eggs
2 tablespoons (30 ml) wholemeal flour
freshly ground black pepper
pinch sea salt
2 oz (50 g) butter
2 large pickled gherkins, very finely chopped
either 2 tablespoons (30 ml) vinegar from the gherkin jar
or 2 tablespoons (30 ml) white wine vinegar (the gherkin vinegar
    is best if you have enough)

Scrub the parsnips. Don't peel them but trim the thin root parts and the thick stem-ends. Simmer the parsnips in lightly salted water for 20 minutes. Drain them, and while they are still warm, gently peel off the thin outer skin. Cut them in half lengthways and carefully cut out the woody cores, keeping the other parts completely intact.

Beat the eggs, flour, salt and pepper together. Lay the parsnip halves on a plate and pour over the egg mixture. Make sure the parsnips are well-coated on both sides. Melt half the butter in a frying pan on a low to moderate heat. Lay in the parsnips and cook them till both sides are golden brown. Remove and lay them

on a flat, warm serving dish. Raise the heat under the pan and
put in the remaining butter. When it has melted, put in the
gherkins and vinegar. Swirl everything around and let the
resulting sauce bubble. Spoon it over the parsnips.

¥   ¥   ¥

Pâtés make superb first courses. If you eat cheese, you can make
them with curd cheese. Mushrooms make one with a good rich
flavour, while green peas and sorrel make a light, refreshing one
for summer.

Mushroom and watercress pâté

2 oz (50 g) flat mushrooms
4 oz (125 g) watercress (about 2 bunches)
1 oz (25 g) butter
1 medium onion, finely chopped
4 oz (125 g) curd cheese
few drops Tabasco sauce
for serving:
hot brown toast

Finely chop the mushrooms and watercress. Melt the butter in a
frying pan on a low heat. Put in the onion and cook it until
it is soft. Raise the heat, add the mushrooms and cook them
briskly for 1 minute. Mix in the watercress and stir it around
until it goes limp. (Only about ½ minute.) Put all the contents of
the pan into a blender with the cheese and the Tabasco sauce.
Work them until you have a smooth pâté. (You will have to give
the mixture about 4 quick whizzes, stopping between each one to
stir everything around.) Put the pâté into one earthenware bowl
or into four individual soufflé dishes or ramekins and chill until
firm. Hand the toast separately.

Pea and sorrel pâté

2 lb (900 g) peas, weighed in their shells
2 oz (50 g) butter
20 chopped sorrel leaves

2 tablespoons (30 ml) chopped parsley
2 tablespoons sour cream
for serving:
hot brown toast *or* Scotch oatcakes

Shell the peas. Melt the butter in a saucepan on a low heat. Stir
in the peas, cover them and let them cook gently for 12 minutes.
Stir in the sorrel, cover again and cook for 2 minutes more.
Pound the peas, butter and sorrel to a paste with a pestle and
mortar or with a wooden spoon in a bowl. (If you would rather
have a smoother texture, work them in a blender.) Mix in the
parsley and sour cream. Press the mixture into 4 small ramekins
or soufflé dishes and chill until firm. Again, hand brown toast or
oatcakes separately.

Avocado pears and curd cheese make a simple, smooth, pale
green pâté that preserves their individual flavour.

Avocado pâté

1 ripe avocado pear
4 oz (125 g) curd cheese
1 clove garlic, crushed with a pinch sea salt
2 tablespoons (30 ml) chopped parsley
grated rind and juice ½ lemon
for serving:
brown toast *or* plain wholemeal biscuits

Peel and stone the avocado and mash it to a smooth purée.
Thoroughly mix it with the cheese, garlic, parsley and lemon rind
and juice. Press the mixture into 4 small ramekins or soufflé
dishes and chill until firm. Hand the brown toast or wholemeal
biscuits separately.

Make a firm mustardy cheese that uses mustard and cress like a
savoury herb. Chilled, it can be served like a pâté.

Mustard and cress cheese

2 boxes mustard and cress

1 oz (25 g) butter
1 small onion, finely chopped
4 oz (125 g) curd cheese
2 teaspoons (10 ml) strong granular mustard such as Urchfont
  Full Strength
for serving:
wholemeal or granary scones or brown toast

Melt the butter in a frying pan on a low heat. Stir in the onion
and cook it until it is soft. Cut in the cress and cook it for about
½ minute until it just begins to wilt. Take the pan from the heat
and thoroughly mix in the cheese and mustard. Put the mixture
into 4 small ramekins or soufflé dishes and chill until firm. Hand
the toast or scones separately.

Aubergines can be baked and puréed and mixed with curd cheese
to make a tasty and refreshing dip for fingers of toast.

Aubergine cheese dip

8 oz (225 g) aubergines (either 2 small ones or one medium sized)
little oil for greasing foil
2 tablespoons (30 ml) olive oil for cooking
1 small onion, finely chopped
1 clove garlic, finely chopped
1 tablespoon (15 ml) tomato purée
4 oz (125 g) curd cheese
juice ½ lemon
2 tablespoons (30 ml) chopped chervil or parsley

Preheat the oven to Reg 6/400°F/200°C. Wrap the aubergines
together in lightly oiled foil and bake them for 30 minutes. Cut
them in half lengthways and scoop out all the flesh. Chop it
finely. Heat the oil in a saucepan on a low heat. Stir in the onion
and garlic, cover them and cook them gently for 5 minutes. Stir
in the aubergine pulp and cook it, uncovered, until most of the
moisture has evaporated. Stir in the tomato purée, take the pan
from the heat and let the mixture cool. Cream the cheese in a
bowl and beat in the aubergine mixture and lemon juice. Chill
the dip slightly and pile it into 4 small serving bowls. Scatter the

chervil or parsley over the top and serve it with hot fingers of
wholemeal or granary toast.

You can also use eggs as a base for pâtés.

Sorrel, mushroom and egg pâté

4 hard-boiled eggs
6 oz (175 g) flat mushrooms
8 sorrel leaves
1 teaspoon (5 ml) mustard powder
2 oz (50 g) butter
for serving:
brown toast is best with this one

Chop the eggs, mushrooms and sorrel. Melt the butter in a frying
pan on a moderate heat. Stir in the mushrooms and sorrel and
cook them for 1 minute. Keeping the pan on the heat, stir in the
eggs. When everything is well mixed, remove the pan from the
heat and stir in the mustard. Put the mixture into a blender and
whizz until you have a smooth pâté. (You will probably have to
stop several times and move the mixture around to get it quite
smooth.) Press into 4 small soufflé dishes or ramekins and chill
until firm.

If you don't eat cheese or eggs, the tiny brown Chinese lentils
make excellent pâtés when mixed with a little tahini.

Brown lentil and apple pâté

4 oz (125 g) brown Chinese lentils
½ pint (275 ml) water
1 bayleaf
sea salt and freshly ground black pepper
2 small (or 1 really large) Bramley apples
4 tablespoons (60 ml) olive oil
1 medium onion, finely chopped
2 tablespoons (30 ml) tahini

Put the lentils into a saucepan with the water and bayleaf,
seasoning them well. Cover and set on a low heat. Bring them to
the boil and simmer gently for 1 hour, by which time all the water

should be absorbed and the lentils tender. Remove the bayleaf
and mash the lentils well, using a potato masher if you have
one or a heavy wooden spoon or pestle. Peel, core and finely chop
the apples. Heat the oil in a saucepan on a low heat and mix
in the onion and apples. Cover and cook them gently for 10
minutes or until the apples can be beaten to a pulp. Thoroughly
mix in the lentils. Take the pan from the heat and mix in the
tahini. Press the mixture into an earthenware bowl or four
individual soufflé dishes or ramekins and chill until firm.

Brown lentil and mushroom pâté

4 oz (125 g) brown Chinese lentils
½ pint (275 ml) water
1 bayleaf
sea salt and freshly ground black pepper
4 oz (125 g) flat mushrooms
4 tablespoons olive oil
1 medium onion, finely chopped
1 clove garlic, finely chopped
1 tablespoon (15 ml) tahini
1 tablespoon (15 ml) chopped thyme
2 tablespoons (30 ml) chopped parsley
lemon juice (from one lemon or less)

Cook the lentils as for the apple pâté and mash them. Finely chop
the mushrooms. Heat the oil in a saucepan on a low heat. Put
in the onion and garlic and cook them until they are just turning
golden. Raise the heat to moderate and put in the mushrooms.
Cook them for 2 minutes, stirring. Take the pan from the heat
and mix in the lentils, thyme, parsley and tahini. Gradually add
the lemon juice, tasting as you go to get the right amount. Press
the mixture into 4 small soufflé dishes or ramekins and chill until
firm.

Lastly a special pâté for Christmas

Brown lentil and cranberry pâté

4 oz (125 g) brown lentils

½ pint (275 ml) water
1 bayleaf
sea salt and freshly ground black pepper
4 oz (125 g) cranberries
3 tablespoons (45 ml) olive oil
1 medium onion, finely chopped
1 large clove garlic, very finely chopped
2 teaspoons (10 ml) chopped thyme
1 tablespoon (15 ml) tahini
2 tablespoons (30 ml) brandy
for serving:
hot brown toast

Cook the lentils and mash them as for the apple pâté. Chop the cranberries. Heat the oil in a frying pan on a low heat. Stir in the onion and garlic and cook until golden. Mix in the lentils, cranberries and thyme and keep stirring until the cranberries are cooked and almost melting into the lentils (about 3 minutes). There is no danger of anything sticking as long as you keep everything on the move as the juice will run from the cranberries to moisten the lentils. Remove the pan from the heat and beat in the tahini and brandy. Press the pâté into 4 small soufflé dishes or ramekins and chill until firm. Hand the brown toast separately.

Soups

A tasty bowl of soup makes a welcoming start to any meal. Use winter roots and vegetables with warming, earthy flavours for the colder days, and make lighter flavoured and sometimes even chilled soups for the summer.

I have always relied mostly on vegetables to provide both the base and the flavour for all kinds of soup, whether they were coarse, blended or sieved, or served as a clear stock containing firm pieces of chopped vegetable. They are excellent for everyday and for special occasions, and the recipes here, though all vegetarian, could find their place in any kind of cookbook.

There is only one significant difference in making soup for a vegetarian meal, and that is the kind of stock that you use. How are you going to make one with enough flavour not only for soups, but suitable for every kind of culinary purpose? I have tried various methods and the one below was the best from all aspects. It is simple and cheap to make, is a middling golden colour, and has a strong vegetable-y flavour that is not over-biased in any one direction.

Basic vegetable stock

First of all, take the biggest saucepan or flameproof casserole you possess – 12 pints (7 litres) if you have one, or even more. Put in the following essentials:

2 medium onions, cut in half but not peeled
2 medium carrots, scrubbed and cut in half lengthways
2 sticks of celery, broken into short lengths, and a few celery leaves
    (in the summer, when no celery is available, use a few lovage
Brussels sprout trimmings
large bouquet garni which includes 2 bayleaves

2 teaspoons (10 ml) black peppercorns

2 tablespoons (30 ml) tamari sauce (this provides both flavour and some protein)

After this, half-fill your pot with trimmings or small pieces of any vegetable you have around, such as:

potato and celeriac peelings

trimmed ends of leeks

any turnip, swede or parsnip trimmings or any small root vegetables halved or quartered

tough outer leaves of green cabbages

cauliflower, kale, spinach or spring green stalks

brussels sprout trimmings

outer pieces of runner beans

pea and bean pods

(It is a good idea to keep a polythene stock-bag in the refrigerator and collect all your bits in it over a couple of days.) Pour in water to about 2 in (6 cm) from the top of the saucepan, and include any liquid you may have over from cooking white beans. Don't add brown-bean stock, it can be rather bitter. Cover the pan, set it on a moderate heat and bring the water to the boil. Turn the heat down and simmer for two hours. Cool the stock and strain it. Put it in a polythene container near the top of the refrigerator and it will keep for a week or more.

ঙ ঙ ঙ

Now you are ready to begin. First of all, let's start with simple soups that don't have to be sieved or blended. The vegetables are chopped, softened in butter or oil and then simmered with all kinds of flavourings in a stock thickened with wholemeal flour or with sieved potatoes.

Mushroom soup is many people's favourite. Use dark, flat tasty mushrooms and spice them with curry powder; or use a dark beer for a soup that tastes as dark as it looks.

Curried mushroom soup

8 oz (225 g) dark, flat mushrooms

1 oz (25 g) butter, *or* 4 tablespoons (60 ml) olive oil
1 large onion, finely chopped
1 clove garlic, finely chopped
2 teaspoons (10 ml) hot Madras curry powder
1 tablespoon (15 ml) wholemeal flour
1½ pints (850 ml) stock
1 bayleaf
lemon juice to taste (up to half a lemon)

Finely chop the mushrooms. Melt the butter or heat the oil in a saucepan on a low heat. Stir in the mushrooms, onion, garlic and curry powder. Cover, and let them sweat for 5 minutes. Stir in the flour and cook for 1 minute. Stir in the stock and bring it to the boil. Add the bayleaf, and simmer gently, uncovered, for 15 minutes. Add the lemon juice a little at a time, tasting as you go. Remove the bayleaf just before serving.

Mushroom and ale soup

6 oz (175 g) dark, flat mushrooms
1 oz (25 g) butter *or* 4 tablespoons (60 ml) olive oil
1 large onion, finely chopped
1 tablespoon (15 ml) wholemeal flour
1 tablespoon (15 ml) tomato purée
1 pint (575 ml) stock
½ pint (275 ml) draught dark mild ale (or substitute bottled brown ale)
1 bayleaf
2 tablespoons (30 ml) chopped parsley

Finely chop the mushrooms. Melt the butter or heat the oil in a heavy saucepan on a low heat. Stir in the mushrooms and onion, cover them and let them sweat for 10 minutes. Stir in the flour and cook for 1 minute. Stir in the tomato purée and then the stock and ale. Bring them to the boil, stirring. Add the bayleaf and the parsley and simmer, uncovered, for 15 minutes. Remove the bayleaf before serving.

Leeks have been used for soups and pottages since Saxon times

and they are still available for a good half of the year and maybe
more. Chop them up and cook them fairly quickly in unblended
soups to bring out all their flavour. The first leek soup below is
a light, refreshing lemony one for every day. The other two are
rather more special, with white wine or with Stilton cheese to give
them a heady tang.

Leek and lemon soup

12 oz (350 g) leeks
1 oz (25 g) butter, *or* 4 tablespoons (60 ml) olive oil
1 tablespoon (15 ml) wholemeal flour
2 teaspoons (10 ml) mustard powder
1½ pints (850 ml) stock
2 thinly pared strips lemon rind
juice 1 lemon
2 tablespoons (30 ml) chopped parsley

Finely chop the leeks. Melt the butter or heat the oil in a saucepan on a low heat. Stir in the leeks, cover them and let them
sweat for 10 minutes. Stir in the flour and mustard and cook
them for 1 minute. Stir in the stock, bring it to the boil, and add
the lemon rind. Simmer the soup, uncovered, for 15 minutes.
Add the lemon juice and parsley and remove the strips of lemon
rind.

If you think the amount of wine a little too extravagant in this
one, use ¼ pint (150 ml) instead and make up the rest with stock.

Leek and white wine soup

12 oz (350 g) leeks (white and green parts)
1 oz (25 g) butter *or* 4 tablespoons (60 ml) olive oil
1 tablespoon (15 ml) wholemeal flour
1 pint (575 ml) stock
½ pint (275 ml) dry white wine
1 tablespoon (15 ml) English Vineyard mustard
2 tablespoons (30 ml) chopped parsley

Finely chop the leeks. Melt the butter or heat the oil in a saucepan on a low heat. Stir in the leeks, cover them and let them

sweat for 10 minutes. Stir in the flour and let it cook for 1 minute. Stir in the stock, bring it to the boil, stirring, and add the wine and mustard. Simmer, uncovered, for 15 minutes. Add the parsley just before serving so it looks and tastes nice and fresh.

Leek and Stilton soup

8 oz (225 g) leeks
1 oz (25 g) butter
1 tablespoon (15 ml) wholemeal flour
1½ pints (850 ml) stock
4 oz (125 g) soft Stilton cheese

Finely chop the leeks. Melt the butter or heat the oil in a sauce-Stir in the leeks, cover them and let them sweat for 7 minutes. Stir in the flour, let it cook for 1 minute and stir in the stock. Bring it to the boil and simmer for 10 minutes, uncovered. Grate the Stilton (or crumble it if it's too soft to grate) and cream it in a bowl with a wooden spoon. Gradually work in the hot soup, keeping the mixture smooth. Return it to the saucepan and reheat without boiling.

ॐ   ॐ   ॐ

Chopped watercress can be used like a herb in some soups, just to give flavour; or you can use a whole bunch of it for a clear water-cress soup.

Watercress and orange soup

1 bunch watercress
1 oz (25 g) butter *or* 4 tablespoons (60 ml) olive oil
1 large onion, finely chopped
1 tablespoon (15 ml) wholemeal flour
1½ pints (850 ml) stock
1 tablespoon (15 ml) mixed chopped marjoram and thyme
1 tablespoon (15 ml) chopped parsley
juice of 2 medium oranges with grated rind of 1

Finely chop the watercress. Melt the butter or heat the oil in a saucepan on a low heat. Stir in the onion and cook it gently until it is brown. Stir in the flour and cook it for 1 minute. Stir in the stock and bring it to the boil. Add the herbs and orange rind and simmer for 5 minutes. Add the watercress and simmer for 5 minutes more. Stir in the orange juice and reheat if necessary before serving.

꽃　　꽃　　꽃

Miso soups are an essential part of diets that contain no animal products at all. Here is a way of using miso and cabbage to make a rich dark soup.

Cabbage and miso soup

1 small green winter cabbage
4 tablespoons (60 ml) olive oil
2 medium onions, finely chopped
1 clove garlic, finely chopped
2 tablespoons (30 ml) miso
2 pints (1.150 L) stock
2 tablespoons (30 ml) chopped savory
lots of freshly grated nutmeg

Finely chop the cabbage. Heat the oil in a saucepan on a low heat. Stir in the onions and garlic, cover them and let them sweat for 10 minutes. Mix in the miso and stir in the stock. Bring it to the boil, add the savory and grate in the nutmeg. Then put in the cabbage. Cover and simmer for 20 minutes.

꽃　　꽃　　꽃

For a complete change here is a refreshing soup made from Brussels sprouts and yoghurt, with a hint of lemon.

Brussels sprout and yoghurt soup

1 lb (450 g) Brussels sprouts
1 oz (25 g) butter
1 large onion, finely chopped

1½ pints (850 ml) stock
2 thinly pared strips lemon rind
1 carton natural yoghurt
2 teaspoons (10 ml) wholemeal flour
4 tablespoons (60 ml) chopped parsley

Trim and finely chop the sprouts. Melt the butter in a saucepan on a low heat. Stir in the sprouts and onion, cover them and let them sweat for 10 minutes. Pour in the stock and bring it to the boil, then add the lemon rind. Cover and simmer gently for 20 minutes. Blend the flour and yoghurt together (this stops the yoghurt from curdling). Remove the lemon rind from the soup and stir in the yoghurt and parsley. Reheat gently and serve.

Use runner beans, green peppers and savory for a soup that tastes of late summer.

Runner bean and green pepper soup

1 lb (450 g) runner beans
2 medium-sized green peppers
1 oz (25 g) butter *or* 4 tablespoons (60 ml) olive oil
1 medium onion, finely chopped
1 tablespoon (15 ml) wholemeal flour
1¼ pints (725 ml) stock
1 tablespoon (15 ml) chopped savory
¼ pint (150 ml) dry white wine

Finely chop the beans. Core, de-seed and chop the peppers. Melt the butter or heat the oil in a saucepan on a low heat. Stir in the beans and onion, cover them and let them sweat for 10 minutes. Stir in the flour and cook it for 1 minute. Stir in the stock. Bring it to the boil and add the peppers and savory. Simmer, uncovered, for 10 minutes. Pour in the wine and reheat to serve.

This is another summery soup, spiced sweetly with dill seeds and made slightly tangy with curd cheese.

Cucumber and lettuce soup

heart of 1 large Webb's lettuce
1 small (or ½ large) cucumber
1 oz (25 g) butter
1 large onion, finely chopped
1 teaspoon (5 ml) dill seeds
1 tablespoon (15 ml) wholemeal flour
1½ pints (850 ml) stock
2 tablespoons (30 ml) chopped parsley
2 oz (50 g) curd cheese
juice 1 lemon

Finely chop the lettuce heart. Wipe the cucumber but do not peel it. Quarter it, cut out the seeds and then chop it into small dice. Melt the butter in a saucepan on a low heat, put in the onion and the dill seeds and cook them until the onion is soft. Raise the heat to moderate and put in the cucumber and lettuce. When the lettuce has wilted, stir in the flour and then the stock. Bring the stock to the boil, add the parsley, and simmer, uncovered, for 15 minutes. Work the cheese and lemon juice together in a bowl and gradually add 6 tablespoons (90 ml) of the hot soup. Pour the resulting mixture back into the saucepan and mix it in well. Reheat gently, without boiling, to serve.

꙳   ꙳   ꙳

A good way of using up left-over boiled potatoes is to sieve them and use them instead of flour to slightly thicken unblended soups. If you are cooking potatoes especially for the purpose, always boil them in their skins and peel them afterwards. They are excellent for oniony soups.

Celery and onion soup thickened with potato

6 oz (175 g) celery
1 medium onion
3 oz (75 g) potatoes (cooked)
1 oz (25 g) butter *or* 4 tablespoons (60 ml) olive oil
1½ pints (850 ml) stock

sea salt and freshly ground black pepper to taste
1 bayleaf
8 chopped sage leaves
¼ pint (150 ml) dry cider

Finely chop the celery and onion. Rub the potatoes through a sieve. Melt the butter or heat the oil in a saucepan on a low heat. Stir in the celery and onion, cover them and let them sweat for 10 minutes. Remove the pan from the heat and gradually work in the potato. Stir in the stock. Set the pan back on the heat and bring it gently to the boil, stirring. Season, add the sage and bayleaf and simmer, uncovered, for 15 minutes. Remove the bayleaf, pour in the cider and reheat.

This is a rich, nut-brown version of French onion soup.

Onion and potato soup

12 oz (350 g) onions
4 oz (125 g) cooked potatoes
1 oz (25 g) butter *or* 4 tablespoons (60 ml) olive oil
1½ pints (850 ml) stock
1 large bayleaf
sea salt and freshly ground black pepper to taste
1 tablespoon (15 ml) grated Parmesan cheese (optional but it makes it nicer)
¼ pint (150 ml) sherry

Finely chop the onions. Rub the potatoes through a sieve. Melt the butter or heat the oil in a saucepan on a low heat. Stir in the onions and cook them, uncovered, until they are golden, stirring from time to time. Take the pan from the heat and work in the sieved potatoes and then the stock. Season to taste and add the bayleaf. Bring the soup to the boil and let it simmer, uncovered, for 10 minutes. Remove the bayleaf, stir in the cheese and sherry and reheat to serve.

※　　　※　　　※

Red lentils easily become soft and make good, thick unblended soups if they are simmered for long enough. Make a rich, nutty one with browned onions. It is very substantial, so serve it before a light meal or a salad. It could in fact be served as a complete meal like the pottages (see pottage chapter).

Red lentil soup with browned onion

8 oz (225 g) red lentils
3 tablespoons (45 ml) olive oil
2 large onions, thinly sliced
1 large clove garlic, finely chopped
2 pints (1¼ l) stock
1 bayleaf
2 teaspoons (10 ml) tamari sauce
3 tablespoons (45 ml) chopped parsley

Wash the lentils in a sieve and drain them well. Heat the oil in a saucepan on a moderate heat. Put in the onions and garlic and brown them fairly quickly, stirring. Pour in the stock and bring it to the boil. Add the lentils and bring to the boil again. Lower the heat and put in the bayleaf. Cover and simmer on the lowest possible heat for 45 minutes. Remove the bayleaf, take the pan from the heat and stir in the tamari sauce and parsley.

You can make creamy soups with avocado pears just by mashing them and mixing them carefully into stock. There are two methods here, one if you eat yoghurt and the other for vegans.

Avocado and lemon soup

2 ripe avocado pears
4 tablespoons (60 ml) olive oil
1 large onion, finely chopped
1 clove garlic, finely chopped
1½ pints (850 ml) stock
grated rind and juice ½ lemon
1 carton natural yoghurt (if you don't use it see the alternative method)
1 tablespoon (15 ml) wholemeal flour

for serving:
2 tablespoons (30 ml) chopped chervil or parsley

Peel the avocados and mash them to as smooth a paste as you can. Heat the oil in a saucepan on a low heat. Stir in the onion and garlic and cook them until the onion is soft.

Yoghurt method: mix in the avocados and gradually stir in the stock to give you a smooth-textured soup. Bring it gently to the boil and add the lemon rind. Simmer gently for 10 minutes and add the lemon juice. Cream the yoghurt with the flour and stir it into the saucepan. Keep stirring on a very low heat until the soup thickens.

Method without yoghurt: after softening the onions, stir in the flour and then add the avocados. Stir in the stock and carry on as above.

Serve the soup (both kinds) scattered with chervil or parsley.

꽃   꽃   꽃

When it comes to blended or sieved soups, you will find that many vegetables make a thick, creamy textured base without the addition of flour, egg-yolks or cream. They can be flavoured with spices and herbs and lemon or orange juice, or you can add curd or cream cheese for both flavour and texture.

If, during the summer, you manage to grow some basil in the herb garden, save it for tomato dishes. With this herb, you can keep all the other ingredients as simple as possible, as its flavour is quite magical.

Tomato, cheese and basil soup

1 lb (450 g) ripe tomatoes
1 oz (25 g) butter
1 medium onion, finely chopped
1 pint (575 ml) stock
8 oz (225 g) curd cheese
3 tablespoons (45 ml) chopped basil

Scald, skin and roughly chop the tomatoes. Melt the butter in a saucepan on a low heat. Stir in the onion, cover, and cook for 5 minutes. Stir in the tomatoes, cover again, and cook for a further 10 minutes. Cool everything slightly and then put the contents of the pan into a blender with the stock and cheese (in two batches if your blender is a small one). Work until you have a smooth, creamy textured soup. Return it to the saucepan, stir in the basil and reheat without boiling. Serve either hot or chilled. N.B. If you chill the soup, still heat it gently after you have added the basil so its flavour can get to work.

Flavour carrots with garlic and put them with tomatoes for a thick, golden autumn soup made when tomatoes are plentiful and carrots getting large.

Carrot and tomato soup

4 oz (125 g) carrots
8 oz (225 g) ripe tomatoes plus two more for garnish
1 oz (25 g) butter *or* 4 tablespoons (60 ml) olive oil
1 medium onion, finely chopped
1 clove garlic, finely chopped
¾ pint (425 ml) stock
bouquet garni
4 tablespoons (60 ml) sherry
for serving:
2 tablespoons (30 ml) chopped parsley and the two tomatoes
   mentioned above

Thinly slice the carrots. Scald, skin and chop the tomatoes. Melt the butter or heat the oil in a saucepan on a low heat. Stir in the carrots, onion and garlic. Cover them and let them sweat for 10 minutes. Add the tomatoes, cover again and cook for a further 2 minutes. Pour in the stock and bring it to the boil. Add the bouquet garni, cover and simmer for 15 minutes. Remove the bouquet garni, cool the soup slightly and work it in a blender or rub it through the fine blade of a *mouli*. Return it to the saucepan, stir in the sherry and reheat. Serve in individual bowls with 2 tomato slices and some chopped parsley floating on top.

When I cook turnips as a vegetable, mustard, lemon and parsley are my favourite flavourers, so here they are in a turnip soup.

Turnip and lemon soup

1 lb (450 g) small white turnips
1 oz (25 g) butter *or* vegetable margarine
1 large onion, finely chopped
1½ pints (850 ml) stock
2 thinly pared strips lemon rind
bouquet garni
2 teaspoons (10 ml) Dijon mustard
juice ½ lemon
4 tablespoons (60 ml) chopped parsley *or* 2 tablespoons (30 ml) parsley and 1 tablespoon (15 ml) chopped lemon thyme

Trim, scrub and finely chop the turnips. Melt the butter or margarine in a saucepan on a low heat. Stir in the turnips and onion, cover them and let them sweat for 10 minutes. Pour in the stock and bring it to the boil. Add the lemon rind and bouquet garni. Cover and simmer for 20 minutes. Cool slightly and remove the bouquet garni and lemon rind. Put the mixture into a blender with the mustard and lemon juice and work until you have a smooth soup; or mix in the mustard and then pass through the fine blade of a mouli sieve. Return the soup to the saucepan, add the lemon and parsley (and lemon thyme if you're using it) and reheat.

❧   ❧   ❧

The seasons for swede and Seville oranges always coincide, and together they make a delicious simple soup.

Swede and Seville soup

12 oz (350 g) swede
1 oz (25 g) butter *or* vegetable margarine
1 large onion, thinly sliced
1½ pints (850 ml) stock
bouquet garni

2 pieces thinly pared Seville orange rind
juice 1 Seville orange

Scrub the swede, trim off the knobbly parts and thinly slice it.
Melt the butter in a saucepan on a low heat. Stir in the swede
and onion. Cover them and let them sweat for 10 minutes. Pour
in the stock and bring it to the boil. Add the bouquet garni and
the orange rind. Cover and simmer for 15 minutes. Remove the
bouquet garni and orange rind and cool the soup slightly. Work
it in a blender or pass it through the fine blade of a mouli sieve
to produce a smooth orange soup. Return it to the saucepan,
add the orange juice and reheat.

Parsnips can be very sweet and heavy, so lighten a parsnip soup
with curd cheese and orange rind.

Parsnip and cheese soup

1 lb (450 g) parsnips
1 oz (25 g) butter
1 large onion, finely chopped
2 pints (1¼ l) stock
bouquet garni
2 oz (50 g) curd cheese
grated rind 1 large orange

Cut the parsnips in half lengthways and remove the woody
cores. Chop the rest finely. Melt the butter in a saucepan on a
low heat. Stir in the parsnips and onion, cover them and let them
sweat for 10 minutes. Stir in the stock and bring it to the boil.
Add the bouquet garni and season lightly if wished. Cover and
simmer for 20 minutes. Remove the bouquet garni and cool the
soup a little. Work it in a blender or pass it through the fine blade
of a mouli sieve. Put the cheese into the rinsed-out saucepan and
cream it with a wooden spoon. Gradually work in the soup.
Stir in the orange rind and reheat gently, without boiling.

Jerusalem artichokes give a soft, creamy colour and texture to blended or sieved soups. Celery alone would need thickening, but here it just makes a good, light contrast in flavour.

Celery and artichoke soup

12 oz (350 g) Jerusalem artichokes
4 large sticks celery
1 oz (25 g) butter *or* vegetable margarine
1 large onion, finely chopped
1½ pints (850 ml) stock
bouquet garni
2 large pickled gherkins, very finely chopped

Peel the artichokes while holding them under water (this stops your hands getting sticky), and thinly slice them. Finely chop the celery. Melt the butter in a saucepan on a low heat. Stir in the artichokes, celery and onion, cover them and let them sweat for 10 minutes. Pour in the stock and bring it to the boil. Add the bouquet garni and simmer, covered, for 20 minutes. Cool the soup slightly and either work it in a blender or rub it through a mouli sieve until it is smooth. Return it to the saucepan, stir in the gherkins and reheat to serve.

Apples and celeriac are an excellent combination in salads, and just as effective in a hot soup. This is another really creamy one.

Celeriac and apple soup

12 oz (350 g) celeriac
2 medium-sized cooking apples
1 oz (25 g) butter *or* vegetable margarine
1 large onion, thinly sliced
1½ pints (850 ml) stock
bouquet garni which includes sage
for serving:
4 tablespoons (60 ml) natural yoghurt (an optional garnish that
   just adds a slightly sharp contrast)

Chop the celeriac into small, thin pieces. Peel, quarter, core and slice the apples. Melt the butter or margarine in a saucepan on a low heat. Mix in the celeriac, apples and onion, cover them and let them sweat for 10 minutes. Pour in the stock and bring it to the boil. Add the bouquet garni, cover and simmer for 20 minutes. Remove the bouquet garni and cool the soup slightly. Work it in a blender or rub it through the fine blade of a mouli sieve. Return it to the saucepan and reheat it. Pour the soup into four serving bowls and float the yoghurt on the top just before taking it to the table.

꙳ ꙳ ꙳

When you make a soup with aubergines, it is best to rub it through a sieve or a mouli sieve so you can remove the larger, bitter-tasting seeds. This soup is a complete contrast to all the thick, rooty ones. It is dark brown and rather like a rich consommé. If you would like to make it a little more substantial, simmer about 2 oz (50 g) broken buckwheat spaghetti in the liquid for 10 minutes before adding the sherry.

Aubergine and tomato soup

2 large aubergines
8 oz (225 g) tomatoes
3 tablespoons (45 ml) olive oil
1 large onion, finely chopped
1 large clove garlic, finely chopped
2 tablespoons (30 ml) chopped marjoram
1¼ pints (725 ml) stock
¼ pint (150 ml) sherry
for optional garnish:
2 firm tomatoes, scalded, skinned, de-seeded and chopped

Preheat the oven to Reg 6/400°F/200°C. Lay the aubergines on the oven rack and bake them for 30 minutes. Cut them in half lengthways, scoop out all the flesh and chop it finely. Scald, skinand chop the tomatoes. Heat the oil in a saucepan on a low heat. Stir in the onion and garlic, cover them, and cook them gently for 5 minutes. Stir in the aubergines, tomatoes and marjoram. Cover again and cook for 10 minutes. Pour in the stock and bring it to the boil. Simmer, covered, for 15 minutes. Rub the soup through a sieve or the fine blade of a mouli sieve. Return it to the rinsed-out pan and add the sherry. Reheat gently, without boiling. Add the chopped tomatoes just before serving.

⁂

Large marrows, baby courgettes and huge golden pumpkins don't make such densely-textured soups as the root vegetables. They are thick enough, though, to need no extra flour or cream and have an almost translucent appearance.

This first soup using these vegetables brings out all the natural flavour of the marrow. If you don't eat cheese, stir in 2 table-spoons (30 ml) chopped savory instead.

Marrow and Cheshire cheese soup

1 small marrow weighing around 2 lb (900 g) (or a 2 lb piece of
  a larger one)
1 oz (25 g) butter
1 large onion, thinly sliced
1 pint (575 ml) stock
freshly ground black pepper
bouquet of savory
2 oz (50 g) grated Cheshire cheese (use white for the best appearance, but the red tastes the same if it's all you can get)

Cut the marrow in half lengthways and scoop out the seeds. Peel it and cut it into small, thin slices. Melt the butter in a saucepan on a low heat. Stir in the marrow and onion, cover them and let them sweat for 10 minutes. Pour in the stock and bring it to the boil. Season with the pepper and add the bouquet of savory. Cover, and simmer for a further 10 minutes. Remove the savory and cool the soup slightly. Work it in a blender or pass it through the fine blade of a mouli sieve. Return it to the pan and stir in the cheese. Reheat so the cheese only just melts and you can still see small flecks of it in the soup.

Marrow is often made into hot, fruity chutneys. Make a fruity curry soup instead.

Curried marrow and sultana soup

1 2 lb (900 g) marrow (or a 2 lb piece from a larger one)
1 oz (25 g) butter *or* 4 tablespoons (60 ml) olive oil
1 large onion, finely chopped
1 large clove garlic, finely chopped
2 teaspoons (10 ml) hot Madras curry powder
2 teaspoons (10 ml) ground cumin (this gives the soup a more
   subtle flavour, but if you don't have any don't let it prevent you
   from making the recipe)
1 pint (575 ml) stock
1 bayleaf
2 oz (50 g) sultanas

Cut the marrow in half lengthways and scoop out the seeds.
Peel it and chop it into small, thin pieces. Melt the butter or
heat the oil in a saucepan on a low heat. Stir in the marrow,
onion, garlic, curry powder and cumin. Cover, and let them sweat
for 5 minutes. Pour in the stock and add the bayleaf. Bring the
stock to the boil stirring, cover and simmer for 10 minutes. Cool
the soup slightly and remove the bayleaf. Work the soup in a
blender or pass it through the fine blade of a mouli sieve. Return
it to the saucepan and stir in the sultanas. Simmer for 2 minutes
to get them nice and plump.

The delicate flavour of courgettes is too good to be masked by
any heavy spices. Use parsley and just a little Parmesan cheese.

Courgette and parsley soup

1 lb (450 g) courgettes
4 tablespoons (60 ml) olive oil
1 large onion, thinly sliced
1 clove garlic, finely chopped
1¼ pints (725 ml) stock
4 tablespoons (60 ml) chopped parsley
freshly ground black pepper
1 tablespoon (15 ml) grated Parmesan cheese (optional)

Wipe and thinly slice the courgettes. Heat the oil in a saucepan
on a low heat. Stir in the onion, garlic and courgettes, cover them

and let them sweat for 10 minutes. Pour in the stock and bring it to the boil. Add the parsley and season with the pepper. Cover, and simmer for 15 minutes. Cool the soup slightly and work it in a blender until it is smooth. (This one is better whizzed in a blender rather than put through a mouli). Return the soup to the pan and, if you are using it, stir in the cheese. Reheat without boiling to just let the cheese melt.

Golden pumpkins make golden autumn soups. This is another very simple one to bring out all the creamy natural flavour and add just a touch of contrasting sharpness.

Pumpkin and caper soup

1 lb (450 g) pumpkin (weighed after peeling and de-seeding)
1 oz (25 g) butter *or* 4 tablespoons (60 ml) olive oil
1 large onion, finely chopped
1¼ pints (725 ml) stock
bouquet garni
1 bayleaf
1½ tablespoons (25 ml) chopped capers
1½ tablespoons (25 ml) chopped parsley
freshly ground black pepper

Chop the pumpkin into small, thin slices. Melt the butter or heat the oil in a saucepan on a low heat. Stir in the pumpkin and onion, cover them and let them sweat for 10 minutes. Pour in the stock and bring it to the boil. Add the bouquet garni and the bayleaf, cover and simmer for 15 minutes. Remove the bouquet and the bayleaf. Cool the soup slightly and work it in a blender or rub it through the fine blade of a mouli. Return it to the saucepan and stir in the capers and parsley. Season with the pepper and simmer gently for 2 minutes to let all the flavour blend.

Broad beans and peas, the fresh summer pulses, benefit from

just a touch of added sharpness, especially when you are relying on vegetable stocks.

Broad bean and lemon soup

2 lb (900 g) broad beans (weighed in their shells)
1 oz (25 g) butter *or* vegetable margarine
1 medium onion, thinly sliced
1½ pints (850 ml) stock
2 thinly pared strips lemon rind
juice 1 lemon
2 tablespoons (30 ml) chopped parsley

Shell the beans and reserve three of the best pods. Melt the butter or margarine in a saucepan on a low heat. Stir in the beans and the onion, cover them and cook them gently for 10 minutes. Pour in the stock and bring it to the boil. Add the reserved pods and lemon rind and simmer, covered, for 20 minutes. Remove the pods and the rind and cool the soup slightly. Work it in a blender or pass it through a mouli sieve so it is thick, creamy and pale green. Return it to the saucepan and stir in the lemon juice. Reheat gently and serve with the parsley sprinkled on the top.

The tarragon vinegar in this pea soup gives flavour but no actual sharpness. It makes the peas taste almost like asparagus.

Pea and lettuce soup

1½ lb (675 g) peas (weighed in their shells)
1 small Density or Webb's lettuce
1 oz (25 g) butter *or* vegetable margarine
1 medium onion, finely chopped
1½ pints (850 ml) stock
bouquet garni
2 teaspoons (10 ml) clear honey
1 tablespoon (15 ml) tarragon vinegar
1 tablespoon (15 ml) chopped tarragon
1 tablespoon (15 ml) chopped parsley

Shell the peas and reserve 4 of the best pods. Chop the lettuce.

Melt the butter or margarine in a saucepan on a low heat. Stir in the peas, reserved pods and onion. Cover them and cook them gently for 5 minutes. Stir in the lettuce and just let it wilt. Pour in the stock and bring it to the boil. Add the bouquet garni, cover and simmer for 15 minutes. Remove the bouquet garni and the pods. Cool the soup a little and put it in a blender with the honey and vinegar. Work it until it is smooth. Return the soup to the saucepan and stir in the tarragon and parsley. Reheat gently to serve.

ụ   ụ   ụ

If you are able to find it in your local delicatessen or cheese specialists, use the strong, hard cheese that is made on the Isle of Islay for this recipe. If not, then use a white Cheshire.

Cauliflower and parsley soup

1 small cauliflower
1½ pints (850 ml) stock
1 medium onion, thinly sliced
2 oz (50 g) chopped parsley
pinch sea salt
freshly ground black pepper
for serving:
3 oz (75 g) grated Isle of Islay (or white Cheshire) cheese

Chop the cauliflower. Put the stock into a saucepan and bring it to the boil. Put in the cauliflower, onion and parsley. Season, cover and simmer for 20 minutes. Cool the soup slightly and work it in a blender or rub it through the fine blade of a mouli sieve. Return it to the saucepan and reheat. Serve in individual bowls with the cheese scattered on top.

This must be one of the easiest soups imaginable if you have a blender. It is certainly one of the most welcome on a hot summer day.

Chilled cucumber and yoghurt soup

1 medium-sized cucumber

4 cartons natural yoghurt
2 tablespoons (30 ml) tomato purée
1 clove garlic, finely chopped
2 teaspoons (10 ml) paprika
1–2 teaspoons (5–10 ml) Tabasco sauce, to taste
for serving:
1 tablespoon (15 ml) chopped coriander or parsley

Wipe, but do not peel the cucumber. Chop it finely. Put it into a blender with the yoghurt, tomato purée, garlic, paprika and Tabasco sauce. Work everything until you have a smooth creamy-looking soup. Chill it and serve it in chilled bowls with the coriander or parsley floating on top.

When the meal is composed mainly of vegetables, very often cooked vegetable accompaniments can seem a little too much of a good thing. They all seem to be incorporated into the main dishes and you don't actually need any others. Potatoes, however, are another matter. They are still the most favoured 'filler' part of any meal, whether your main course consists of cheese, eggs, meat, something nutty or even some of the beans and lentils. Cook them in different ways and they take on completely different textures and flavours, so even when potatoes appear on the table every day there is still plenty of variety.

Whenever you can, always cook potatoes in their skins. The flavour is so much better and also most of their goodness lies just under the surface. We'll deal first with old potatoes.

For plain, boiled potatoes, choose fairly small ones so you can cook them whole or at least only cut in half. Then they stay firm and don't go floury. When they are done, peel them if you like (although this isn't essential), slice them and toss them with butter and chopped herbs, or with some sliced browned onion or chopped spring onions.

Or mash peeled potatoes with butter and a little milk (for a special treat use double cream). You can also make them into a herby purée.

Mashed potatoes and herbs

1½–2 lb (675–900 g) potatoes
2 oz (50 g) butter
8 tablespoons (120 ml) milk
4 tablespoons (60 ml) chopped parsley, chives or watercress
   or 2 tablespoons (30 ml) chopped thyme or spring onions
   or 2 teaspoons (10 ml) chopped sage or rosemary

or a mixture of any herbs
or 1 box mustard and cress
freshly ground black pepper

Boil the potatoes in their skins until they are only just tender.
Drain them, and peel and chop them as soon as they are cool
enough to handle. Put the butter and milk into a saucepan and
set them on a low heat. When the butter has melted, fold in the
herbs and the potatoes and season with the pepper. Cover the
pan and keep it on a low heat for 5 minutes. Mash everything
together well.
Alternatives:
Boil the potatoes with a small, sliced onion and a bayleaf.
Remove the bayleaf but mash the onion with the potatoes.
Flavour the potatoes with 2 tablespoons (30 ml) grated cheese.

Yoghurt and apple make a light-textured, refreshing and unusual
purée of potatoes.

Potatoes mashed with apple and yoghurt

2 lb (900 g) potatoes
1 medium onion, thinly sliced
2 medium-sized *or* 1 enormous Bramley apples
2 tablespoons (30 ml) water
4 tablespoons (60 ml) natural yoghurt
12 chopped sage leaves

Boil the potatoes in their skins with the onion, in lightly salted
water until they are tender. Meanwhile peel, quarter and chop the
apples and put them into a saucepan with the water. Cover and
set them on a low heat until you can beat them to a thick pulp
(10–15 minutes). Drain the potatoes and peel them as soon as
they are cool enough to handle. Put the potatoes, onion and
apples into a saucepan and mash them together. Beat in the
yoghurt and sage to give a light, fluffy purée.

For a change in colour and flavour, you can also boil equal
amounts of potatoes and one of the root vegetables such as

parsnips, turnips or celeriac. Then you can mash them with herbs, fry them to make a potato hash, flecked with small, brown crispy pieces, or make them into round, flat cakes, brush them with beaten egg, and bake them in a hot oven until they are brown.

This spicy dish of mashed potatoes goes well with winter salads.

Hot mashed potato salad

1½ lb (675 g) old potatoes
3 tablespoons (45 ml) olive oil
1 tablespoon (15 ml) white wine vinegar
1 teaspoon (5 ml) Tabasco sauce
2 teaspoons (10 ml) tomato purée

Boil the potatoes in their skins in lightly salted water until they are tender. Drain them, and peel them as soon as they are cool enough to handle. Return them to the saucepan and set it on the lowest heat possible. Quickly mash in the oil, vinegar, Tabasco sauce and tomato purée, being careful not to let any of the mixture stick to the bottom of the pan. Remove from the heat and serve as soon as everything is well mixed.

Mashed potatoes can be made into croquettes of all shapes and sizes, coated with crumbs and deep-fried. In the following recipe they are coloured green with parsley and chives.

Green potato balls

1½ lb (675 g) old potatoes
6 tablespoons (90 ml) double cream
either 3 tablespoons (45 ml) chopped chives
   and 5 tablespoons (75 ml) chopped parsley
or 8 tablespoons (120 ml) chopped parsley
approximately 4 tablespoons (60 ml) seasoned wholemeal flour
1 egg, beaten
approximately 4 tablespoons (60 ml) browned crumbs
deep oil for frying

Boil the potatoes in their skins in lightly salted water until they are tender. Peel them, and mash them while they are still warm. Beat in the cream and herbs. Make the potatoes into small, round balls just a little smaller than a golf ball. Roll them in the flour and coat them in the egg and then the crumbs. Deep fry them in hot oil until they are golden.

Alternative: if you don't use eggs: beat in 1½ oz (40 g) vegetable margarine, coat with the seasoned flour and shallow fry.

🌿   🌿   🌿

Steamed potatoes remain firm and intact, become naturally moist and taste better without any butter. Best for steaming are the small- to medium-sized ones that are mostly available during the first part of the winter. Late in the season they tend to get a little too floury.

Use 1½–2 lb (675–900 g) potatoes, scrub them and cut them into ¼ inch (0.75 cm) slices. (The flavour is best if you leave the skins on.) Season, and steam them, covered, for ½ hour, turning them frequently so they cook evenly. For flavouring put in a bayleaf or a bouquet garni; grate in some nutmeg, or sprinkle in a little curry powder or paprika; steam a sliced, medium-sized onion with the potatoes; or put in some chopped herbs or spring onions.

For a special occasion, make a heady sauce with white wine and fennel seeds, which still needs no added butter or oil.

Steamed potatoes and fennel

1½–2 lb (675–900 g) medium-sized old potatoes
4 1-inch (3 cm) pieces dried fennel stalk
freshly ground black pepper
5 tablespoons (75 ml) dry white wine
½ teaspoon (2.5 ml) dried fennel seeds

Scrub the potatoes and cut them into ¼ inch (0.75 cm) slices. Put them into a vegetable steamer (or into a colander covered with foil) with the pieces of fennel stalk. Cover and steam for 30 minutes, turning them several times. Discard the fennel stalks

and turn the potatoes into a warm serving dish. Put the wine and
fennel seeds into a small saucepan. Bring the wine to the boil and
let it reduce by half. Pour the wine and fennel seeds over the
potatoes.

Braised and simmered potatoes

Like most other vegetables, potatoes can be simmered on top of
the stove or braised in the oven. Here is the basic method.

For every 1½ lb (675 g) scrubbed and sliced or diced potatoes,
melt 1 oz (25 g) butter or heat 4 tablespoons (60 ml) olive oil in
a heavy saucepan (for simmering) or a flameproof casserole (for
braising) on a low heat. Mix in the potatoes, pour in ½ pint (275
ml) stock, season with plenty of sea salt and freshly ground
black pepper and add a bayleaf. Cover, and either simmer on
top of the stove for 30 minutes or put them into an oven preheated to Reg 4/350°F/180°C for 1¼ hours. By the end of the
cooking time the potatoes will be soft and tasty and there will be
just enough liquid left to make a syrupy glaze. Braising makes
for a slightly richer dish than simmering.

Both braised and simmered potatoes are improved tremendously if you put additional flavourings into the pot. Replace the
stock with beer for a change. Soften or brown a sliced onion in
the fat before putting in the potatoes; scatter in some paprika,
mustard powder, or curry powder after the potatoes have been
added; or put in large amounts of chopped herbs or spring
onions.

Braising and simmering are excellent methods of cooking old
potatoes towards the end of their season. There should be plenty
of new spring herbs around at that time for flavouring.

Roast and baked potatoes

What is a roast potato and what is a baked one? Usually, a roast potato is cooked in a pan of butter, oil or dripping and a baked one is cooked plainly, with no fat, in its jacket. There is no definite hard and fast rule, however, and the two terms are often interchanged. This first recipe, just to confuse the issue even more, is a cross between the two methods and is probably the best potato recipe I know of. Use an oven-to-table dish so you can serve the potatoes still surrounded by all the butter and crumbs.

Cut-roasted jacket potatoes

12 small, even-sized potatoes
2 oz (50 g) butter
2 tablespoons (30 ml) dried granary breadcrumbs

Preheat the oven to Reg 6/400°F/200°C. Scrub the potatoes and on one of the flatter surfaces make cuts in them one-eighth-inch (0.25 cm) apart and nearly all the way through. Put the butter into a flat oven-proof dish and put it into the oven to melt. Roll the potatoes in the butter and leave them cut-side up. Put them into the oven for 1 hour, basting occasionally. Scatter the crumbs over the top and baste again. Return them to the oven for 20 minutes.

Even for plain roast potatoes, the skins can be left on. Just scrub them and cut them into chunks about 2 in by 1 in (6 cm by 3 cm) and roast them for 1¼ 1½ hours in butter, margarine, oil or dripping in an oven preheated to Reg 6/400°F/200°C.

Here are two variations on the roast potato theme.

Potato cubes with Parmesan cheese and crumbs

1½ lb (675 g) old potatoes
2 oz (50 g) butter
1 tablespoon (15 ml) grated Parmesan cheese
2 tablespoons (30 ml) browned crumbs

Preheat the oven to Reg 6/400°F/200°C. Put the butter into a roasting pan or large, flat ovenproof dish, and put it into the oven to melt. Scrub the potatoes and cut them into ½ in (1.5 cm) dice. Turn the cubes around in the melted butter and put the dish into the oven for 1 hour, turning them around every 15 minutes. Scatter the cheese and crumbs over the top and return to the oven for a further 15 minutes.

Variation: if you don't eat butter or cheese, use 8 tablespoons (120 ml) oil and scatter over some chopped herbs just before serving.

Roast potatoes with onion rings

1½ lb (675 g) old potatoes
1 large onion
2½ oz (65 g) butter *or* vegetable margarine
2 teaspoons (10 ml) chopped rosemary

Preheat the oven to Reg 6/400°F/200°C. Scrub the potatoes and cut them into ¼ in (0.75 cm) slices. Slice the onion into rings. Use ½ oz (15 g) of the butter or margarine to thickly cover the base of a large, flat ovenproof dish. Evenly scatter in half the onion rings and all the chopped rosemary. Arrange the potato slices on top, overlapping if necessary. Melt the remaining butter in a saucepan or small frying pan on a very low heat without letting it foam. Mix the remaining onion into the pan, not to cook it but to coat it with butter. Spoon the onions and butter evenly over the potatoes. Put the dish into the oven for 1½ hours.

꒞   ꒞   ꒞

Jacket potatoes

Next best in flavour to the cut-roasted potatoes is always the potato baked in its jacket – the simplest way of all and probably the most nutritious.

Use sound, medium-to-large potatoes. Scrub them well and prick them 4 times with a fork. Lay them on a rack in an oven preheated to Reg 6/400°F/200°C and leave them for 1½–2 hours, depending on their size. Their inside should be soft and tasty and the outside lovely and crisp. Don't leave this skin on your plate

when you eat a baked potato – it's the best part. Be extravagant
and spread it with butter and eat it like a biscuit!

One word of warning – if you are cooking anything else in
the oven that gives off a lot of steam, the potato skin will be limp
and not crisp. The worst culprits are lentil loaves, stuffed
vegetables, moist breads and open casseroles.

Once your potatoes are cooked, either serve them whole and
have plenty of butter on the table, or cut them in half lengthways,
scoop out the middles and mash them with butter and various
herbs and flavourers. Try a few of these ideas and then go on to
experiment. The amounts are for 4 medium sized potatoes.

1. Mix in 2 oz (50 g) butter and 4 tablespoons (60 ml) chopped
    parsley and pile the mixture back into the potato shells.
    Scatter 1 tablespoon (15 ml) chopped onion over each potato
    half and return them to the oven for 20 minutes for the onions
    to brown.

2. Mix in 1 oz (25 g) butter and 4 tablespoons (60 ml) chopped
    parsley. Pile the potatoes back into the shells. Scatter with
    chopped onion as above and top with 4 oz (100 g) crumbled
    blue cheese.

3. Mix in 4 tablespoons (60 ml) mixed chopped parsley and
    sage, 4 tablespoons (60 ml) double cream and 2 oz (50 g)
    grated farmhouse Cheddar cheese. Pile the mixture back into
    the shells and top with 2 oz (50 g) cheese. Return the potatoes
    to the oven for the cheese to melt. (This makes more of a
    snack meal than a side dish.)

4. Mix in 4 tablespoons (60 ml) sour cream and 2 teaspoons
    (10 ml) dill seeds. Pile the potatoes back into their shells and
    return to the oven for 20 minutes for the tops to brown.

5. Mix in 5 tablespoons (75 ml) double cream and 1 bunch
    chopped watercress. Return to the oven for 10 minutes to
    heat through.

6. If butter and cream don't come into your diet, mix in 1
    tablespoon (15 ml) tahini and 4 tablespoons (60 ml) dry white
    wine or cider.

Jacket potatoes can also be flavoured as they bake. The following

recipe makes them look like small steam engines with a chimney!
– and also gently flavours them with fennel.

Baked potatoes with fennel stalks

8 medium-sized potatoes (or as many as you need)
8 1½-inch (4 cm) pieces dried fennel stalk (or 1 for each potato)
1 small knob of butter for each potato

Preheat the oven to Reg 6/400°F/200°C. Make a hole in the
upper side of each potato about ½ in (1.5 cm) in diameter and 1 in
(3 cm) deep. Fill the hole with butter and poke in a piece of fennel
stalk. Lay the potatoes on the oven rack and bake them for 1½
hours. About half an hour before the end, push the stalks farther
into the potatoes. Serve the potatoes with the stalk still inserted in
them and a little more butter pressed in if wished.
Alternative: with a sharp knife make a deep slit in one flat side
of each potato going about ¾ of the way through. Insert a bayleaf
as far as you can in the slit and bake the potatoes for 1½ hours.
Serve them with the bayleaves still inside and hand the butter
separately.

Smaller potatoes can be cut in half lengthways and laid, cut-side
down, in an ovenproof dish with a little melted butter or oil.
This way you get the best effects of both roasting and baking with
a firm, crispy skin, a buttery, crisp underneath and a soft, melt-in-
the-mouth texture inside. Again, you can flavour them in a
number of ways.
1. Scatter 2 teaspoons (10 ml) paprika evenly over the dish
   before putting in the potatoes.
2. Cover the base with bayleaves or dried fennel stalks.
3. Lay some rosemary sprigs under the potatoes.
4. Scatter in 2 teaspoons (10 ml) caraway or dill seeds.

To finish our section on old potatoes, here are two recipes for
golden, crinkly-edged potato cakes, one for egg-eaters and the
other for vegans.

Potato and parsley cakes

1½ lb (675 g) potatoes
2 eggs, beaten
4 tablespoons (60 ml) chopped parsley
sea salt and freshly ground black pepper
1½ oz (40 g) butter
6 tablespoons (90 ml) olive oil

Boil half the potatoes in their skins. Drain them, and peel them as
soon as they are cool enough to handle. Mash them well and beat
in the eggs, parsley and seasoning. Peel the remaining potatoes
and grate them immediately into the mashed ones, mixing them
in as you go to stop them discolouring. Heat half the butter and
oil in a heavy saucepan on a low heat. When the butter has
melted, put in the potato mixture in blobs of 1 tablespoon (15 ml)
at a time and flatten them down to flat cakes about ¼ inch (0.75
cm) thick. Cook them until the underside is golden brown, then
turn them over and brown the other side. Remove them and keep
them warm. When half the potato mixture is used up, add the
remaining butter and oil and cook the other half. You should
get about 16 cakes.

Half and half potato cakes

2 lb (900 g) potatoes
2 oz (50 g) butter *or* vegetable margarine
1 teaspoon (5 ml) bicarbonate of soda
4 tablespoons (60 ml) chopped spring onions, chives or Welsh
    onions
sea salt
freshly ground black pepper
2 oz (50 g) butter *or* 8 tablespoons (120 ml) oil for frying

Boil half the potatoes in their skins. Drain them, and peel them
while they are still warm. Mash them well. Peel the remaining
potatoes and grate them into the cooked ones, mixing them in
as you go to prevent them discolouring. Beat in 2 oz (50 g) butter
or margarine, the bicarbonate of soda, spring onions or chives
and seasonings. Heat half the butter or oil in a large frying pan

on a low heat. Put in the potato mixture in 1 tablespoon (15 ml) blobs and flatten these down into flat cakes about ¼ in (0.75 cm) thick. Fry them until the underside is golden brown. Turn them over and brown the other side. Carry on with the rest of the potatoes adding more butter or oil as and when you need it.

New potatoes

Small is beautiful when it comes to new potatoes. The tiniest of all always seem to have the best flavour. Simply wash them before cooking and boil them in lightly salted water until they are just tender. Toss them with melted butter and chopped parsley, mint, chives or fennel, or a mixture of parsley and mint, mint and chives, or fennel and parsley, or try some chervil instead. Like this you have a perfect simple, summer dish.

If you would rather, you can peel them before serving; or you can slice them, especially if they are on the larger side. In both cases they can be folded gently with melted butter and herbs.

Here they are peeled and given a pungent sauce of wine and mint.

New potatoes with wine and mint

1½ lb (675 g) new baby potatoes
1½ oz (40 g) butter
6 tablespoons (90 ml) dry white wine
2 tablespoons (30 ml) chopped mint

Boil the potatoes in their skins until they are only just tender. Drain them, and peel them while they are still warm. Warm the butter and wine together in a saucepan on a low heat. When the butter has melted, turn the potatoes in the resulting sauce and add the mint. Cover and set on the lowest heat possible for 2 minutes for the flavours to penetrate the potatoes.

Sautéd new potatoes

New potatoes are better for sautéing than old ones as they stay nice and firm. Boil them until they are only just tender. Peel them while they are still warm and cut them in half lengthways so you get two flat pieces. Then cut these into halves or quarters depending on the size of the potatoes. Fry them on a moderate heat in a mixture of oil and butter until they are golden brown, moving them around for most of the time.

As an additional touch, sprinkle over a little mustard powder while they are cooking or add some sliced onion or chopped spring onions to the pan.

Grilled new potatoes

Grilling is another tasty way of finishing off boiled new potatoes. Boil them, peel them and cut them in half lengthways to make two flat pieces. Brush these all over with melted butter or with olive oil, and grill them under a preheated, high grill, cut-side up first so they brown. Turn them over and either grill the rounded side plain or spread over some tomato purée, some plain English mustard or one of the spicy kinds, or a mixture of the purée and mustard. You can also scatter over a little paprika, or grated Parmesan cheese.

Simmered new potatoes

If you have a heavy saucepan or casserole with a tight-fitting lid, you can simmer new potatoes in butter and their own steam without any added liquid. Use 1½ oz (40 g) butter to every 1½ lb (675 g) potatoes. Melt the butter, stir in the potatoes, cover and simmer for 30 minutes, shaking the pan occasionally to make sure they cook evenly and don't stick.

Add chopped herbs or 1 teaspoon (5 ml) of a spice such as cumin or paprika for flavour, or cook the potatoes with mushrooms.

New potatoes with mushrooms and lemon

1½ lb (675 g) new baby potatoes
6 oz (175 g) mushrooms (flat ones)
1½ oz (40 g) butter

2 tablespoons (30 ml) mixed chopped thyme and chives
juice ½ lemon

Wash the potatoes. Thinly slice the mushrooms. Melt the butter
in a heavy saucepan (an enamel one is best) on a low heat. Put
in the potatoes and roll them around to coat them with butter.
Put the mushrooms and herbs on top. Cover the pan tightly and
set it on a low heat for 30 minutes, shaking the pan frequently.
Remove the lid, pour in the lemon juice and let it bubble. Serve
as soon as you can.

New-potato salads

Spicy new-potato salads go well with summery meals, and you
can have them both hot and cold. Whichever way, boil the
potatoes and peel them as soon as you can handle them. Then
mix them into the dressing while they are still warm so it soaks
in and flavours and moistens them nicely. Use mayonnaise, or a
simple French dressing flavoured with chopped herbs or a
flavoured mustard.

Here is a hot salad using mayonnaise and white wine.

New potatoes with white wine mayonnaise

1½ lb (675 g) new baby potatoes
¼ pint (150 ml) dry white wine
3 tablespoons (75 g) mayonnaise
2 tablespoons (30 ml) chopped chives

Boil the potatoes in their skins until they are just tender. Drain
them and peel them while they are still warm. Put them back
into the saucepan and pour in the wine. Bring it to the boil on
a moderate heat and let it reduce by half. Gently fold in the
mayonnaise and chives and serve.

This salad can be served hot or cold, but it is still necessary to
heat it first to let all the flavours blend.

Hot potato and raisin salad

1½ lb (675 g) new baby potatoes
2 tablespoons (30 ml) olive oil
1 tablespoon (15 ml) white wine vinegar
1 tablespoon (15 ml) tomato purée
1 teaspoon (5 ml) paprika
1 teaspoon (5 ml) Tabasco sauce
2 tablespoons (30 ml) seedless raisins

Mix the oil, vinegar, tomato purée, paprika and Tabasco sauce
together. Add the raisins and let everything stand for 30 minutes.
Boil the potatoes in their skins until they are just tender. Drain
them, and peel them while they are still warm. Put them back
into the saucepan and gently fold in the dressing and raisins.
Heat the salad through gently on a low heat. Either serve hot or
let the dish cool completely.

This delicious cold potato salad has a spicy, curry-like flavour
combined with the nuttiness of poppy seeds.

Spiced potato salad

1½ lb (675 g) new baby potatoes
1 clove garlic, crushed with a pinch sea salt
1 teaspoon (5 ml) ground cumin
1 teaspoon (5 ml) ground coriander
1 tablespoon (15 ml) poppy seeds
4 tablespoons (60 ml) olive oil
2 tablespoons (30 ml) white wine vinegar

Boil the potatoes in their skins until they are tender. Make the
dressing while they are cooking. Put the garlic, spices and poppy
seeds into a bowl and beat in first the oil and then the vinegar.
Drain the potatoes and let them steam dry. Slice them, without
peeling, while they are still hot. Coat them with the dressing
and let them cool completely. Turn them over just before serving
to distribute the dressing evenly once more.

Salads

No matter how well you cook vegetables and how tasty and attractive you can make them, the best way of serving a good many of them is raw, with a dressing that complements their flavours. While I was preparing this book, I found that the more I made main courses from vegetables, the less I wanted a cooked vegetable accompaniment and the more I fancied, and felt that I actually needed, a salad during some stage of the meal. And so salad recipes were devised for first course, main course and accompaniments. Before I knew where I was they had run away with me and there were over two hundred – almost enough for a complete salad book!

Nearly everyone, however, has their own favourite salad vegetables and combinations of vegetables, and a formula for a dressing that suits their taste and always works. Sometimes, too, you can be restricted by the availability of ingredients, and in general salads seem very much dependent on the inspiration of the moment. So I've decided to give just a few hints on ingredients and dressings for the side salads with definite recipes only for first courses, main courses and the hot and cooked salads which are more unusual.

Side salads

The different combinations of vegetables that can be used for side salads must be endless. Try all the ones that are most commonly served raw, both the familiar and the more exotic, and experiment a little to find out which you like best together. Don't forget, either, to use any fruits that are in season; and if you see anything unusual in the greengrocers that you haven't tried before, buy it and see what you can make with it.

Here are some ideas that may spark off a salad inspiration:
grated raw beetroot and grated apple
Brussels sprouts with satsumas, or grapefruit, with a little sliced
    leek or with pickled onions
white cabbage with celery, grated carrot, green peppers, apples,
    grapes, pears, orange or grapefruit
red cabbage with grated beetroot, apples, coarsely grated carrot
Chinese cabbage and grapes.
grated carrots and chopped green peppers
grated carrot and grated swede
cauliflower and celery or apples
equal parts of celery and celeriac, both chopped
celeriac, white cabbage and apples
celery and red and green peppers
chicory with orange or grapefruit
cress and tomatoes
raw courgettes, very thinly sliced, with raw mushrooms or
    tomatoes
curly endive or the less curly Batavia with red peppers
Florence fennel with green peppers and apples
a firm summer lettuce with chopped cucumber and a chopped
    lemon, or with raspberries, redcurrants or blackberries
lettuce and sorrel
raw mushrooms with mustard and cress
raw young green peas and thinly sliced new carrots in mayonnaise
watercress with green peppers, tomatoes, orange, mustard and
    cress or winter radish
grated turnip and grated apple; grated turnip and watercress
radishes, dandelions and watercress, using radish leaves as well

Additions:

Besides your main ingredients, make your salad even better by
adding any of these in fairly small quantities:
nuts – particularly peanuts and chopped walnuts
sesame seeds
poppy seeds

dried fruits – currants, raisins, chopped dried apricots, chopped dates

pickles – large Hungarian gherkins, dill cucumbers, pickled onions, pickled walnuts, capers (all chopped)

a very little diced or grated cheese

Dressings:

The basic French dressing is made from oil (olive is the best) and an acid (either vinegar or citrus juice).

There is not really one type of vinegar that is better than the rest. Each has its own particular flavour so try to choose the one that goes best with your main ingredients. Tarragon vinegar is the mildest and is best with vegetables that have a delicate flavour and with salads that contain fruits such as raspberries or pears. White wine vinegar is probably the most universal as it has no really pronounced flavour and goes with almost any vegetable. I tend to put red wine vinegar into salads made from red vegetables (red cabbage and beetroot) but it is also excellent with the more robust lettuces and with curly endive. Cider vinegar is perfect for any salad that contains apples, and also for white cabbage, celery and celeriac. Use malt vinegar carefully and only with the more robust salad ingredients as it can overpower the delicate ones.

The proportions that I normally use for the simple dressing base are:

4 tablespoons (60 ml) olive oil

2 tablespoons (30 ml) vinegar

   or juice 1 lemon

   or juice ½ large sweet orange (Spanish ones are best)

   or juice 1 medium-sized Seville orange

   or (if I'm lucky enough to find them) juice 2 limes

If you find this a little sharp you can safely add 1–2 tablespoons (15–30 ml) more oil.

Once you have your base, flavour it with small amounts of other ingredients that go with your main vegetables.

I rarely make a salad without garlic and for the proportions above use 1 really large clove or 2 small ones, crushing them with a pinch of sea salt, with the point of a small, sharp knife.

If you think garlic would not go with the rest of the meal then try other members of the onion family:

thinly sliced shallots

thinly sliced small onions

thinly sliced leeks (up to 1 leek is enough)

chopped chives

chopped spring onions, scallions or Welsh onions

If you have not crushed the garlic with salt add a pinch of sea salt on its own. The other essential ingredient (unless you are using a hot spice) is freshly ground black pepper.

These are all you really need to make an acceptable dressing for any salad, but don't let the ideas stop there, for there are more flavourers waiting to be used:

1 teaspoon (5 ml) paprika (good with tomatoes, red and green peppers)

1 teaspoon (5 ml) curry powder (try with cauliflower, salads that contain apples and dried apricots, chicory)

1 teaspoon (5 ml) cinnamon (try with white cabbage, celery and salads that contain apples and pears)

1 teaspoon (5 ml) mustard powder (try with Brussels sprouts, curly endive, grated turnips)

2 teaspoons (10 ml) of the milder whole-grain mustards or 1 teaspoon (5 ml) of the stronger (chosen carefully these go with almost anything)

1 tablespoon (15 ml) dry white wine (try with grape and orange salads)

1 tablespoon (15 ml) dry red wine (try with red cabbage and beetroot salads)

1 tablespoon (15 ml) tomato purée (try with any salad that contains red and green peppers)

1 teaspoon (5 ml) Tabasco sauce (use this in conjunction with paprika)

1 tablespoon (15 ml) Worcester sauce (good with Brussels sprouts, cheesy salads and cabbage and celery; NOT with

pineapple – some strange chemical effect supercharges the
hotness)

1 tablespoon (15 ml) tamari sauce (gives a rich, caramel-type
flavour to any salad)

any combination of seasonal herbs chosen to go with your
main dish and with the salad vegetables, using up to 4
tablespoons (60 ml) of the milder herbs and 2 tablespoons
(30 ml) of the stronger

1 tablespoon (15 ml) tahini for a nutty flavour (add this carefully and gradually)

1 tablespoon (15 ml) peanut butter (add this like tahini)

1 tablespoon (15 ml) curd or cream cheese or some crumbled
or grated blue cheese.

2 teaspoons (10 ml) dill or caraway seeds (try dill with
cucumber, caraway with cabbage).

For a change from the basic oil and vinegar dressing use 6
tablespoons (90 ml) natural yoghurt or 4 tablespoons (60 ml)
yoghurt beaten with 2 tablespoons (30 ml) oil. Flavour as you
would a French dressing.

An excellent dressing can also be made by mashing 2 ripe
bananas with 4 tablespoons (60 ml) cider vinegar and some
crushed garlic. Use it for watercress, green peppers, celery, white
cabbage and carrot salads and those that contain apples.

For a creamy but still refreshing flavour, mix 4 tablespoons
(60 ml) sour cream with the juice of ½ lemon, season with pepper
and add garlic crushed with sea salt. A very little soft brown
sugar can also be added to this one. (About ½ teaspoon, 2.5 ml).

Wherever a recipe states mayonnaise, use a home-made one as
the flavour is so much better than the bought kinds. If you don't
use eggs, here is a recipe for a mayonnaise made with soya flour
which can be used wherever mayonnaise is stated.

Soya mayonnaise

1 tablespoon (15 ml) soya flour
2 teaspoons (10 ml) mustard powder
¼ pint (150 ml) warm water

8 tablespoons (120 ml) olive oil
2 tablespoons (30 ml) white wine vinegar or cider vinegar

Put the flour and mustard into a small saucepan. Using a wooden spoon, gradually stir in the water. Set the pan on a very low heat and keep stirring until the mixture boils. With the constant agitation this will take about 10 minutes. Simmer on the lowest heat possible, stirring frequently but not all the time, for 5 minutes. Let the mixture cool. Put this base-sauce into a bowl and gradually beat in first the oil and then the vinegar. Lastly mix in any herbs or spices that you fancy for your salad.

N.B. Should the oil curdle the sauce, leave it standing for about half an hour and then whisk it furiously as though you were punishing it! Carry on with the rest of the oil and it should blend in perfectly.

❧   ❧   ❧

Cooked salads

You can also make side salads by cooking certain vegetables in olive oil and then adding the sharp part of the dressing.

Try it with broad beans and make a refreshing, summery dressing with yoghurt and lemon.

Broad bean and lemon salad

2 lb (900 g) broad beans (weighed before shelling)
3 tablespoons (45 ml) olive oil
½ carton natural yoghurt
juice 1 lemon
2 tablespoons (30 ml) chopped parsley

Shell the beans and put them into a heavy saucepan with the oil. Cover them and set them on a low heat for 15 minutes, stirring occasionally. Take the pan from the heat and let the beans cool a little. Mix in the yoghurt, lemon juice and parsley and let the salad get quite cold before serving. On a really hot day serve it slightly chilled.

Mint and white wine vinegar are all that you need to go with fresh young peas and new carrots.

Cooked carrot, pea and mint salad

1 lb (450 g) new carrots
1 lb (450 g) peas (weighed before shelling)
2 sprigs mint
6 tablespoons (90 ml) olive oil
3 tablespoons (45 ml) white wine vinegar
3 tablespoons (45 ml) chopped mint

Thinly slice the carrots. Shell the peas and reserve 4 of the best pods. Put the oil into a saucepan and warm it on a low heat. Mix in the carrots, peas, pods and mint sprigs. Cover, and simmer gently for 15 minutes, stirring occasionally. Take the pan from the heat, remove the pods and mint sprigs and stir in the vinegar and chopped mint. Let the salad get quite cold before serving.

In this recipe, marrow is cooked with oil and tomatoes to give it a sharp thick red sauce with an Italian flavour.

Marrow salad in tomato sauce

1 small marrow weighing 1½–2 lb (675–900 g)
4 tablespoons (60 ml) olive oil
1 large onion, thinly sliced
1 large clove garlic, finely chopped
8 oz (225 g) ripe tomatoes, scalded, skinned and chopped
1 tablespoon (15 ml) tomato purée
either 1 tablespoon (15 ml) chopped thyme
   or 1 tablespoon (15 ml) chopped basil (this is best if it's available)
2 tablespoons (30 ml) white wine vinegar

Peel the marrow and cut it in half lengthways. Scoop out the seeds and slice each half into pieces ¼ in (0.75 cm) thick. Heat the oil in a large saucepan on a low heat, stir in the onion and garlic and cook them gently for 10 minutes, covered. Add the tomatoes and simmer, still covered, for 5 minutes more. Stir in the tomato purée and thyme or basil and then mix in the marrow.

Cover and simmer for 10 minutes, stirring occasionally. Stir in the vinegar and either serve the salad hot or turn it out to cool completely.

Preserve the delicate flavour of sweetcorn and French beans with wine and a little chopped savory.

Corn and French bean salad

2 corn cobs
12 oz (350 g) French beans
4 tablespoons (60 ml) olive oil
1 medium onion, thinly sliced
1 tablespoon (15 ml) chopped savory
4 tablespoons (60 ml) dry white wine

Cut the corn from the cobs. Top and tail the beans and break them into 1 in (3 cm) lengths. Heat the oil in a saucepan on a low heat. Stir in the corn, beans, onion and savory. Cover them and cook them gently for 15 minutes, stirring occasionally. Pour in the wine and bring it to the boil. Turn the salad into a bowl and let it cool completely before serving.

ş   ş   ş

Hot side salads

Any of the combinations of ingredients and flavourers that are used for ordinary cold side salads can be used for hot ones. Start off by cooking the vegetables quickly with the oil and then add the vinegar or fruit juice. Let it bubble and take the pan from the heat. It's best to prepare hot salads just before you serve them as the vegetables go limp and slightly watery and all their individual character disappears if they are kept warm too long. They are, however, so quick to make that you can easily do it between courses without any panic if all the ingredients are prepared and collected together beforehand.

When it comes to flavourers, put garlic, dill or caraway seeds, ground spices, sliced onions and dried fruits into the pan with the vegetables and add any other flavourers with the second part of the dressing. Nuts go into the pan just before the vinegar and sesame seeds can be added either with the vegetables or, as in the following recipe, toasted first.

Hot Brussels sprout and sesame seed salad

1 lb (450 g) small, nutty, Brussels sprouts
2 tablespoons (30 ml) sesame seeds
4 tablespoons (60 ml) olive oil
1 large clove garlic, finely chopped
2 tablespoons (30 ml) white wine vinegar

Trim and thinly slice the sprouts. Put the sesame seeds into a heavy frying pan without any oil. Set them on a moderate heat and move them around constantly until they brown and start to pop and jump about. Add the oil to the pan and let it heat up. Put in the sprouts and garlic and move them around on the heat for 1 minute. Pour in the vinegar and let it bubble. Remove the pan from the heat and serve the salad as soon as you can.

White cabbage and pears make a mild-flavoured, refreshing salad that goes superbly with nuts and mild cheese.

Hot white cabbage and pear salad

½ medium-sized white cabbage
2 large, very firm Conference pears (or 4 small ones)
6 allspice berries
10 black peppercorns
4 tablespoons (60 ml) olive oil
1 medium onion, thinly sliced
1 large clove garlic, finely chopped
1 tablespoon (15 ml) chopped fresh tarragon, or 2 teaspoons (10 ml)
   crumbled dried tarragon (during the winter)
2 tablespoons (30 ml) tarragon vinegar

Shred the cabbage. Quarter and core the pears and cut them into pieces about 1 in (3 cm) long and ½ in (1.5 cm) wide. Crush the allspice and peppercorns together. Heat the oil in a frying pan on a low heat. Stir in the onion and garlic and cook them until the onion is soft. Raise the heat to moderate and mix in the cabbage, pears, tarragon, crushed spices and dried tarragon, if you are using it. Stir them around on the heat for 2 minutes so the cabbage just begins to wilt. Pour in the vinegar and let it bubble, and mix in the fresh tarragon. Take the pan from the heat and serve the salad as soon as possible.

Here is a robust and rich salad with red cabbage, red wine vinegar and sour cream.

Hot red cabbage, apple and caraway salad

½ medium-sized red cabbage
2 medium-sized cooking apples
2 tablespoons (30 ml) red wine vinegar
2 tablespoons (30 ml) sour cream
3 tablespoons (45 ml) olive oil
1 large clove garlic, finely chopped
2 teaspoons (10 ml) caraway seeds

Shred the cabbage finely. Quarter, core and slice the apples. Mix the vinegar and cream together. Heat the oil in a large frying pan or paella pan on a moderate heat. Put in the cabbage, garlic and caraway seeds and stir them around on the heat for about 2 minutes, so the cabbage just begins to darken and wilt. Pour in the vinegar and sour cream, stir them around on the heat and let them bubble. Serve as soon as you can.

Carrots, leeks, currants and mustard sound quite incongruous, but in a hot salad they work.

Hot carrot and leek salad

8 oz (225 g) carrots
8 oz (225 g) leeks
2 tablespoons (30 ml) white wine vinegar
2 teaspoons (10 ml) English Vineyard mustard
4 tablespoons (60 ml) olive oil
2 oz (50 g) currants

Slice the carrots paper thin. Wash and thinly slice the leeks. Mix the vinegar and mustard together. Heat the oil in a frying pan on a high heat. Put in the carrots, leeks and currants and move them around in the pan for 2 minutes. Stir in the vinegar and mustard, let them bubble and serve immediately.

Celery and apples go together hot or cold.

Hot celery and apple salad

1 small head celery
2 medium-sized cooking apples
4 tablespoons (60 ml) sour cream
juice 1 lemon
1 teaspoon (5 ml) soft brown sugar
4 tablespoons (60 ml) olive oil
1 large clove garlic, finely chopped
2 tablespoons (30 ml) finely chopped celery leaves

Chop the celery. Quarter, core and thinly slice the apples. Mix the cream, lemon juice and sugar together. Heat the oil in a large frying pan or paella pan on a high heat. Put in the celery, apples and garlic and move them around on the heat for $\frac{1}{2}$ minute so they heat through but the celery stays crunchy and the apples firm. Stir in the sour cream mixture and let it bubble. Serve the salad immediately with the chopped celery leaves scattered over the top.

For a complete change, cucumber, fennel (the herb) and spring onions make a hot salad in late spring or summer.

Hot cucumber and spring onion salad

1 large cucumber
6 large spring onions
2 tablespoons (30 ml) white wine vinegar
1 teaspoon (5 ml) mustard powder
4 tablespoons (60 ml) olive oil
2 tablespoons (30 ml) chopped fennel

Wipe the cucumber and cut it into round slices about $\frac{1}{8}$ in

(3 mm) thick. Chop the spring onions into ½ in (1.5 cm) lengths, using both white and green parts. Mix the vinegar and mustard together. Heat the oil in a large frying pan on a high heat. Put in the onions and cucumber and stir them around until the onions just start to soften. Mix in the chopped fennel and quickly stir in the vinegar. Let it bubble and take the pan from the heat.

Making a hot salad is a very similar process to the Chinese methods of stir-frying and stir-braising, so it is not surprising that Chinese cabbage is ideally cooked this way. Here is a simple recipe with orange.

Hot Chinese cabbage and orange salad

½ medium-sized Chinese cabbage (slice it lengthways into 2)
2 large oranges
2 tablespoons (30 ml) white wine vinegar
4 tablespoons (60 ml) olive oil
1 large clove garlic, finely chopped

Chop the cabbage into 1 in (3 cm) pieces. Cut the rind and pith from one of the oranges. Cut it into lengthways quarters and slice it thinly. Squeeze the juice from the other orange and mix it with the vinegar. Put the oil and garlic into a large frying pan and set it on a moderate heat. When the oil is warm, add the cabbage and move it around until it just begins to wilt. Pour in the orange juice and vinegar and let them bubble. Quickly mix in the sliced orange and serve the salad immediately.

Curly endive is one of my favourite salad vegetables. It's like a more robust and flavoursome lettuce and can be used in the winter instead of the delicate cabbage lettuces that are not really worth having. It is also far better for hot salads. As an alternative you can use the less curly batavia for this salad.

Hot endive salad

1 small curly endive (or ½ large one – they are often rather enormous!)

2 tablespoons (30 ml) white wine vinegar
1 teaspoon (5 ml) Tabasco sauce
4 tablespoons (60 ml) olive oil
1 large clove garlic, finely chopped

Break the endive into separate leaves. Mix the vinegar and Tabasco sauce together. Heat the oil and garlic in a large frying pan on a high heat until the garlic just begins to brown. Mix in the endive and stir it around for ½ minute. Pour in the vinegar and Tabasco sauce, let them bubble and serve the salad immediately.

The next salad, with Florence fennel, makes an excellent side dish, or it could be served as a first course before a substantial meal such as one based on pasta.

Hot fennel salad with sesame seeds and lemon

2 medium-sized bulbs fennel weighing together around 1 lb (450 g)
4 tablespoons (60 ml) olive oil
1 large clove garlic, finely chopped
2 tablespoons (30 ml) sesame seeds
grated rind and juice 1 lemon

Chop the fennel. Heat the oil in a frying pan on a high heat. Put in the fennel, garlic and sesame seeds and cook them quickly, moving them around all the time, until they begin to brown. Add the lemon rind and juice. Let the juice bubble and serve as soon as you can.

This orange and tomato salad goes well with egg dishes and quiches.

Hot orange and tomato salad

2 medium oranges
1 lb (450 g) firm tomatoes
2 tablespoons (30 ml) white wine vinegar
2 teaspoons (10 ml) Dijon mustard
4 tablespoons (60 ml) olive oil

1 large clove garlic, finely chopped
2 tablespoons (30 ml) chopped lemon thyme, or thyme

Remove the peel and pith from the oranges, cut them in half lengthways and thinly slice them. Slice the tomatoes into rounds. Mix the vinegar and mustard together. Heat the oil in a large frying pan on a high heat. Put in the garlic and let it brown. *Quickly* stir in the oranges, tomatoes and herbs and heat them through without letting them soften. Stir in the vinegar mixture and bring it to the boil, then serve the salad immediately.

🌿   🌿   🌿

First-course salads

When cooked vegetables make up the main meal, start off with a refreshing salad. This first one is good and substantial, ideal served before pottage dishes or before omelets or scrambled eggs. You could even serve it as a light lunch or double all the ingredients and make it into a main meal.

Avocado, orange and celery salad

2 avocado pears
3 Spanish oranges
2 large sticks celery
4 tablespoons (60 ml) olive oil
1 clove garlic, crushed with a pinch sea salt
1 tablespoon (15 ml) chopped thyme
lettuce leaves for serving

Cut the pears in half and remove the stones. Peel each half and then cut each one in half lengthways again. Thinly slice each piece crossways. Cut the peel and pith from 2 of the oranges, cut them into lengthways quarters and slice them. Finely chop the celery. Put the pears, oranges and celery into a bowl. Squeeze the juice from the remaining orange and mix it with the oil, garlic and thyme. Fold the dressing into the salad and let it stand for 15 minutes. Arrange some lettuce leaves on 4 serving plates and pile the salad on top.

When nuts are the main feature of a salad use freshly shelled ones, if you have the time. This one was made the first time with Kent Cobs that were practically straight from the tree. The tahini makes it really substantial, but the grapes provide a refreshing contrast.

Nutty grape and cabbage salad

½ medium-sized green cabbage
4 oz (125 g) white grapes
1 tablespoon (15 ml) tahini
2 tablespoons (30 ml) tarragon vinegar
4 oz (125 g) freshly shelled Kent Cobs or hazel nuts

Shred the cabbage. Halve and de-seed the grapes and put them into a bowl with the cabbage. Gently work the tahini into the tarragon vinegar and mix them into the salad. Divide it between 4 small bowls and scatter the nuts over the top.

Carrots make an unusual filling for melon, and the melon juice itself provides a moist, fruity dressing that is sufficient on its own.

Melon, carrot and sesame salad

1 large, ripe honeydew melon
8 oz (225 g) carrots
1 tablespoon (15 ml) tahini
2 tablespoons (30 ml) sesame seeds
1 oz (25 g) currants

Cut the melon into quarters and scoop out the seeds. Scoop out about half the flesh from each quarter, chop it finely and put it into a bowl with any juice that has collected. Grate in the carrots and mix in the tahini, sesame seeds and currants. Put the mixture back into the melon quarters and re-shape them into wedges.

Carrots go surprisingly well with all kinds of fruit. Here is a completely different salad with grapefruit and yoghurt.

Carrot, grapefruit and yoghurt salad

8 oz (225 g) carrots
2 large grapefruit
2 oz (50 g) raisins
1 large clove garlic, crushed with a pinch sea salt
freshly ground black pepper
2 cartons natural yoghurt

Peel the grapefruit, divide into segments and chop. Grate the carrots and put them into a bowl with the grapefruit and raisins. Mix the garlic and pepper into the yoghurt and then fold it into the rest of the ingredients. Serve in small bowls.
N.B. This salad is best served very cold. If the yoghurt is taken straight from the refrigerator and the salad is served immediately it will be just right. If not, chill the whole lot together and serve it in bowls of room temperature.

Raw cauliflower makes a crunchy first-course salad if it is left in whole fleurettes and softened very slightly first by marinating in a lemony dressing.

Raw cauliflower coated in cheese

1 small to medium cauliflower
4 tablespoons (60 ml) olive oil
juice ½ lemon
8 oz (225 g) curd cheese
2 tablespoons (30 ml) wheatgerm

Use the head of the cauliflower only and break it into small fleurettes. Mix the oil and lemon juice together and marinate the cauliflower in this dressing for 2 hours, turning it several times. Lift it out with a perforated spoon (and save the dressing for another salad). Spread the curd cheese over the white part of each fleurette. Lay the fleurettes on a serving dish and sprinkle the wheatgerm over the top.

Celery, celeriac and sesame seeds make a nutty and substantial salad.

Celery, celeriac and sesame seed salad

6 oz (175 g) celeriac
4 large sticks celery
4 tablespoons (60 ml) sesame seeds
2 tablespoons (30 ml) tamari sauce
2 tablespoons (30 ml) cider vinegar
4 tablespoons (60 ml) olive oil
2 medium-sized tart eating apples (use ones with red-tinged skins
    for a super appearance)

Grate the celeriac and chop the celery. Mix them in a bowl with the sesame seeds. Beat the tamari sauce, vinegar and oil together and fold them into the salad. Either divide it between 4 small bowls or put it into 1 large one. Quarter and core the apples and thinly slice them lengthways. Arrange them round the salad and serve immediately.

Celeriac is a good vegetable for hot salads. Here we have the hot celeriac spooned over fresh lettuce, with a tarragon-flavoured dressing coating them both.

Hot and cold celeriac salad

8 oz (225 g) celeriac
1 lettuce
2 teaspoons (10 ml) Dijon mustard
4 tablespoons (60 ml) tarragon vinegar
4 tablespoons (60 ml) olive oil
1 clove garlic, finely chopped
1 box mustard and cress

Cut the celeriac into matchstick pieces. Tear the lettuce into small pieces and arrange them in 1 large salad bowl or 4 small ones. Mix the mustard and vinegar together. Heat the oil in a frying pan on a moderate heat. Put in the celeriac and garlic and cook them for five minutes, moving them around constantly. The celeriac should just soften but not colour. Pour in the vinegar mixture and let it bubble. Cut up the mustard-and-cress, mix it in and spoon everything over the lettuce.

A hot, nutty dressing made with walnuts makes an excellent dressing for fresh, raw fennel.

Raw fennel with hot walnut and lemon dressing

2 medium-sized bulbs fennel weighing together about 1 lb (450 g)
4 oz (125 g) walnuts
4 tablespoons (60 ml) olive oil
1 large clove garlic, finely chopped
juice 2 lemons (or 1 really large, juicy one)

Chop the fennel and divide it between 4 small serving bowls. Finely chop the walnuts. Heat the oil in a frying pan on a high heat, put in the walnuts and garlic and brown them quickly, moving them around all the time. Pour in the lemon juice and let it bubble. Spoon all the contents of the pan over the fennel and serve the salads immediately.

This salad is hot and cold again, but the main vegetable, the salsify, is cooked completely so you get a lovely contrast between its soft, melty texture and the crisp batavia. The buttery, lemony dressing coats everything deliciously.

Salsify salad

1 lb (450 g) salsify *or* black scorzonera
½ batavia (or 1 cabbage lettuce if none is available)
2 oz (50 g) butter
4 tablespoons (60 ml) chopped parsley
juice 1 lemon
Alternative: Jerusalem artichokes make a good substitute for salsify

Scrub the salsify and cut it into 6 in (25 cm) lengths (or smaller if you are using a small saucepan). Cook it in boiling salted water for 15 minutes. Drain it, and peel it while it is still warm. Cut it into ½ in (1.5 cm) slices. Tear the batavia or lettuce into small pieces and arrange it in 4 serving bowls. Melt the butter in a saucepan on a very low heat, so it doesn't foam. Add the parsley and lemon juice and fold in the salsify. Let it heat through and spoon it over the batavia.

This next salad, with succulent mushrooms and light cucumber, makes a surprisingly satisfying first course.

Mushroom and cucumber salad

1 lb (450 g) very fresh open mushrooms
½ small cucumber (or ¼ large one)
4 tablespoons (60 ml) natural yoghurt
2 tablespoons (30 ml) olive oil
1 tablespoon (15 ml) chopped capers
grated rind 1 lemon
3 tablespoons (45 ml) chopped parsley
1 bunch watercress or 1 small lettuce for serving

Thinly slice the mushrooms. Cut the cucumber into quarters lengthways and slice each quarter. Beat the yoghurt, oil, capers, lemon rind and 2 tablespoons (30 ml) of the parsley together. Fold them into the mushrooms and cucumber and let the salad stand for 30 minutes. Arrange a bed of lettuce or watercress on 4 small serving plates and spoon the salad on top. Scatter over the remaining parsley.

Although the last salad can be served at any time of the year, cucumber and yoghurt always seem very summery, so add some strawberries to complete the picture.

Strawberry and cucumber salad

1 carton natural yoghurt
1 large cucumber
1 large clove garlic, crushed with a pinch sea salt
freshly ground black pepper
8 oz (225 g) strawberries

Put the yoghurt into a bowl. Cut 12 thin slices from the cucumber for garnish and grate the rest into the yoghurt. Mix in the garlic and pepper. Reserve 8 small strawberries, quarter the rest and mix the quartered ones into the salad. Put the salad into 4 small serving bowls and garnish with the reserved cucumber slices and strawberries.

In July, August and September you can buy the more robust flavoured ridge cucumbers, that can be chopped or sliced and put into side-salads hot or cold, and into main course dishes. They can also be hollowed out and stuffed to make a first course. They come in all degrees of width and length. For the following recipe, I found two fairly short ones, but you could also use 1 really long one cut in half. Keep about ¼ in (0.75 cm) of the seeds in the cut end to make the boat shape. If you find the skins of ridge cucumbers a little bitter (they may be towards the end of the season), peel them first.

Ridge cucumbers stuffed with Caerphilly and walnuts

2 ridge cucumbers about 6 in (18 cm) long and quite fat
6 oz (175 g) Caerphilly cheese
3 oz (75 g) chopped walnuts

Cut the cucumbers in half lengthways, scoop out the seeds and discard them. Scoop out the flesh, leaving 4 thin shells, and chop it. Grate the cheese into a bowl and mix in the walnuts and chopped cucumbers. Press the mixture back into the shells and serve.

Should you be successful in growing basil, and have some left over from your tomato soup, use it in tomato salads to give a sweet and pungent flavour. Here the tomatoes are put with peaches in a creamy dressing which is matched by the creamy-coloured almonds.

Peach, almond and tomato salad

4 small peaches
4 oz (125 g) almonds
12 oz (350 g) firm tomatoes
2 tablespoons (30 ml) chopped basil
4 tablespoons (60 ml) double cream
2 tablespoons (30 ml) white wine vinegar
or, instead of the cream and vinegar, 6 tablespoons soya mayonnaise made with white wine vinegar
1 teaspoon (5 ml) paprika

freshly ground black pepper
1 large clove garlic, crushed with a pinch sea salt

Chop the peaches. Blanch and split the almonds. Chop the tomatoes. Put them in a bowl with the basil. Mix together the cream and vinegar (or soya mayonnaise), the paprika, pepper and garlic, and fold them into the salad. Serve from 1 large bowl or in 4 small ones.

A pineapple adds a touch of luxury to any table. Make salads that contain it as simple as possible to preserve all the flavour.

Pineapple, tomato and peanut butter salad

1 small pineapple
4 large, firm tomatoes
4 tablespoons (60 ml) crunchy peanut butter
1 large clove garlic, crushed with a pinch sea salt
1 tablespoon (15 ml) chopped thyme

Cut the husk from the pineapple. Cut the flesh into 8 rings and stamp out the cores. Finely chop 2 of the tomatoes and mix them with the peanut butter, garlic and thyme. Slice each of the remaining tomatoes into 4 rings. Spread the peanut butter mixture evenly over each pineapple slice and put a tomato ring in the centre of each one.

The first, new, tart apples of the season are ideal for salads. (At other times of the year, cookers are often the best.) And when apples first arrive, there are plenty of English green peppers around. The lovage isn't essential but do use it if you have some in the garden to give a spicy, celery-like flavour.

New apple, green pepper, peanut and raisin salad

2 large George Cave (or any other early green) apples
2 medium-sized green peppers
4 oz (125 g) peanuts
4 oz (125 g) raisins
2 teaspoons (10 ml) poppy seeds

1 tablespoon (15 ml) chopped lovage
2 tablespoons (30 ml) cider vinegar
2 tablespoons (30 ml) olive oil
1 large clove garlic, crushed with a pinch sea salt
freshly ground black pepper

Quarter, core and chop the apples. Core and chop the peppers.
Put them into a bowl with the peanuts, raisins, poppy seeds and
lovage. Mix the vinegar, oil, garlic and pepper together and fold
the dressing into the salad. Serve it in 4 small bowls.

Kent Cobs are not sold only in Kent (although we do have a large
share of them). The new ones reach most parts of the country
and are fresh, white and milky. It is well worth spending some
time shelling enough for a salad. This simple recipe brings out
the best in fresh nuts.

Simple cob-nut salad

8 oz (225 g) Kent Cobs (weighed before shelling)
1 small firm lettuce (Density or Webbs)
4 sticks new celery
2 tablespoons (30 ml) sour cream and 2 tablespoons (30 ml) cider
    vinegar (or 4 tablespoons (60 ml) soya mayonnaise made with
    cider vinegar)

Shell the nuts. Shred the lettuce and chop the celery. Mix these
two together and divide them between 4 small bowls. Mix the
sour cream and vinegar together and fold them into the salads.
Scatter the nuts on top.

Grapefruit can be bought all the year round. It makes a first
course in itself or can be combined with other ingredients into
salads both simple and complicated. Here is a simple one. Use
either ordinary or soya mayonnaise.

Grapefruit and watercress mayonnaise

2 grapefruit
2 bunches watercress

4 tablespoons (60 ml) mayonnaise
1 tablespoon (15 ml) Worcestershire sauce or Yorkshire Relish

Peel the grapefruit, pull them into segments and chop each one
into three or four pieces, depending on their size. Chop half the
watercress and put it in a bowl together with the grapefruit and
any juices that have run from it. (These will combine with the
mayonnaise to make the dressing.) Mix the mayonnaise and
Worcestershire sauce together and fold them into the grapefruit
and watercress. Arrange the remaining watercress on 4 serving
plates and spoon the salad on top.

This salad uses bananas to make a sort of dip for the pieces of
pepper and watercress.

Pepper, watercress and banana salad

2 medium-sized green peppers
1 bunch watercress
2 ripe bananas
2 green chillis
6 tablespoons (90 ml) olive oil
3 tablespoons (45 ml) cider vinegar
2 teaspoons (10 ml) tomato purée
1 clove garlic, crushed with a pinch sea salt

Core and chop the peppers. Break the watercress into small
pieces. Mash the bananas. Core the chillis and chop them very
finely. Mix them into the bananas. Put the watercress and peppers
into a bowl. Combine the oil, vinegar, tomato purée and garlic to
make the dressing. Mix 2 tablespoons (30 ml) of the dressing into
the bananas and fold the rest into the peppers and watercress.
Divide the peppers and cress between 4 small serving plates.
Spoon the banana mixture in the centre of each one.

The large-rooted winter radishes are more fiery than the spring
and summer ones. They are also a little tougher so slice them
very thinly or chop them into tiny dice. They go very well with
grated horseradish and, conveniently enough, their seasons coin-

cide. The contrast to these strong flavours is given here by the creamy dressing and mild Derby cheese.

Winter radish and Derby salad

4 winter radishes weighing together around 1 lb (450 g)
1 carton sour cream
2 tablespoons (30 ml) white wine vinegar
2 teaspoons (10 ml) grated horseradish
4 oz (100 g) grated white Derby cheese

Scrub the radishes and cut each one in half lengthways. Cut them into very thin slices. Mix the cream, vinegar, horseradish and cheese together and fold them into the radishes. Serve the salad in small bowls.

Here is a way of combining two other winter ingredients – curly endive and Seville oranges.

Seville cheese salad

4 oz (125 g) curd cheese
grated rind and juice 1 Seville orange
1 clove garlic, crushed with a pinch sea salt
½ a curly endive
24 cob or hazel nuts

Cream the cheese in a bowl and work in the orange rind and juice and the garlic. Break the endive into leaves and arrange them in 4 small bowls or on 4 small serving plates. Put a blob of the cheese mixture on top of each one and top each with 6 hazel nuts.

ℨ   ℨ   ℨ

Main course salads

Main course salads are refreshing and welcome at all times of the year and, like all salads, depend very much on individual tastes and moods. To make them irresistible, buy all kinds of unusual cheeses and different nuts and crunchy seeds. Mix them together or serve them separately in portions large enough to satisfy the heartiest eaters. If you find the amounts given here too little or too great, adjust them accordingly.

Main course salads probably look most attractive if they are served from one large bowl, but often, with the crunchier vegetables especially, different people like different amounts. There are those (myself included!) who can easily crunch their way through platefuls, whereas others (perhaps those who are not quite so used to them) can only manage a little. As it is important that everyone eats their fair share of the protein part of the meal (be it nuts or cheese) it might be a good idea to serve the main vegetable part in one large bowl so everyone can take as much (or as little) as they wish, and the rest in small individual bowls or on small plates. There is, however, no definite rule, so find a way to best suit the occasion and the eaters.

Accompany the following salads with hot or cold potato dishes, a savoury bread or a salad made from one of the pulses.

Avocado pears are one of the few vegetables that can actually make up a complete meal without the addition of any other kind of protein. Here are two salads using them, the first with mushrooms in a lemony dressing.

Avocado and mushroom salad

8 oz (225 g) mushrooms
juice 2 small lemons (or 1 large one)
6 tablespoons (90 ml) olive oil
2 teaspoons (10 ml) Dijon mustard
1 clove garlic, crushed with a pinch sea salt
3 boxes mustard and cress
4 firm avocado pears
2 tablespoons (30 ml) chopped parsley

Thinly slice the mushrooms. Mix the lemon juice, oil, garlic and mustard together for the dressing and fold it into the mushrooms. Leave them to stand for 30 minutes, turning them several times. Stone and peel the avocados and cut them into long, thin, lengthways slices. Arrange a bed of cress on 4 serving plates, and arrange the avocado slices on top. Mix the parsley into the mushrooms and spoon them over the avocados.

This avocado salad is filled out with cottage cheese, but if you are a vegan it is not absolutely essential, and the dollops of flavoured cheese may be left out.

Avocado and cottage cheese salad

4 firm avocado pears
2 bunches watercress
2 boxes mustard and cress
dressing:
   1 tablespoon (15 ml) tomato purée
   1 clove garlic, crushed with a pinch sea salt
   1 teaspoon (5 ml) paprika
   6 tablespoons (90 ml) olive oil
   3 tablespoons (45 ml) white wine vinegar
8 oz (225 g) cottage cheese
1 tablespoon (15 ml) tomato purée
1 teaspoon (5 ml) paprika
1 teaspoon (5 ml) Tabasco sauce

Chop the watercress and cut all the mustard and cress from the boxes. Put the tomato purée for the dressing into a small bowl and beat in the garlic, 1 teaspoon (5 ml) paprika, oil and vinegar. Mix half the dressing into the cresses. Mix the cottage cheese with the second tablespoon (15 ml) tomato purée, second teaspoon (5 ml) paprika and Tabasco sauce. Halve and stone the avocados, cut them into quarters lengthways and peel them. Arrange a base of the cress salad on 4 serving plates. Arrange the cheese and the pieces of avocado attractively on top. Spoon the remaining dressing over the avocados only.

Sunflower seeds can be used like nuts in salads. Try this one for a superb combination of colours and flavours.

Sunflower and pomegranate salad

8 oz (225 g) small, nutty Brussels sprouts

8 large sticks white celery
2 pomegranates
¼ pint (150 ml) mayonnaise (egg or soya)
8 oz (225 g) sunflower seeds

Thinly slice the Brussels sprouts, chop the celery and put them together in a bowl. Take the seeds from the pomegranates and put them in a separate bowl. Spoon 2 tablespoons (30 ml) of the mayonnaise into the pomegranate seeds and the rest into the celery and Brussels sprouts. Scatter the pomegranate seeds on top of the main salad. Either scatter the sunflower seeds on top of these, or hand them separately in small dishes.

This next salad is given its special individuality by the cinnamon.

Cob-nut, date and cinnamon salad

8 oz (225 g) shelled cob or hazel nuts
2 oz (50 g) chopped dates (weighed without stones)
4 large sticks celery
½ small white cabbage
2 medium-sized cooking apples
either 1 carton sour cream and 2 tablespoons (30 ml) cider vinegar
or ¼ pint (150 ml) soya mayonnaise made with cider vinegar
1 clove garlic crushed with a pinch sea salt
freshly ground black pepper
1 teaspoon (5 ml) ground cinnamon

Mix the nuts and dates together. Chop the celery and finely shred the cabbage: quarter, core and slice the apples, and put all together in a salad bowl. Beat the cream and vinegar together and add the garlic, pepper and cinnamon. (Or mix the last three into the soya mayonnaise.) Fold the dressing into the salad. Either scatter the nuts and dates on top or serve them separately.

Here a selection of delicate coloured vegetables and fruit contrast with brown nuts and sultanas.

White winter salad with walnuts

¼ medium-sized white cabbage
½ small cauliflower
4 sticks white celery
4 oz (125 g) white grapes
2 tart eating or small mellow cooking apples
¼ pint (150 ml) mayonnaise (egg or soya)
1 tablespoon (15 ml) chopped thyme
8 oz (225 g) walnuts
3 oz (75 g) sultanas

Shred the cabbage finely and chop the cauliflower and celery. Halve and de-seed the grapes. Quarter, core and thinly slice the apples. Put all these into a large salad bowl and mix in the mayonnaise and thyme. Mix the walnuts and sultanas together and either scatter them over the top of the salad or serve them in separate dishes.

It is always important to make salads look attractive, so wherever you can use contrasting and matching colours, as in this red and white recipe. If you can't buy Red Windsor cheese, choose a mild white one such as Lancashire or Derby rather than a discordant orange or yellow.

Red and white cheese salad

½ small white cabbage
1 medium-sized beetroot weighing around 6 oz (175 g)
2 pomegranates (if available, not absolutely essential)
8 oz (225 g) Red Windsor cheese
dressing:
4 tablespoons (60 ml) sour cream
2 tablespoons (30 ml) red wine vinegar
6 allspice berries
6 black peppercorns
1 clove garlic, crushed with a pinch sea salt

Shred the cabbage finely and put it into a salad bowl. Grate the beetroot and add this. Take the seeds from the pomegranates and add these. Mix everything together. Cut the cheese into ½ in

(1 cm) dice. Beat the sour cream and vinegar together. Crush the allspice berries and peppercorns. Add these to the cream and vinegar with the garlic and fold the dressing into the salad. Either scatter the cubes of cheese over the top or serve them separately.

Here is a completely different red and white salad made of crunchy crimson cabbage with sweet and savoury toppings.

Winter cheese and coconut salad

½ medium-sized red cabbage
8 oz (225 g) beetroot
1 carton sour cream
4 tablespoons (60 ml) red wine vinegar
3 juniper berries
3 allspice berries
1 large clove garlic, finely chopped
1 large pinch sea salt
6 oz (175 g) fresh coconut
12 black olives
4 oz (125 g) black grapes
12 oz (350 g) cottage cheese

Shred the cabbage finely. Grate the beetroot. Put them together in a salad bowl. Mix the sour cream and vinegar together. Crush the spices, garlic and salt together and mix them into the dressing. Fold it into the salad and let the bowl stand for 30 minutes.

Grate the coconut. Stone and quarter the olives and mix them into the coconut. Halve and de-seed the grapes and mix them into the cheese. Arrange half the salad on four serving plates and arrange the coconut and cheese mixtures on top. Serve the rest of the salad separately.

Alternative: if you don't eat cheese, use twice as much coconut and twice as many olives. Keep the grapes but mix them into the salad.

In this slimming but very substantial salad, cottage cheese again makes up one of the main ingredients.

Hazel-nut and carrot salad

6 oz (175 g) shelled hazel-nuts (fresh if possible)
8 oz (225 g) grated carrots
8 oz (225 g) cottage cheese
4 tablespoons (60 ml) cider vinegar
for serving:
watercress, mustard and cress or lettuce (or a mixture)

Mix the hazelnuts, carrots, cottage cheese and vinegar together and pile them on top of the green cresses or lettuce. It couldn't be easier, but it tastes no less good for that.

Chopped cauliflower is far less crunchy to eat than you might think. The white parts almost melt in your mouth. Cashew nuts are creamy flavoured and slightly sweet so the creamy dressing and the mild cheese in this salad make excellent accompaniments. The angelica isn't essential but it does add a little extra touch if you have some in the herb garden.

Cauliflower, Caerphilly and cashew salad

1 medium-sized cauliflower
6 oz (175 g) Caerphilly cheese
6 oz (175 g) cashew nut pieces
either 4 tablespoons (60 ml) double cream *and* 2 tablespoons (30 ml) white wine vinegar
or 6 tablespoons (90 ml) soya mayonnaise
½ teaspoon (2.5 ml) mustard powder
2 tablespoons (30 ml) chopped angelica leaves (optional extra)

Finely chop the cauliflower and dice the cheese. Put them both into a bowl with the cashew nuts. Mix the cream, vinegar and mustard powder together (or mix the mustard powder with the soya mayonnaise) and stir them into the salad. Scatter the angelica leaves over the top.

Cauliflower goes well with curry spices as long as they are not too strong. This salad uses yellow turmeric and has mango chutney for a touch of sweetness.

Two-flower and chutney salad

1 large cauliflower
2 large Cox's apples
6 tablespoons (90 ml) olive oil
2 tablespoons (30 ml) cider vinegar
1 clove garlic, crushed with a pinch sea salt
1 tablespoon (15 ml) mango chutney (or any fruity home-made chutney)
1 teaspoon (5 ml) ground turmeric
8 oz (225 g) sunflower seeds

Finely chop the cauliflower. Quarter, core and chop the apples and put them with the cauliflower in a bowl. Mix the oil, vinegar, garlic, chutney and turmeric together and fold them into the salad. Either scatter the sunflower seeds on top or serve them in separate dishes. (Serving them separately may not be necessary as raw cauliflower is very easily eaten so everyone will probably take roughly the same amount.)

Chinese cabbage needs to be sharpened slightly with fruit and spicy dressings.

Chinese cabbage, cheese and grape salad

10 large Chinese cabbage leaves
8 oz (225 g) white grapes
8 oz (225 g) red Cheshire cheese (red makes a good contrasting colour)
dressing:
1 egg yolk
1 teaspoon (5 ml) Dijon mustard
4 fl oz (125 ml) olive oil
1 tablespoon plus 1 teaspoon (20 ml in all) tarragon vinegar
1 tablespoon (15 ml) chopped tarragon

Break the cabbage leaves into small pieces. Halve and de-seed the grapes. Dice the cheese. Put all these into a salad bowl. Put the egg yolk into a small mixing bowl and work in the mustard. Gradually add 1 tablespoon (15 ml) of the oil. Beat in 1 teaspoon

(5 ml) of the vinegar and then gradually add the rest of the oil.
Beat in the remaining vinegar and the chopped tarragon. Fold
the dressing into the salad.

Here are two endive salads, one with cheese and one without.
If endive is unobtainable use a cos lettuce instead.

Endive, red pepper and Edam salad

1 large curly endive
2 medium-sized red peppers
8 oz (225 g) Edam cheese
4 tablespoons (60 ml) olive oil
2 tablespoons (30 ml) cider vinegar
1 large clove garlic, crushed with a pinch sea salt
1 teaspoon (5 ml) paprika
1 teaspoon (5 ml) Tabasco sauce
2 teaspoons (10 ml) dill seeds
1 really large or two medium-sized Bramley apples

Break the endive into small pieces. Core and chop the peppers.
Dice the cheese into $\frac{1}{2}$ in (1 cm) pieces. Put the endive into one
bowl and the peppers and cheese into another. Mix the oil,
vinegar, garlic, paprika, Tabasco sauce and dill seeds together
to make the dressing and fold half into the endive and half into
the peppers and cheese. Arrange the endive on 4 serving plates
and pile the cheese and peppers in the middle of each one.
Quarter and core the apples and cut them into thin lengthways
slices. Arrange them around the cheese and serve immediately.

Endive, apricot and peanut salad

1 large curly endive
4 tablespoons (60 ml) olive oil
grated rind and juice 1 medium orange
2 tablespoons (30 ml) white wine vinegar
1 tablespoon (15 ml) tomato purée
1 large clove garlic, crushed with a pinch sea salt
4 oz (125 g) dried apricots
8 oz (225 g) peanuts (roasted, not salted)

Break the endive into small pieces and put it in a bowl. Mix the oil, orange rind and juice, vinegar, tomato purée and garlic together and fold the resulting dressing into the salad. Finely chop the apricots and mix half of these and half the peanuts into the endive. Divide the salad between 4 serving plates and scatter the remaining peanuts and apricots over the top.

Fennel tastes so good and is sometimes so difficult to find in provincial shops that it is always best served as simply as possible so you can appreciate its lovely aniseedy flavour. Walnuts and garlic seem to go with it naturally. Add just a few olives so the salad is flecked with colour and flavour, and top it with a mild cream cheese.

Fennel, cream cheese and walnut salad

2 large bulbs fennel together weighing 1–1½ lb (450–675 g)
8 green olives
4 tablespoons (60 ml) olive oil
1 clove garlic, crushed with a pinch sea salt
freshly ground black pepper
8 oz (225 g) Somerset soft cheese (or any other sweet cream cheese)
8 oz (225 g) chopped walnuts

Chop the fennel. Stone and chop the olives, and put them in a bowl with the fennel. Mix the oil, vinegar, garlic and pepper together and stir them into the salad. Arrange the salad on 4 serving plates. Put a blob of cheese on the top of each one and surround it with walnuts.

New potatoes make an attractive filling salad. Put them with cheese for a main course.

New potato and cheese salad

1½ lb (675 g) new baby potatoes
3 tablespoons (45 ml) olive oil
1 tablespoon (15 ml) white wine vinegar
1½ tablespoons (25 ml) Worcestershire sauce or Yorkshire Relish

8 oz (225 g) grated white Derby or Lancashire cheese
1 large Webb's lettuce
1 lb (450 g) firm tomatoes
1 box mustard and cress

Wash the potatoes and boil them in their skins. While they are cooking, mix the oil, vinegar and Worcestershire sauce together. Drain the potatoes and peel and slice them as soon as they are cool enough to handle. Fold them into the dressing, taking care not to break them up too much. Fold in the cheese and let the salad get completely cool. Separate the lettuce into leaves and arrange these on a flat serving dish. Slice the tomatoes into rounds. Just before serving, mix the cress into the potato salad and then pile it on top of the lettuce. Arrange the tomato slices round the edge.

Main course salads don't have to be complicated to be good. The following ones are simplicity itself.

Brussels sprouts and Stilton salad

1 lb (450 g) small, nutty Brussels sprouts
8 oz (225 g) Stilton cheese
1 clove garlic, crushed with a pinch sea salt
6 tablespoons (90 ml) mayonnaise

Trim the sprouts and thinly slice them. Dice the Stilton into very small pieces. Mix the sprouts and Stilton in a bowl. Mix the garlic into the mayonnaise and fold it into the salad.

Red Leicester and tomato salad

8–12 oz (225–350 g) Red Leicester cheese
1 lb (450 g) tomatoes
8 pickled onions
10 chopped sorrel leaves
4 tablespoons (60 ml) olive oil
2 tablespoons (30 ml) malt vinegar

Dice the cheese into ½ in (1 cm) pieces. Chop the tomatoes into pieces a similar size. Finely chop the pickled onions. Put all these into a bowl with the sorrel. Blend the oil and vinegar together and mix them into the salad.

This is one of the most beautiful looking and tasting salads you could possibly wish for. If ever you wanted to persuade someone that a salad is not just a few lettuce leaves, this should be the way to do it.

Pineapple, salted almond and watercress salad

8 oz (225 g) almonds
1 tablespoon (15 ml) sea salt
6 tablespoons (90 ml) olive oil
1 medium to large pineapple
2 bunches watercress
2 tablespoons (30 ml) white wine vinegar
1 clove garlic, crushed with a pinch sea salt
1 teaspoon (5 ml) paprika

Blanch the almonds and squeeze them out of their skins. Scatter the sea salt on a piece of doubly-folded kitchen paper. Heat 4 tablespoons (60 ml) of the oil in a heavy frying pan on a moderate heat. Put in the almonds and fry them until they are a rich, golden brown, moving and turning them all the time. Lift them onto the salted paper and turn them in the salt, then let them cool.

Cut the husk from the pineapple. Slice the flesh into rings and stamp out the cores. Chop the flesh into chunks about ¾ in (2 cm) square. Chop the watercress and put it into a bowl with the pineapple. Mix the remaining oil with the vinegar, garlic and paprika and fold them into the pineapple and watercress. Arrange this salad on 4 serving plates and scatter the almonds equally over each portion.

My last salad is the best of all, whatever your normal eating habits. Serve it at any time and for any course. It's the most marvellous pick-me-up and refresher I know. If you have a hangover, have stayed out too late, eaten too much or over-worked make it up in large quantities, varying the proportions of ingredients as you like. Have it for lunch, or have it in the evening and go to bed early – next morning you'll be as right as rain!

All-in-together salad

½ small white cabbage
4 large sticks celery
1 medium-sized cooking apple
1 large Spanish orange
4 satsumas or clementines
6 oz (175 g) peanuts
4 oz (125 g) raisins
4 tablespoons (60 ml) olive oil
2 tablespoons (30 ml) cider vinegar
1 large clove garlic, crushed with a pinch sea salt
freshly ground black pepper

Shred the cabbage. Chop the celery. Quarter, core and chop the apple. Cut the rind and pith from the orange; cut the rest into lengthways quarters and slice them thinly. Pull the satsumas or clementines into segments. Put everything into a large salad bowl with the peanuts and raisins. Mix the oil, vinegar, garlic and pepper together and fold them into the salad.

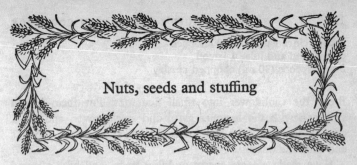

Nuts, seeds and stuffing

The recipes in this section contain no dairy products and no pulses, and yet every one of them is filling and delicious.

Nuts are an important source of protein in vegetarian diets and as well as featuring in salads can be put into cooked dishes in all kinds of ways. But there are no nut cutlets here as I have tried to use nuts, in conjunction with other vegetables, in ways that leave them a recognisable part of the meal. Nut dishes can be surprisingly inexpensive to make. Although by the pound their price is high, you need relatively few to fill you up and satisfy. With some of the richer ones, such as pine nuts, you even have to be careful not to use too many as their flavour when cooked can be quite over-powering. Nuts are an ingredient few non-vegetarians make the most of and I am glad that this book has made me discover how good they can be.

Cauliflower always makes good meatless meals and it goes really well with nuts. A simple way of making a nutty cauliflower dish is to cook the vegetable until it is just tender and then brown it quickly with some peanuts or blanched almonds. This recipe takes the idea a little further to make a nutty mould good enough for the best of dinner parties.

Cauliflower and nut mould

2 small or 1 medium-sized cauliflowers
bouquet garni
6 tablespoons (90 ml) stock
3 oz (75 g) almonds
3 oz (75 g) walnuts
2 tablespoons (30 ml) sesame seeds
4 tablespoons (60 ml) olive oil

1 large clove garlic, finely chopped
grated rind and juice 1 lemon
2 tablespoons (30 ml) chopped parsley

Break the cauliflower into small fleurettes. Put them into a saucepan with the bouquet garni and stock, cover, and set it on a moderate heat for 20 minutes. Blanch and split the almonds and chop the walnuts.

Have ready a large, warm pudding basin, and heat a round serving plate. Heat the oil in a frying pan on a high heat. Put in the cauliflower and garlic and brown them quickly, then transfer them to the pudding basin. Lower the heat under the pan to moderate. Put in the nuts and sesame seeds and brown them, moving them around constantly. Quickly add the lemon rind and juice and parsley. Mix all the contents of the pan into the cauliflower. Press everything down fairly hard and cover the top of the basin with a warm, flat plate. Leave the mould in a warm place for 1 minute and then turn it out onto the plate. It should hold together and look perfect as you take it to the table, but it collapses as soon as it is cut so serve it quickly.

Nuts can be tossed into any type of cooked green cabbage and then heated through fairly quickly. They go well with the Primo cabbages that are available in the summer and the autumn and that can be made into cooked salad dishes (to be served hot) by simmering in an oil and vinegar dressing. Another good Primo cabbage dish can be made when the first new cooking apples come into season. They will cook down to a fairly sharp pulp that binds the cabbage almost like kneaded butter. At any other time of the year, make it with a hard white cabbage and Bramley apples.

Primo cabbage with apples and peanuts

1 medium-sized Primo cabbage
1 large clove garlic, finely chopped
3 tablespoons (45 ml) olive oil
2 tablespoons (30 ml) white wine vinegar

freshly ground black pepper
2 Grenadier or other new cooking apples
8 oz (225 g) peanuts

Shred the cabbage. Put it into a saucepan with the garlic, oil,
vinegar and pepper. Cover the pan and set it on a low heat for
10 minutes. While it is cooking, peel, quarter, core and slice the
apples. Stir them into the pan with the peanuts. Cover the pan
again and cook for 5 minutes more.

Here is a beautiful, shiny green dish of spinach flecked with
golden cashews. These are another nut which can be very rich
so I have only used 6 oz (175 g). If you find this too little, then
the amount can easily be increased to 8 oz (225 g).

Spinach and cashew nuts

2 lb (900 g) spinach
1½ oz (40 g) butter *or* vegetable margarine
6 oz (175 g) cashew nut pieces

Break the stems from the spinach and put the leaves into a saucepan with only the water that clings to them after washing. Cover
and set the pan on a low heat for 15 minutes, stirring the spinach
occasionally. Drain it well and press down hard to extract as
much liquid as possible. Turn it onto a board and chop it finely.
Melt the butter or margarine in a frying pan on a moderate heat.
Put in the cashew pieces and fry them until they are a golden
brown, moving them around constantly. Mix the spinach into
the nuts and keep cooking for a further 2 minutes, still moving
everything around. An ideal accompaniment to this dish is baked
or grilled tomato halves.

The texture of aubergines makes them almost meals in themselves. Any more nuts in this dish would make it far too rich.

Aubergine and nut crumble

4 medium-sized aubergines

1 tablespoon (15 ml) sea salt
1 lb (450 g) tomatoes
4 tablespoons (60 ml) olive oil
2 large onions, thinly sliced
1 large clove garlic, finely chopped
½ pint (275 ml) stock
1 tablespoon (15 ml) tomato purée
1½ oz (40 g) pine nuts
2 oz (50 g) chopped walnuts
2 tablespoons (30 ml) sesame seeds
4 tablespoons (60 ml) wheatgerm

Slice the aubergines into ½ in (1 cm) rounds. Put them into a colander and sprinkle them with the salt. Leave them to drain for 30 minutes, wash them with cold water and pat them dry with kitchen paper.

Preheat the oven to Reg 6/400°F/200°C. Slice the tomatoes into rounds. Heat half the oil in a frying pan on a moderate heat. Put in the aubergine slices and cook them through, turning them once. (You will probably have to do this in 2 batches and add a further tablespoon (15 ml) of oil with the second batch.) Remove the aubergines and set them aside. Lower the heat under the pan and put in the remaining oil. Put in the onions and garlic and cook them until the onions are soft. Pour in the stock and bring it to the boil. Stir in the tomato purée and take the pan from the heat. Put half the aubergine slices in the bottom of a large pie dish and cover them with half the onions and stock. Lay on half the tomatoes and scatter in all the pine nuts and walnuts evenly. Lay on the remaining tomatoes and then the rest of the aubergines. Spoon in all the remaining onions and stock. Mix the sesame seeds and wheatgerm together and sprinkle them over the top. Bake the crumble for 30 minutes.

Aubergines can also be stuffed with various fillings. This recipe is based on the Middle Eastern dish called Imam Bayeldi. The almonds give a soft creamy flavour, but for a pungent change you can use 3 oz (75 g) pine nuts instead. There will then be no need to blanch and sliver them.

Aubergines full of almonds and tomatoes

8 small aubergines, each weighing around 4 ozs (100–125 g)
1 tablespoon (15 ml) fine sea salt
1½ lbs (675 g) tomatoes
4 oz (125 g) almonds
4 tablespoons (60 ml) olive oil
1 large onion, finely chopped
1 large clove garlic, finely chopped
2 oz (50 g) currants
2 tablespoons (30 ml) chopped parsley
1 teaspoon (5 ml) ground cumin
1 teaspoon (5 ml) ground coriander
8 tablespoons (120 ml) water

Cut each aubergine in half lengthways and scoop out all the flesh. Salt the shells and the flesh and put them in a colander to drain for 30 minutes. Scald and skin the tomatoes. Cut 8 of the smaller ones into 4 slices each (or if they are all large, cut 4 of them in half lengthways and then slice them in 4). De-seed and chop the rest. Blanch and sliver the almonds. Preheat the oven to Reg 4/350°F/180°C. Rinse the aubergines shells and flesh with cold water and pat them dry with kitchen paper. Discard the large seeds and finely chop the flesh. Heat 3 tablespoons (45 ml) olive oil in a frying pan on a low heat. Put in the aubergine shells and cook them until they are soft and pliable. Remove them and set them aside. Mix in the onion and garlic and cook them until the onion is soft. Mix the chopped aubergine into the pan and cook everything for 2 minutes more. Stir in the chopped tomatoes and currants and cook them until the tomatoes are soft and pulpy, stirring frequently. Mix in the almonds, parsley, cumin and coriander and take the pan from the heat. Carefully fill the cooked shells with the mixture and arrange the tomato slices on top. (2 on each half). Pack the aubergines in a wide-based casserole in a single layer. Mix the remaining tablespoon (15 ml) oil with the water and pour them round the aubergines. Cover the casserole and put it into the oven for 45 minutes. Serve with steamed brown rice.

N.B. If you haven't got a casserole big enough, use 2 and pour

1 tablespoon (15 ml) oil and 6 tablespoons (90 ml) water into each.

❧   ❧   ❧

The following two dishes are made in the Chinese style, and as Chinese meals often consist of a selection of smaller dishes rather than one large one they are given in half the quantities needed to make a main meal for 4 people. Serve these two together or one of these and one of the Chinese-style dishes in the pulses section. Accompany them with Chinese egg-fried rice or fried rice with turmeric.

Sweet and sour almonds with green peppers and pineapple

4 oz (125 g) almonds
1 medium-sized green pepper
½ small pineapple
1 tablespoon (15 ml) cornflour
2 teaspoons (10 ml) tamari sauce
5 tablespoons (75 ml) cider vinegar
1 tablespoon (15 ml) clear honey
3 tablespoons (45 ml) olive oil
1 large onion, finely chopped
1 large clove garlic, finely chopped

Blanch and split the almonds. Core the pepper and chop it into ½ in (1 cm) squares. Dice the pineapple. Blend the cornflour, tamari, vinegar and honey together. Heat the oil in a frying pan on a low heat. Put in the onion, garlic and green pepper and cook them until the onions are golden. Mix in the almonds and pineapple. Pour in the cornflour and let it simmer, stirring, until it thickens to a thick, glossy sauce.

Chinese cauliflower, carrots and cashews

1 very small cauliflower
4 oz (125 g) carrots
1 tablespoon (15 ml) cornflour

4 tablespoons (60 ml) dry sherry
½ pint (275 ml) stock
2 teaspoons (10 ml) tamari sauce
3 tablespoons (45 ml) olive oil
1 large onion, thinly sliced
1 large clove garlic, finely chopped
4 oz (125 g) cashew nut pieces
½ oz (15 g) fresh ginger root, grated or 1 teaspoon (5 ml) ground
   ginger (use the fresh ginger if you can find any – it's so much
   better)

Chop the cauliflower, keeping the fleurette shapes but making
the pieces very small (½–¾ in or 1–2 cm). Slice the carrots paper
thin. Put the cornflour in a bowl and gradually mix in the sherry,
stock and tamari. Heat the oil in a large frying pan on a
high heat. Put in the cauliflower, carrots, onion and garlic and
stir them around on the heat until they begin to brown. Lower
the heat to moderate. Stir in the cornflour mixture and then
the cashews and ginger. Cover the pan and keep it on the moderate heat for 10 minutes.

❧   ❧   ❧

It's good to wander through woods in early November, stamping
on the green, spiny chestnut shells and coming home loaded
with glossy brown nuts. Chestnuts have a flavour and texture
completely different from those of other nuts and it is well worth
having a peeling session for the delicious final dish. Always
remember, though, to give yourself enough time to get it done.
You can serve chestnuts whole, or you can mash them to a
purée to make stuffings and savoury loaves.

   They are the same size and shape as Brussels sprouts and the
two together can make a meal in themselves as well as a side dish.
Serve the following recipe with a savoury rice.

Brussels sprouts, onions and chestnuts

1 lb (450 g) Brussels sprouts
½ lb (225 g) button onions
1 lb (450 g) chestnuts

1 oz (25 g) butter
½ pint (275 ml) stock
freshly grated nutmeg
2 tablespoons (30 ml) chopped thyme

Nick the tops from the chestnuts and put them into a saucepan of water. Cover them, bring them to the boil and simmer for 10 minutes. Peel them, leaving them immersed until you get to them. (Otherwise the skins will harden back on.) Trim the sprouts. Peel the onions. Melt the butter in a saucepan on a low heat. Put in the onions and cook them until they are beginning to look transparent. Mix in the Brussels sprouts and chestnuts. Pour in the stock and bring it to the boil. Add the nutmeg and thyme. Cover the pan and keep it on a moderate heat for 20 minutes. All the stock should be absorbed and the vegetables and chestnuts just tender with a rich, slightly brown glaze.

This loaf is moist and savoury and excellent with a light salad and baked potatoes.

Chestnut and celery loaf

1 lb (450 g) chestnuts
1½ oz (40 g) butter or vegetable margarine
4 large sticks celery, finely chopped
1 large onion, finely chopped
1 clove garlic, finely chopped
¼ pint (150 ml) stock
grated rind and juice 1 lemon
1 tablespoon (15 ml) chopped parsley
1 tablespoon (15 ml) chopped thyme
1 tablespoon (15 ml) chopped marjoram
little more butter or margarine for greasing a 2 lb (900 g) loaf tin

Preheat the oven to Reg 4/350°F/180°C. Nick the tops from the chestnuts and put them into a saucepan of water. Set them on a moderate heat, bring them to the boil and simmer them for 20 minutes. Peel them, leaving them immersed until you come to each one. Chop them finely. Melt 1 oz (25 g) of the butter or margarine in a frying pan on a low heat. Put in the celery, onion and garlic and cook them until they are golden. Pour in the stock and bring it to the boil. Mix in the chestnuts, cover the pan and simmer for 10 minutes. Mix in the remaining butter or margarine and the lemon rind and juice. Take the pan from the heat and mix in the herbs. Press everything into the greased loaf tin. (The mixture will not fill it but is just too much for the 1 lb size.) Bake the loaf for 1 hour. Check after the first 30 minutes to see if it is drying too much; if so, cover the tin with foil. Turn the loaf onto a flat plate to serve.

As with Brussels sprouts, a few chestnuts are often added to red cabbage to make a side dish. Here they make a complete meal of beautiful, warming, contrasting colours – deep purple cabbage and golden nuts.

Chestnuts with red cabbage

8 prunes
¼ pint (150 ml) dry red wine
1¼ lb (565 g) chestnuts
½ lb (225 g) button onions (or, if not available, 2 thinly sliced
  medium onions)
1 small red cabbage
2 medium-sized cooking apples
4 tablespoons (60 ml) olive oil
2 tablespoons (30 ml) red wine vinegar

Soak the prunes in the wine for at least 4 hours. Stone and chop them. Nick the tops from the chestnuts and put them into a pan of cold water. Bring them to the boil and simmer them for 10 minutes, covered. Peel them, leaving them immersed until you get to each one.

Preheat the oven to Reg 6/400°F/200°C. Peel the onions. Shred the cabbage. Peel, quarter, core and slice the apples. Heat the oil in a flameproof casserole on a low heat. Put in the onions and cook them until they look transparent, turning them frequently. Stir in the chestnuts, cabbage, apples and prunes. Pour in the wine and vinegar and bring them to the boil. Cover the casserole and put it into the oven for 45 minutes. Serve with jacket-baked potatoes.

Here we have light-tasting cabbage and celery in wine, to contrast with a rich chestnut purée.

Savoy stuffed with chestnuts

1 large Savoy cabbage
1¼ lb (565 g) chestnuts
4 tablespoons (60 ml) olive oil
1 large onion, finely chopped
1 large clove garlic (or 2 small), finely chopped
4 large sticks celery, finely chopped
¼ pint (150 ml) dry white wine
1 tablespoon (15 ml) chopped thyme
1 tablespoon (15 ml) chopped marjoram

Nick the tops from the chestnuts, put them into a saucepan of water, cover them and bring them to the boil. Simmer them for 10 minutes. Peel them, leaving them immersed until you get to each one. Preheat the oven to Reg 5/375°F/190°C. Discard the tough outer leaves of the cabbage. Cut the main part in half lengthways and scoop the middle leaves leaving 2 shells about ½ in (1.5 cm) thick. Chop the scooped-out part. Chop the chestnuts finely.

Heat half the oil in a frying pan on a low heat. Put in half the onion, garlic and celery and cook them until they are golden. Mix in half the chestnuts and half the wine. Work everything together and mix in half the herbs. Take the pan from the heat and fill the cabbage halves with the chestnut mixture. Heat the remaining oil in a really large flameproof casserole on a low heat. Put in the remaining onion, garlic and celery and cook them until the onion is just beginning to soften. Stir in the shredded cabbage and add the remaining wine. Bring it to the boil and set the stuffed cabbage halves on top of the mixture, pushing in the bases so they are well-surrounded. Cover the casserole and put it into the oven for 45 minutes. Serve the cabbage halves on

the bed of celery and shredded cabbage, cutting each one in half
again at the table and giving a quarter to each person.

If you can find a fairly small pumpkin, then make one half into
a golden melt-in-the-mouth container for a tasty stuffing in which
the seeds are used as well.

Stuffed pumpkin

½ a 4½–5 lb (2–2¼ k) pumpkin, cut in half lengthways
2 oz (50 g) hazel nuts
1 oz (25 g) pine kernels
3 tablespoons (45 ml) olive oil
1 large onion, finely chopped
3 oz (75 g) granary or wholemeal breadcrumbs
1 tablespoon (15 ml) mixed chopped thyme and savory
1 tablespoon (15 ml) tomato purée
¼ pint (150 ml) stock
little oil for greasing

Preheat the oven to Reg 4/350°F/180°C. Discard the centre pith
of the pumpkin but reserve the seeds. Grind the hazel nuts and
pine nuts in a blender, grinder or nut mill. Heat the oil in a frying
pan on a moderate heat. Put in the pumpkin seeds and cook them
until they are golden, moving them around most of the time.
Remove them and set them aside. Lower the heat, put in the
onion and cook it until it is soft. Take the pan from the heat and
work in the milled nuts and breadcrumbs. Mix in the pumpkin
seeds, herbs and tomato purée and bind everything with the
stock. Put the mixture in the centre of the pumpkin. Lightly
brush the exposed cut surface of the pumpkin with a little oil.
Set it in an oiled baking tin and put it into the oven for 1½ hours.
Lift the pumpkin onto a warm serving dish and take it to the
table whole. Use a sharp knife and cut the pumpkin into large
wedges rather like those of a melon, keeping the stuffing in place
as best you can.
N.B. Although the skin of the pumpkin gets surprisingly soft and

tender when cooked for so long do warn people that it's best not eaten.

Marrow is another vegetable that can be filled with flavoursome stuffings. You can either fill the whole thing or cut it into rings and steam them before stuffing them separately and finishing them quickly under the grill. As marrow is light and fresh, it makes a perfect surrounding for a nutty filling.

Marrow with walnut and tomato stuffing

1 fairly small marrow weighing around 2½ lb (1.125 k), not too thick
1 sprig thyme
4 oz (125 g) walnuts
1 lb (450 g) firm tomatoes
1 oz (25 g) butter or vegetable margarine
1 large onion, finely chopped
1 clove garlic, finely chopped
2 oz (50 g) granary or wholemeal breadcrumbs
6 tablespoons (90 ml) dry white wine
1 tablespoon (15 ml) tomato purée
1 tablespoon (15 ml) chopped thyme

Cut the marrow into 12 rings about ½–¾ in (1–2 cm) thick. Peel them and scoop out their seeds. Steam them with the thyme sprig in a vegetable steamer or a colander covered with foil for 10 minutes. Lift them out and let them steam dry. Lay them on a flat, heatproof dish. (You may have to use 2 dishes or eventually cook them in two batches.)

Grind the nuts in a blender, grinder or nut mill. Scald and skin ½ lb (225 g) of the tomatoes. Squeeze out the seeds into a sieve, hold them over a bowl and rub with a wooden spoon to extract the juice. Finely chop the tomato flesh. Melt the butter or margarine in a frying pan on a low heat. Stir in the onion and garlic and cook them until they are golden. Take the pan from the heat and work in the nuts, crumbs, tomato purée, wine, thyme and reserved tomato juice. Gently mix in the chopped tomatoes. Press this mixture into the marrow rings. Cut the remaining tomatoes into thick slices. Preheat the grill to high, put under the dish of marrow and cook for 2 minutes or until the tops of the fillings are browned. Carefully turn the slices using a palette knife or fish-slice. Lay 1 large tomato slice or 2 small ones on top of each round. Put the dish back under the grill for a further 2 minutes.

꙳ ꙳ ꙳

Mushrooms make substantial vegetarian meals. Find two small marrows, fill them with curried mushrooms and serve a complete marrow boat to each person.

Marrow stuffed with curried mushrooms

2 small marrows weighing 1½ lb (675 g) each
2 bayleaves
1 lb (450 g) mushrooms
4 tablespoons (60 ml) olive oil
1 large onion, finely chopped
1 large or 2 small cloves garlic, finely chopped
2 teaspoons (10 ml) hot Madras curry powder
2 teaspoons (10 ml) fenugreek seeds (not absolutely essential but gives an unusual bitter flavour)
1 teaspoon (5 ml) ground turmeric
4 oz (125 g) granary or wholemeal breadcrumbs
3 tablespoons (45 ml) chopped parsley
¼ pint (150 ml) stock
little oil for basting
for serving:
Curry and lemon sauce made with 1 pint (575 ml) stock (see under sauces)

Cut the tops off the marrows, scoop out the seeds and peel them. Put a bayleaf inside each one. Steam the marrows and the caps in a large colander covered with foil for 20 minutes turning them once. (A vegetable steamer would probably be too small and even with a colander you may have to steam each marrow separately.) Carefully lift out the marrows and turn them on end so they drain well.

Preheat the oven to Reg 6/400°F/200°C. Finely chop the mushrooms. Heat the oil in a frying pan on a low heat. Stir in the onion, garlic, curry powder, fenugreek seeds and turmeric and cook them until the onion is soft. Raise the heat to moderate and mix in the mushrooms. Cook them for 1 minute stirring. Pour in the stock and bring it to the boil. Take the pan from the heat and work in the breadcrumbs and parsley. Put the pan back on the heat and stir for 1 minute so the breadcrumbs get thoroughly moistened. Take the pan from the heat and let everything cool a little. Press the stuffing into the marrows and anchor the tops with cocktail sticks. Brush the marrows with oil and put them into a roasting tin. Bake them for 30 minutes.

To serve: lay the marrows side by side on a really large serving dish. Cut them in half lengthways at the tables and give a complete half to each person. Hand the sauce separately.

❦ ❦ ❦

Here are three dishes which rely on miso to provide the protein part of the meal. Brussels sprouts are a filling little vegetable and a simple miso and nutmeg sauce is all that is necessary to make them into a complete meal. Serve them with a savoury rice.

Brussels sprouts with miso sauce

2 lb (900 g) Brussels sprouts
2 tablespoons (30 ml) olive oil
2 teaspoons (10 ml) soya flour
2 tablespoons (30 ml) miso
¾ pint (425 ml) stock
little freshly grated nutmeg
large pinch ground mace
2 tablespoons (30 ml) chopped parsley

Trim the sprouts. Heat the oil in a saucepan on a low heat. Stir in the flour and keep stirring until the mixture bubbles. Mix in the miso and blend in the stock. Season with the nutmeg and mace. Bring the sauce to the boil and add the sprouts. Cover and simmer for 20 minutes. Add the parsley just before serving.

Miso always seems to be cold-weather food, so here are two warming, hearty dishes made with root vegetables. The first has a nutty crumble topping.

Root vegetable crumble

12 oz (350 g) parsnips
1 lb (450 g) carrots
8 oz (225 g) white turnips
8 oz (225 g) swede
2 medium onions
1 oz (25 g) vegetable margarine
1 pint (575 ml) stock
2 tablespoons (30 ml) tomato purée
2 tablespoons (30 ml) grated horseradish
topping:
2 oz (50 g) vegetable margarine
2 oz (50 g) ground walnuts
2 oz (50 g) sesame seeds
2 oz (50 g) wheatgerm
4 tablespoons (60 ml) chopped mixed herbs

Preheat the oven to Reg 4/350°F/180°C. Chop the parsnips, carrots, turnips and swede into ½ in (1.5 cm) dice. Thinly slice the onions. Melt the margarine in a large flameproof casserole on a low heat, stir in all the vegetables, cover them and let them sweat for 10 minutes. Pour in the stock and bring it to the boil. Stir in the tomato purée and horseradish. Cover the casserole and put it into the oven for 30 minutes. Melt the margarine for the topping in a frying pan on a low heat. Stir in the milled walnuts, sesame seeds, wheatgerm and herbs and set the pan aside. Take the vegetables from the casserole and put them into a large pie dish. Spoon the topping evenly over the top and bake the crumble for 30 minutes.

The pastry for this pie is made with self-raising flour to give a really light and crumbly texture. Underneath are soft and tender root vegetables in a rich sauce.

Root vegetable and miso pie

½ lb (225 g) carrots
½ lb (225 g) swede
½ lb (225 g) white turnips
½ lb (225 g) parsnips
2 tablespoons (30 ml) olive oil
1¼ pints (700 ml) stock
2 tablespoons (30 ml) miso
1 tablespoon (15 ml) tomato purée
2 tablespoons (30 ml) grated horseradish
10 chopped sage leaves
4 tablespoons (60 ml) chopped parsley
for the pastry:
8 oz (225 g) wholemeal self-raising flour
pinch sea salt
freshly ground black pepper
4 oz (125 g) vegetable margarine
cold water to mix

Make the pastry and set it aside to chill. Thinly slice the carrots. Cut the swede and turnips into small, thin pieces about the same size as the carrot slices. Cut the parsnips in half lengthways and remove the woody cores. Thinly slice the main parts.

Put all the vegetables into a saucepan with the oil and ¾ pint (425 ml) stock. Cover and set on a moderate heat for 20 minutes, stirring occasionally. Preheat the oven to Reg 6/400°F/200°C. Put the miso into a small bowl and work in the tomato purée. Gradually mix in the remaining ½ pint (275 ml) stock and then the horseradish, sage and parsley. Mix this sauce into the cooked vegetables and then turn them all into a large pie dish. Cover them with the pastry and bake the pie for 30 minutes. Serve with a bright green vegetable such as Brussels tops, spring greens or curly kale and jacket-baked potatoes.

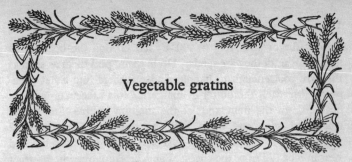

Vegetable gratins

Vegetables served in a creamy, flavoured sauce can make first-course or side dishes in both vegetarian and non-vegetarian meals, and if you cook a selection of them and serve them with potatoes, rice or wholemeal pasta they provide a meal in themselves.

Flavour the sauce with different kinds of cheese, mustards, tomato purée, herbs, spices and orange and lemon juice. Top the dish with browned crumbs, sesame seeds, chopped nuts, wheatgerm or oatmeal.

If you don't eat milk or cheese, make a bechamel sauce with soya flour (*see* under sauces) and flavour it in the same way as the milky sauces. Alternatively you can make a lighter, more translucent sauce with stock or a mixture of stock and wine.

Most of the vegetables in gratin dishes have to be cooked first. The simplest and best way to do this is to steam them, perhaps with a bouquet garni or a bayleaf. Alternatively, you can simmer them gently in a very little water with perhaps a knob of butter or margarine.

The recipes below use various methods of pre-cooking. Beetroot are always best if you boil them. Any other method would take far too long. This is one of the stock and wine sauces, and the winey effect is supercharged by the flavour of the wine-matured cheese.

Beetroot with red wine sauce and red cheese

8 small round beetroot
1 oz (25 g) butter *or* vegetable margarine
1 tablespoon (15 ml) wholemeal flour
¼ pint (150 ml) dry red wine
¼ pint (150 ml) stock
4 oz (125 g) red Windsor cheese

Preheat the oven to Reg 6/400°F/200°C. Boil the beetroot in their skins until they are tender. Drain them, peel them as soon as they are cool enough to handle, and put them into a flat oven-proof dish. Melt the butter or margarine in a saucepan on a low heat. Stir in the flour and let the mixture bubble. Stir in the stock and wine and bring them to the boil. Simmer for 2 minutes, stirring frequently. Take the pan from the heat and beat in 3 oz (75 g) of the cheese. Pour the sauce over the beetroot and scatter the remaining cheese on top. Put the dish into the oven for 25 minutes.

Mace is a lovely light flavourer for nutty Brussels sprouts and the onion sauce in this recipe makes a creamy contrast.

Brussels sprouts with onion sauce

1 lb (450 g) Brussels sprouts
1 oz (25 g) butter
1 large onion, finely chopped
1 tablespoon (15 ml) wholemeal flour
½ pint (275 ml) milk
½ teaspoon (2.5 ml) ground mace
3 tablespoons (45 ml) browned crumbs

Preheat the oven to Reg 6/400°F/200°C. Trim the sprouts. Put 1 in (3 cm) of water into the bottom of a saucepan and bring it to the boil. Put in the sprouts, cover them and cook them for 2 minutes on a moderate heat. Drain them and put them in a flat, oven-proof dish. Melt the butter in a saucepan on a low heat. Stir in the onion and cook it until it is soft. Stir in the flour and let the mixture bubble. Take the pan from the heat and stir in the milk. Replace the pan on a moderate heat and bring the sauce to the boil, stirring. Add the mace and simmer gently for 2 minutes. Pour the sauce over the Brussels sprouts and scatter the browned crumbs over the top. Put the dish into the oven for 30 minutes.

In this recipe the carrots are simmered first with butter and honey to make them sweet and rich. They are finished with a creamy orange sauce and topped with nutty sesame seeds.

Carrots in tomato and garlic sauce

1½ lb (675 g) carrots
2 oz (50 g) butter
1 teaspoon (5 ml) clear honey
1 clove garlic, very finely chopped
1 tablespoon (15 ml) wholemeal flour
1 tablespoon (15 ml) tomato purée
½ pint (275 ml) milk
freshly grated nutmeg
3 tablespoons (45 ml) sesame seeds

Preheat the oven to Reg 6/400°F/200°C. Scrub the carrots. If they are fairly small, leave them whole; if long and thin, cut them into 2 in (6 cm) lengths; and if they are wide, halve or quarter them lengthways as well. Put them into a saucepan with 1 oz (25 g) of the butter and the honey and just cover them with water. Cover them with a lid and set them on a moderate heat for 20 minutes. If there is still any liquid left in the saucepan, take off the lid and continue cooking until the carrots are glazed. Transfer them to a flat, ovenproof dish and don't wash the saucepan. Put the second oz (25 g) of butter in it and set it on a low heat. Add the garlic and let it soften but not brown. Stir in the flour and let the mixture bubble and then stir in the tomato purée. Take the pan from the heat and stir in the milk. Grate in some nutmeg. Set the pan back on the heat and bring the sauce to the boil, still stirring. Simmer it gently for 2 minutes and pour it over the carrots. Scatter the sesame seeds over the top and put the dish into the oven for 30 minutes.

The old favourite, cauliflower cheese, is another favourite gratin dish. Here the sauce is lightened with stock and made spicy with Worcestershire sauce.

Worcestershire and Cheshire cauliflower

1 large cauliflower

1 bayleaf
1 oz (25 g) butter
1 tablespoon (15 ml) wholemeal flour
¼ pint (150 ml) stock
¼ pint (150 ml) milk
2 tablespoons (30 ml) Worcestershire sauce or Yorkshire Relish
4 oz (125 g) grated farmhouse Cheshire cheese

Preheat the oven to Reg 6/400°F/200°C. Break the cauliflower into small fleurettes. Put them into a vegetable steamer (or in a colander covered with foil) with the bayleaf and steam them for 15 minutes so they are just tender. Lift them out and put them into a flat, ovenproof dish. Melt the butter in a saucepan on a moderate heat. Stir in the flour and let the mixture bubble. Take the pan from the heat and stir in the stock and milk. Replace the pan on the heat and bring the sauce to the boil, stirring. Let it simmer gently for 2 minutes. Take the pan from the heat and beat in the Worcester sauce and 3 oz (75 g) of the cheese. Pour the sauce over the cauliflower and scatter the rest of the cheese over top. Put the dish into the oven for 30 minutes.

Leeks, Dijon mustard and white wine are a perfect combination. Again stock makes a lighter textured sauce.

Leeks with wine and mustard sauce

1½ lb (675 g) fairly thin leeks
1 oz (25 g) butter or vegetable margarine
1 tablespoon (15 ml) wholemeal flour
¼ pint (150 ml) stock
¼ pint (150 ml) dry white wine
2 teaspoons (10 ml) Dijon mustard
2 tablespoons (30 ml) chopped parsley
3 tablespoons (45 ml) coarse oatmeal

Preheat the oven to Reg 6/400°F/200°C. Wash the leeks well and cut them into 2½ in (8 cm) lengths. Put them into a vegetable steamer (or a colander covered with foil) and steam them for 15 minutes, turning them once. Transfer them to a flat, oven-proof dish. Melt the butter or margarine in a saucepan on a moderate heat. Stir in the flour and let the mixture bubble. Take the pan from the heat and stir in the stock, wine and mustard. Bring the sauce to the boil, stirring, and let it simmer gently for 2 minutes. Mix in the parsley and pour the sauce over the leeks. Scatter the oatmeal over the top and put the dish into the oven for 30 minutes, or until the oatmeal is golden brown.

Cook mushrooms in a lemon butter and coat them with a savoury sauce flavoured with mustard seed.

Lemon mushrooms with mustard and cress

1 lb (450 g) button mushrooms
1½ oz (40 g) butter
juice 1 lemon
1 teaspoon (5 ml) mustard seeds
1 tablespoon (15 ml) wholemeal flour
½ pint (275 ml) milk
1 box mustard and cress
2 tablespoons (30 ml) wheatgerm

Preheat the oven to Reg 6/400°F/200°C. If the mushrooms are tiny, leave them whole; if large, then halve or quarter them. Melt 1 oz (25 g) of the butter in a saucepan on a moderate heat. Put in the mushrooms and turn them in the butter for 2 minutes. Pour in the lemon juice and let it bubble and reduce almost completely. Lift the mushrooms out into either 1 large flat ovenproof dish or 4 small heatproof dishes, leaving any buttery liquid in the saucepan. Put in the remaining butter and melt it on a moderate heat. Stir in the mustard seeds and the flour and let the flour bubble. Take the pan from the heat and stir in the milk. Bring the sauce to the boil, stirring, and let it simmer for 2 minutes. Take the pan from the heat and fold in the mustard and cress. Pour the sauce over the mushrooms and scatter the wheatgerm over the top. Put the dish or dishes into the oven for 30 minutes or until the wheatgerm is golden brown.

Cheese

Yes, say cheese every day, for it really can be served at every meal – breakfast included if you like! There are so many different flavours, textures and colours that no matter how many kinds you try, there will be others just waiting to be sliced into. Some are best for eating plain and others will melt deliciously into cooked dishes or can be cubed and tossed in to heat through quickly.

When you're buying cheese, try to steer clear of the factory made types in their sweaty, plastic wrappers. If it is English cheese, then look for the farmhouse varieties and have them cut straight from the block if possible. Search round in delicatessens, specialist real cheese shops and on market stalls to see how many different types you can find. When you discover one you have never had before, buy it and try it. Have it plain first and then think about how it can be put into cooked dishes and which are the flavours it will best go with. Try it on toast or with raw vegetables in salads, scattered over cooked ones or grated into an omelet.

You don't always have to rely on shops for cheese – it can sometimes turn up in the most extraordinary places. I stopped once in a garage in Wiltshire on the way home from the West Country, only to find on the counter a wooden platter of cheese that had been made on a farm a few miles away. That is the sort of opportunity that with cheese you should never miss.

Self-sufficiency and so-called 'backyard dairying' are becoming increasingly popular and cheese-making in the home kitchen is no more unusual. If you know of anyone who keeps goats or one or two cows and makes their own cheese see if you can buy regularly from them. Or better still, have a go at making it yourself and attend one of the courses that are now being arranged!

A hard goat cheese is my own particular favourite and I always make sure I have some in store. However, this is as yet by no means readily available and so the recipes below are all made with cheeses that you should be able to find at least in delicatessens and cheese shops and very often also in chain stores and supermarkets.

The first two recipes are based on cooked vegetables, and in smaller quantities would make ideal side-dishes. In each case the cheese added at the end matches the colour of the vegetables, and their individual, rather special, flavours make the dishes both perfect meals that are simple and cheap for every day and also impressive enough for a formal dinner.

The light, cidery flavour in this one goes well with the savoury Derby cheese.

Artichokes, leeks and sage Derby cheese

1 lb (450 g) Jerusalem artichokes
1 lb (450 g) leeks
1 oz (25 g) butter
1 teaspoon (5 ml) mustard powder
½ pint (275 ml) dry cider
1 bayleaf
8 oz (225 g) grated sage Derby cheese

Peel and thinly slice the artichokes. (Hold them under water while you peel them otherwise your hands will get very sticky.) Wash and thinly slice the leeks. Melt the butter in a large saucepan on a moderate heat. Stir in the mustard and let the mixture bubble for ½ minute. Stir in the cider and bring it to the boil. Mix in the artichokes and leeks and tuck in the bayleaf. Cover the pan and keep it on a moderate heat for 45 minutes. All the liquid should be absorbed and the artichokes just tender. Remove the bayleaf. Preheat the grill to high. Put half the artichokes and leeks into a fairly high-sided heatproof serving dish. Lay on half the cheese, the remaining vegetables and then the rest of the cheese. Put the dish under the grill for 2 minutes so that the top cheese melts and sets very slightly.

This is a winey red and white dish of cheese and red cabbage, with beetroot to give a contrasting flavour and texture.

Red cabbage, beetroot and red Windsor cheese

12 oz (350 g) red cabbage
1 raw beetroot weighing 4–6 oz (125–175 g)
1 large Bramley apple
1 oz (25 g) butter
1 medium onion, thinly sliced
4 crushed juniper berries
½ teaspoon (2.5 ml) caraway seeds
4 tablespoons (60 ml) dry red wine
3 tablespoons (45 ml) red wine vinegar
8 oz (225 g) red Windsor cheese

Preheat the oven to Reg 4/350°F/180°C. Shred the cabbage. Peel the beetroot and chop it into matchstick pieces. Peel, quarter, core and slice the apple. Melt the butter in a flameproof casserole on a low heat. Stir in the onion and apple and cook them until the onion is soft. Mix in the cabbage, beetroot, crushed juniper berries and caraway seeds. Pour in the wine and vinegar and bring them to the boil. Cover the casserole and put it into the oven for 1½ hours. Grate the cheese. Put half the cabbage mixture into a fairly high-sided, heatproof serving dish. Put in a layer of half the cheese, then the remaining cabbage and top with the rest of the cheese. Return the dish to the oven for 10 minutes or put it under a high grill for a shorter time so that the cheese just melts.

The pointed, pale spring cabbages have a light and refreshing texture. Cook one very simply, with spring onions, and toss in cubes of tasty cheese just before serving.

Spring cabbage and spring onions with savory and cheese

1 large spring cabbage (both inner and outer parts)
12 spring onions
2 tablespoons (30 ml) chopped savory

½ pint (275 ml) stock
8 oz (225 g) farmhouse Cheddar cheese

Shred the cabbage. Chop the onions into 1 in (3 cm) lengths. Put both onions and cabbage into a saucepan with the savory and stock, cover and set on a moderate heat for 20 minutes, stirring once or twice. Cut the cheese into ½ in (1.5 cm) dice. Toss it into the cabbage just before serving so it heats through but doesn't melt. Serve with plainly boiled new potatoes in their jackets, tossed in butter, mint and parsley.

The leeks in this recipe are cooked even more simply and then coated in a hot salad dressing. You can buy the Ilchester Applewood smoked Cheddar cheese in most delicatessens, but if you can't find it use a strong farmhouse Cheddar.

Hot salad of leeks and cheese

1 lb (450 g) thin white leeks
8 oz (225 g) Applewood smoked Cheddar cheese (or plain farmhouse Cheddar)
4 tablespoons (60 ml) olive oil
2 tablespoons (30 ml) white wine vinegar
1 teaspoon (5 ml) Dijon mustard
1 clove garlic, crushed with a pinch sea salt
2 tablespoons (30 ml) chopped parsley

Cut the leeks into ¾ in (2 cm) lengths. Cut the cheese into ½ in (1 cm) dice. Steam the leeks for 15 minutes, turning them once. While they are cooking mix the oil, vinegar, mustard and garlic together and gently warm them in a saucepan. Transfer the leeks to a hot serving dish and gently mix in the cheese. Fold in the hot dressing and scatter the parsley over the top.

When cauliflower cheese was first made in this country, Cheshire was the favourite cheese to use for it. The white kind used here makes the dish really attractive.

Cauliflower and Cheshire cheese

1 large cauliflower

1 bayleaf
8 oz (225 g) white Cheshire cheese
2 eggs, beaten
2 teaspoons (10 ml) Worcestershire sauce or Yorkshire Relish
little butter for greasing

Break the cauliflower into small fleurettes and put it into a sauce-pan with the bayleaf and ¾ in (2 cm) water. (Use some of the inner leaves as well if they are sound). Cover the saucepan and set it on a low heat for 15 minutes, so the cauliflower is just tender. Preheat the oven to Reg 6/400°F/200°C. Transfer the cauliflower to a lightly buttered, flat, heatproof serving dish. Grate the cheese and mix 6 oz (175 g) with the eggs and Worcester sauce. Spoon the mixture evenly over the cauliflower and scatter the remaining cheese over the top. Put the dish into the oven for 20 minutes or until the top is golden brown.

This method of cooking cauliflower is similar to Chinese stir-braising, although the final dish is not at all Oriental in character.

Special cauliflower with cheese and pine nuts

1 large cauliflower plus the best of its inner leaves
1 oz (25 g) butter
2 oz (50 g) pine nuts
1 clove garlic, finely chopped
juice 1 lemon
8 tablespoons (120 ml) stock
1 tablespoon (15 ml) chopped lemon thyme
8 oz (225 g) grated farmhouse Cheddar cheese

Break the cauliflower into fleurettes the size of the small centre ones. This will mean dividing the large outer ones into several pieces. Do it by cutting the stem and breaking the flower part. Chop the centre part of the stem and the reserved leaves. Melt the butter in a large frying pan on a high heat. Put in all the cauliflower, the pine kernels and garlic. Stir them around on the heat until they begin to brown. Pour in the lemon juice and stock and bring them to the boil. Mix in the lemon thyme. Cover the pan tightly and set it on a low heat for 10 minutes. Transfer everything to a heatproof serving dish and scatter the cheese over the top. Preheat the grill to high and put the dish underneath for the cheese to melt.

Here, celery and button onions are stir-braised in a tomato-flavoured sauce. The cheese is added at the last minute so the white cubes stay firm and make a good contrast in colour.

Stir-braised celery and button onions with Caerphilly

8 oz (225 g) button onions
1 small head celery – the stalks and 4 tablespoons (60 ml) chopped
    celery leaves
3 tablespoons (45 ml) olive oil
1 large clove garlic, finely chopped
$\frac{1}{4}$ pint (150 ml) stock
2 tablespoons (30 ml) tomato purée
1 tablespoon (15 ml) chopped thyme
8 green olives, stoned and chopped
10 oz (275 g) Caerphilly cheese

Peel the onions. Chop the celery stalks into $\frac{3}{4}$ in (2 cm) pieces. Heat the oil in a large frying pan on a low heat. Mix in the onions, celery stalks and garlic and cook them until the onions are transparent and just beginning to brown. Stir everything around frequently. Raise the heat to moderate, pour in the stock and bring it to the boil. Mix in the tomato purée, thyme, celery leaves and olives. Cover the pan and keep it on a moderate heat for 10 minutes. Mix in the cheese and serve immediately. (If you want to prepare this in advance you can cook the dish completely except for adding the cheese. Then leave it standing for as long as you like; heat it up and add the cheese just before serving.)

Stir-frying is another Chinese method. It is even quicker and simpler than stir-braising. Double Gloucester with chives is now one of the most readily available of the unusual cheeses, but if you can't find it use a farmhouse double Gloucester.

This dish, unlike the one above, must be prepared at the last minute.

Stir-fried Brussels sprouts and Gloucester cheese

1 lb (450 g) Brussels sprouts
10 oz (275 g) double Gloucester cheese with chives
4 tablespoons (60 ml) olive oil
1 large clove garlic, finely chopped
8 tablespoons (120 ml) stock
2 teaspoons (10 ml) Urchfont full strength mustard (or any other strong granular mustard not too highly spiced)

Trim and thinly slice the sprouts. Cut the cheese into ½ in (1.5 cm) dice. Heat the oil in a frying pan on a high heat. Put in the sprouts and garlic and stir them around for 1 minute. Pour in the stock and bring it to the boil. Mix in the mustard and keep cooking until the liquid is almost completely reduced. Mix in the cheese and immediately take the pan from the heat and serve.

Potatoes and cheese together make really substantial meals. All you need to accompany them is a refreshing salad or a bright green lightly-cooked vegetable. Use genuine Italian mozzarella for this one if you can possibly find it as it has a creamier texture than the other varieties. If not, you should be able to find Scottish or Danish.

Button onions and potatoes with mozzarella cheese

1 lb (450 g) button onions
1½ lb (675 g) potatoes
2 oz (50 g) butter
1½ pints (850 ml) stock
freshly ground black pepper
sea salt
freshly grated nutmeg
2 tablespoons (30 ml) wholemeal flour
2 tablespoons (30 ml) grated Parmesan cheese
4 tablespoons (60 ml) chopped parsley
10 oz (275 g) mozzarella cheese

Peel the onions. Scrub the potatoes and cut them into ½ in (1.5 cm) dice Melt 1 oz (25 g) of the butter in a large saucepan on a low heat. Put in the onions and cook them, turning frequently, until they look transparent. Mix in the potatoes and when they are well coated with butter, pour in the stock. Season with the pepper, salt and nutmeg. Bring the stock to the boil, cover and simmer for 20 minutes. Strain the onions and potatoes and reserve all the stock. You should have around 1 pint (575 ml).

Melt the remaining butter in a saucepan on a moderate heat. Stir in the flour and let the mixture bubble. Keep stirring for 1 minute. Take the pan from the heat and stir in the reserved stock. Replace it, bring it back to the boil and simmer for 1 minute more. Stir in the Parmesan cheese and take the pan from the heat again. Fold in the onions, potatoes and parsley. Put half the mixture into a really large pie dish or heatproof serving dish. Slice the mozzarella very thinly and lay half on top. Put in the remaining vegetables and top with the rest of the cheese. Preheat the grill to high. Put the dish underneath for the top to brown.

This dish is far simpler and lighter but just as tasty. It is an excellent way of using old potatoes towards the end of their season, when the first spring onions come into the shops.

Potatoes layered with cheese and spring onions

1½ lb (675 g) fairly small old potatoes
12 medium-sized spring onions, finely chopped
8 oz (225 g) grated farmhouse Cheddar cheese
freshly ground black pepper
freshly grated nutmeg
little sea salt if required
little butter for greasing

Preheat the oven to Reg 6/400°F/200°C. Boil the potatoes (whole if possible) in their skins until they are just tender. Drain them and slice them, without peeling, into ¼ in (0.75 cm) rounds. Put a layer of one third of the potatoes into the bottom of a greased pie dish or serving dish. Season them with the pepper, nutmeg and salt and then scatter over one third of the onions and one third of the cheese. Continue with 2 more similar layers, ending with cheese. Put the dish into the oven for 10 minutes so the cheese just melts down into the potatoes.

Aubergines, courgettes, yoghurt and eggs make this dish quite filling, so a smaller amount of cheese is used just to help flavour the tasty topping.

Vegetable moussaka

1 lb (450 g) aubergines
2 teaspoons (10 ml) sea salt
1 lb (450 g) courgettes
1 lb (450 g) tomatoes
6 tablespoons (90 ml) olive oil
1 large onion, thinly sliced
1 large or 2 small cloves garlic, finely chopped
1 teaspoon (5 ml) ground cinnamon
1 tablespoon (15 ml) grated Parmesan cheese
topping:
2 tablespoons (30 ml) wholemeal flour
4 eggs, beaten
1 carton natural yoghurt
3 oz (75 g) grated farmhouse Cheddar cheese

Slice the aubergines into ¼ in (0.75 cm) rounds. Put them into a colander and sprinkle them with the salt. Leave them to drain for 30 minutes, then rinse under the cold tap and pat dry. Preheat the oven to Reg 6/400°F/200°C. Thinly slice the courgettes. Scald, skin and chop the tomatoes. Heat 2 tablespoons (30 ml) of the oil in a frying pan on a low heat. Put in the onion and garlic and cook them until the onion is beginning to soften. Mix in the courgettes and continue cooking until they are soft, moving everything about frequently. Add the tomatoes and stir in the cinnamon. Simmer, uncovered for 2 minutes, and set the pan aside.

Heat half the remaining oil in another frying pan on a moderate heat. Put in the aubergines and brown them on both sides. Do this in 2 batches, or more if necessary, adding more oil as you go. Put half the cooked aubergine slices in the bottom of a really large pie dish or fairly deep oven-proof serving dish.

Sprinkle over half the Parmesan cheese. Put in all the courgette and tomato mixture and sprinkle over the remaining cheese. Top with the remaining aubergines. Beat all the ingredients for the topping together and pour them over the vegetables. Bake for 30 minutes until the top is firm and golden.

This dish has a topping of a completely different kind – golden yellow, lightly risen potatoes, crisp on the outside and fluffy in the middle. Underneath is a steamy, tasty, pale green mixture of vegetables and cheese.

Celeriac, celery and sage Derby shepherd's pie

1 lb (450 g) celeriac
4 large sticks celery
1 oz (25 g) butter
1 large onion, thinly sliced
¼ pint (150 ml) dry cider
6 oz (175 g) sage Derby cheese, grated
topping:
1½ lb (675 g) potatoes
freshly ground black pepper
2 eggs, separated

Preheat the oven to Reg 6/400°F/200°C. Scrub the potatoes and boil them in their skins until they are tender. While they are cooking peel the celeriac and chop it into pieces about 1 in (3 cm) square and very thin. Slice the celery. Melt the butter in a large frying pan or saucepan on a low heat. Stir in the celeriac, celery and onion, cover them and let them sweat for 10 minutes. Pour in the cider and bring it to the boil. Simmer for 1 minute, uncovered Put half the vegetables into a large pie dish and add all the cheese, in an even layer. Put the rest of the vegetables on top. Drain the potatoes when they are ready and let them steam dry. Peel them as soon as they are cool enough to handle and mash them or rub them through a sieve. Season them with the pepper and beat in the egg yolks. Stiffly whip the egg whites and fold them quickly into the potatoes. Pile the mixture on top of the pie dish, smooth

it over and then make patterns on the top with a fork. Bake the
pie for 45 minutes.

ᛃ   ᛃ   ᛃ

Cottage cheese is light and slimming, ideal for lunch and supper
dishes. Plain, it can be a little uninteresting, so mix in seasonings
and flavourings, chopped vegetables, fruits and herbs to liven it
up. Serve it cold in the summer; in the winter mix in something
hot and spicy and heat it through in the oven.

The following recipes can be cooked in individual heatproof
dishes or in 1 fairly large pie dish. Serve them alone, on toast or
with a baked potato and a salad. In smaller quantities, baked in
individual ramekins, they can also be served as a first course.

Cottage cheese and tomato bake

1 lb (450 g) cottage cheese
2 tablespoons (30 ml) tomato purée
2 teaspoons (10 ml) made English mustard
1 lb (450 g) firm tomatoes
2 boxes mustard and cress
2 tablespoons (30 ml) browned crumbs (optional)

Preheat the oven to Reg 6/400°F/200°C. Put the cheese into a
bowl and mix in the tomato purée and made mustard. Put half
the mixture into a large pie dish. Slice the tomatoes into rounds
and lay half on top of the cheese. Cut the mustard and cress and
arrange it evenly over the tomatoes. Smooth on the rest of the
cheese and top with the remaining tomatoes. Scatter the crumbs
on top and put the dish into the oven for 30 minutes.

Cottage cheese and watercress bake

1 lb (450 g) cottage cheese
2 tablespoons (30 ml) Worcestershire sauce or Yorkshire Relish
2 large bunches watercress
1 lb (450 g) firm tomatoes

Preheat the oven to Reg 6/400°F/200°C. Mix the sauce into the cheese. Chop the cress and tomatoes and mix in these as well. Pile the mixture into a heatproof serving dish and put it into the oven for 20 minutes.

Cottage cheese and green pepper bake

1 lb (450 g) cottage cheese
2 medium-sized green peppers
1 lb (450 g) tomatoes
1 clove garlic, very finely chopped
2 teaspoons (10 ml) paprika
1 teaspoon (5 ml) Tabasco sauce
for serving:
granary or wholemeal toast

Preheat the oven to Reg 6/400°F/200°C. Put the cheese into a large pie dish or oven-proof dish. Core and finely chop the peppers. Chop the tomatoes. Mix them into the cheese with the garlic, paprika and Tabasco sauce. Put the dish into the oven for 20 minutes.

Cottage cheese and beetroot bake

1 lb (450 g) cottage cheese
2 medium-sized cooked beetroot, weighing together 10–12 oz (275–350 g)
2 tablespoons (30 ml) grated horseradish
4 teaspoons (20 ml) made English mustard
2 boxes mustard and cress

Preheat the oven to Reg 6/400°F/200°C. Put the cheese into a bowl. Grate in the beetroot. Add the horseradish and mustard and mix everything together well. Put the mixture into a pie-dish or other ovenproof dish and bake for 20 minutes. Scatter the cress over the top just before serving.

Eggs

Eggs are one of the most versatile ingredients a cook possesses, whether the meals she is preparing are vegetarian or not. They can be made into both savoury and sweet dishes, boiled, poached, fried, scrambled or baked, and served hot or cold, to produce meals that vary tremendously in appearance, texture and flavour. Eggs are the universal stand-by. They can stretch meals in emergencies or be prepared in a matter of minutes when you come home later than you had planned and have to rush out again in half an hour. They can be served for lunch or for supper and can be made into first courses or used in the main dish at dinner time.

Omelets

Omelets can be made from any number of eggs, depending on how many people you have to feed and the occasion at which they are being served. They can be made from a plain, beaten egg mixture folded round a vegetable filling, or the vegetables can be actually mixed into the beaten eggs so all the ingredients together form a thick, savoury cake.

If you are making a filled omelet, use one egg per person for a first course and two for a main meal. Beat each person's eggs separately with a little sea salt and freshly ground black pepper; for extra flavour add some chopped herbs, chives or spring onions, a little made English mustard, or grated farmhouse Cheddar or Parmesan cheese. The filling can be made up of just one vegetable such as sliced and sautéed mushrooms or lightly cooked asparagus, French beans or broccoli, or it can be a quick mixture of whatever you have handy in the refrigerator. Make the filling for all your omelets together and always have it prepared and keeping hot before you start cooking the eggs.

As for what to cook the omelet in, if you make them frequently it's well worth-while investing in a fairly large, round sided omelet pan. If you don't have one, use a heavy frying pan.

Cook single-egg omelets that are going to be filled in $\frac{1}{4}$ oz (10 g) butter, and two-egg ones in $\frac{1}{2}$ oz (15 g) butter, and use a moderate heat. This will brown the underneath and give you a fairly fluffy texture, whilst being slow enough to set the top at the same time. Melt the butter and let the foam subside and then pour in the beaten eggs. Tip the pan in all directions whilst the omelet is cooking and lift the edges of the setting eggs so as much of the mixture as possible gets to the sides and bottom. When the underside is brown and the top only just set, lay your filling on one half of the omelet and fold the other half over the top. Then carefully slide the omelet onto a warm serving dish and keep it warm while you make the others.

You can fill these plain omelets with all kinds of vegetables, and this makes them excelent for emergency meals. Here is an example that can be varied at will.

Savoury-filled omelet

for 4 omelets:
8 eggs
little sea salt and freshly ground black pepper
4 tablespoons (60 ml) chopped parsley
4 tablespoons (60 ml) chopped celery leaves (if available)
up to 2 oz (50 g) butter
for filling:
4 sticks celery
4 oz (125 g) mushrooms
6 firm tomatoes
1 oz (25 g) butter
1 medium onion, thinly sliced
1 clove garlic, finely chopped

Make the filling first. Finely chop the celery and thinly slice the mushrooms. Scald, skin and roughly chop the tomatoes. Melt 1 oz (25 g) butter in a frying pan on a low heat. Mix in the onion, garlic and celery and cook them until they are golden. Raise the heat to moderate and mix in the mushrooms. Cook them for

1½ minutes and then mix in the tomatoes. Remove the pan from the heat and keep the filling warm while you prepare the omelets.

Beat the eggs in 4 batches of 2. Add 1 tablespoon (15 ml) each of parsley and celery leaves, salt and black pepper to each. Melt ½ oz (15 g) of the butter in an omelet pan on a moderate heat. Pour in the first lot of beaten egg mixture and cook, tipping the pan and lifting the edges to let the mixture get to the sides and base. When the underside is brown and the top almost set put ¼ of the filling onto one half of the omelet. Fold the other side over the top and carefully slide the omelet onto a warm serving plate. Keep it warm while you prepare the rest. Add more butter to the pan as you need it. You may not have to use the whole amount.

These leek and cheese omelets differ slightly from the basic method in that both sides are browned. The leeks are used as a flavouring in the mixture and also as the filling.

Leek and cheese omelet

for 4 omelets:
6 medium-sized straight leeks
2 oz (50 g) butter
8 eggs
4 teaspoons (20 ml) made English mustard
4 tablespoons (60 ml) chopped parsley
6 oz (175 g) grated farmhouse Cheddar cheese

Cut two of the leeks in half lengthways and thinly slice them. Cut the other four into lengths of about 4 in (12 cm). Steam these for 15 minutes. Melt ½ oz (15 g) of the butter in a frying pan on a low heat. Put in the sliced leeks and cook them until they are soft. Beat the eggs in 4 batches of 2 and into each mix in ¼ of the softened leeks, 1 teaspoon (5 ml) of mustard, 1 tablespoon (15 ml) chopped parsley and quarter of the cheese.

Melt another ½ oz (15 g) of the butter in an omelet pan on a low heat. Pour in the mixture for 1 omelet and spread it out so it is about ¼ in (0.5 cm) thick. When the underneath is brown, turn the omelet over. Lay one of the steamed leeks on one side and,

when the second side is brown, fold over the other half. Slide
the omelet onto a warm serving plate and keep it warm while you
cook the rest.

When your eggs and filling are mixed together, it's best to half
cook the omelet on top of the stove and then finish it off under
a high grill. This gets you out of turning it over, which, with
something so thick that is only half set, could be disastrous.

You can serve this kind of omelet hot, or you can let it cool
completely, cut it into wedges and take it on a picnic.

Use either six or eight eggs, providing your pan is big enough.
Any of the amounts in the recipes below can be altered up or
down. Generally, if you have a fairly substantial filling, use six
eggs, eight if you have a lighter one. But there is no hard and fast
rule.

This is a real spring omelet using fresh green tangy leaves and
spring onions. Eat it hot, or cut it into wedges for a spring picnic.

Sorrel and mushroom omelet

16 sorrel leaves
8 dandelion leaves
4 oz (125 g) flat mushrooms
12 spring onions
8 eggs
sea salt
freshly ground black pepper
2 tablespoons (30 ml) chopped mixed herbs
1 oz (25 g) butter

Chop the sorrel and dandelion leaves. Thinly slice the mushrooms.
Chop the onions. Beat all the eggs together with the seasonings
and herbs. Melt the butter in an omelet pan on a modern heat.
Put in the sorrel, dandelion, mushrooms and onions and stir
them around on the heat for $1\frac{1}{2}$ minutes.

Preheat the grill to high. Pour the eggs and herbs into the
omelet pan and mix them into the filling. Cook the omelet, lifting
the setting edges and tipping the pan to let as much of the mix-

ture as possible get to the sides and base. When the underneath is golden brown transfer the pan to the grill so the omelet is about 2 in (6 cm) away from the heat. Leave it until the top is risen and golden brown and the middle is set through. (If you're not quite sure, test it with a fine skewer.)

In this omelet, the mustard and cress is used to give flavour, like a savoury herb, and it also provides a fairly substantial filling.

Tomato, cheese and cress omelet

8 eggs
4 oz (100 g) grated farmhouse Cheddar cheese
sea salt
freshly ground black pepper
2 boxes mustard and cress
2 tablespoons (30 ml) chopped parsley
6 firm tomatoes
$\frac{3}{4}$ oz (20 g) butter
1 large onion, thinly sliced

Beat the eggs with the cheese, seasonings, cress and parsley. Cut each tomato into 4 slices. Melt the butter in an omelet pan on a low heat. Put in the onion and cook it until it is golden. Stir in the egg mixture. Preheat the grill to high. Raise the heat under the pan to moderate, spread the mixture evenly over the pan and cook it until the underside is brown. Put the pan under the grill until the top is just set. Arrange the tomato slices on top and put the pan back under the grill until the spaces between the tomatoes are browned and the omelet is set through. (Test it with a fine skewer, if you're not quite sure.)

Bananas are an ingredient that can be either sweet or savoury. When you fry them they go soft and melty. So do aubergines, so put them together to make an unusual and delicious omelet flavoured, if you can get it, with nutty chervil.

Aubergine and banana omelet

2 medium-sized aubergines

2 teaspoons (10 ml) fine sea salt
1 large banana
1½ oz (40 g) butter
1 small onion, thinly sliced
6 eggs
4 tablespoons (60 ml) chopped chervil or parsley

Dice the aubergines and put them into a colander. Sprinkle them
with the salt and leave them to drain for 30 minutes. Wash them
with cold water and dry them with kitchen paper. Peel and slice
the banana. Melt ½ oz (15 g) of the butter in an omelet pan on a
low heat. Mix in the onion and cook it until it is golden. Cool
it a little and then beat it with the eggs and chervil. Put the
remaining butter into the pan and melt it on a moderate heat. Put
in the aubergines and banana and cook them, stirring, for 2
minutes. Mix them into the eggs. Pour everything back into the
pan and set it on a low heat. Preheat the grill to high. When the
omelet is golden brown underneath and beginning to set, transfer
the pan to the high grill and cook it until the omelet is firm right
through and the top golden brown and puffy.

Potatoes and eggs together make a meal in themselves. Serve both
of these potato omelets with lots of green vegetables or a substantial side salad. Nothing else will be needed.

Old potato omelet

2 medium-sized old potatoes
4 tablespoons (60 ml) olive oil
1 large onion, thinly sliced
1 large clove garlic, finely chopped
6 eggs
sea salt
freshly ground black pepper
4 tablespoons (60 ml) chopped parsley

Scrub and thinly slice the potatoes. Heat the oil in a large omelet
pan on a low heat. Put in the potatoes, onion and garlic and cook

them until they are golden brown, moving them around and turning them frequently. Beat the eggs with the seasonings and parsley. Preheat the grill to high. Pour the eggs into the pan and make sure they cover and get all round the potatoes. Cook the omelet until the underside is golden brown, lifting the edges and tipping the pan so as much egg as possible gets to the sides and base. Transfer the pan to the grill so the egg is about 2 in (6 cm) away from the heat, and cook the omelet until the top is set, browned and slightly risen.

New potato omelet

for 4 individual omelets:
16 new baby potatoes
8 eggs
4 tablespoons (60 ml) chopped parsley
up to 2 oz (50 g) butter
1 large onion, thinly sliced
1 large clove garlic, finely chopped
6 oz (175 g) grated farmhouse Cheddar cheese

Boil the potatoes in their skins until they are tender. Drain them and peel them while they are still warm. Cut each one in half lengthways to give two flat pieces. Beat the eggs in 4 batches of 2, dividing the parsley evenly between them. Melt ½ oz (15 g) of the butter in an omelet pan on a moderate heat. Put in the onion, and garlic and potatoes, rounded side down. Cook until everything is just beginning to brown. Remove 24 of the potato halves and three-quarters of the onions. Turn over the remaining 8 potato halves and arrange them evenly in the pan. Pour two beaten eggs with parsley over and around the potato halves. Preheat the grill to high. Cook the omelet, tipping the pan and lifting the sides occasionally, until the top is firm. Scatter the cheese over the top and put the pan under the grill. Cook until the cheese is melted and bubbly and the omelet is puffing up. Slide the omelet onto a warm plate and keep it warm while you cook the others in the same way.

❧ ❧ ❧

Soufflé omelets

Soufflé omelets are a little more complicated to make. The eggs are separated and the whites beaten until they are stiff to give a light and fluffy texture to the finished dish. Because of the bulk of the beaten whites, it is only possible to cook 4 eggs at a time in an omelet pan, so the amounts given below will provide a main course for only 2 people or a first course for four. For a main meal for 4 people, double all the ingredients and either use 2 pans or keep one omelet warm while you cook a second. Soufflé omelets can easily be kept warm and will not flop like an ordinary soufflé.

The soufflé omelets below each have a different savoury topping. On the first, it is the same as the filling. With the others you have crispy-fried onion rings for a contrast in texture.

Mushroom soufflé omelets

8 oz (225 g) open mushrooms
1½ oz (40 g) butter
1 medium onion, finely chopped
1 tablespoon (15 ml) chopped parsley
1 tablespoon (15 ml) chopped thyme
4 large eggs, separated

Finely chop the mushrooms. Melt 1 oz (25 g) butter in a frying pan on a low heat. Put in the onion and cook it until it is soft. Raise the heat to moderate. Put in the mushrooms and herbs and cook them for 2 minutes, stirring frequently. Remove the pan from the heat and cool the mixture a little, then mix half of it with the egg yolks.

Stiffly whip the egg whites and fold them into the yolk mixture with a metal spoon. Heat ½ oz (15 g) butter in an omelet pan on a moderate heat. Preheat the grill to moderate. While the butter in the pan is still foaming, put in the omelet mixture and spread the top evenly with a flat knife or palette knife. Cook the omelet for 1 minute. Put the pan under the grill for the top to set and just turn brown. Slide the omelet out onto a large plate. Reheat the remaining mushroom mixture and spoon it over the top.

Curried onion soufflé omelet

4 eggs, separated
1 oz (30 g) butter
1 medium onion, finely chopped
2 teaspoons (10 ml) curry powder
1 tablespoon (15 ml) chopped parsley
for topping:
1 medium onion, sliced into rings
1 egg, beaten
2 teaspoons (10 ml) curry powder
2 tablespoons (30 ml) wholemeal flour
deep fat for frying

Melt ½ oz (15 g) butter in a frying pan on a low heat. Stir in
the chopped onion and 2 teaspoons (10 ml) curry powder and
cook them gently until the onion is soft. Allow to cool a
little, then mix with the egg yolks. Add the parsley. Stiffly
whip the egg whites and fold them into the yolk mixture with a
metal spoon. Melt ½ oz (15 g) butter in an omelet pan on a
moderate heat. Preheat the grill to moderate. Pour the egg mixture into the omelet pan and smooth the top with a flat knife or
palette knife. Cook the omelet for 1 minute. Put the pan under
the grill and cook until the top is brown and set.
Topping:
Prepare this while the onion and curry powder filling is cooking.
Dip the onion rings into the beaten egg. Mix 2 teaspoons (10 ml)
curry powder and the flour together and put them into a bowl.
Put in the onion rings and turn them in the flour until they are
well coated. While the omelet is cooking, deep fry them in hot oil
until they are brown and crisp. Scatter the crisp onion rings over
the omelet before serving.

Mustard and cress soufflé omelet

4 eggs, separated
1 oz (25 g) butter
1 medium onion, finely chopped
1 teaspoon (5 ml) mustard powder
1 teaspoon (5 ml) mustard seeds

1 box mustard and cress
topping:
1 medium onion, sliced into rings
1 egg, beaten
2 tablespoons (30 ml) wholemeal flour
1 teaspoon (5 ml) mustard powder
deep fat for frying

Melt ½ oz (15 g) butter in a frying pan on a low heat. Put in the chopped onion, 1 teaspoon (5 ml) mustard powder and the mustard seeds and cook them until the onions are soft. Allow them to cool a little then mix them into the egg yolks and add the mustard and cress. Stiffly whip the egg whites and fold them into the yolk mixture with a metal spoon. Melt the remaining butter in an omelet pan on a moderate heat. Preheat the grill to moderate. Pour the egg mixture into the omelet pan and smooth the top with a flat knife or palette knife. Cook the omelet for 1 minute. Transfer the pan to the grill and carry on cooking until the top is set and golden brown.

Topping:
Prepare this while the onion and mustard filling is cooking. Dip the sliced onion into the beaten egg. Put the flour and the mustard powder together into a bowl and turn the onions in them to get them well-coated. Deep fry the onion rings in hot oil until they are crisp and golden. Scatter them over the omelet to serve.

Soufflés

One step on from soufflé omelets are soufflés proper. All the ones here are best made in a 6 in (15 cm) diameter soufflé dish. To prepare it you will need some greaseproof paper about 3 in (10 cm) longer than the circumference. Folded double it should double the height of the dish.

Thickly butter the dish and the part of the paper that will extend above it. Sprinkle the buttered paper thickly with browned crumbs and tip any excess into the dish. Add a few more and move the dish about so they stick to the butter. You can tip any loose ones out if you like, but I prefer to leave them in to give the soufflé a lovely crispy crumby base.

Tie the prepared paper round the dish with fine cotton string. Sellotape and nylon string disintegrate disastrously in the oven, but artists' masking tape is very effective if you can steal some! Always have your dish prepared before you start to make the soufflé, so the mixture can be poured in quickly.

When the soufflé comes out of the oven, cut the string and gently pull the paper away from the risen filling, using a rounded knife to help you if necessary. Then take it to the table as soon as possible. If you can, time your meal perfectly by putting the soufflé into the oven just before you serve the first course. You will then be able to eat this at leisure, take a relaxed saunter to the oven and remove your impressive-looking masterpiece. (Well, that's the ideal situation anyway!)

The conventional way of making a soufflé mixture is with a basic thick bechamel sauce made with flavoured (or infused) milk. All you do is put the milk into a saucepan with the flavourings and set it on a really low heat while your prepare the rest of the ingredients. It will take about 10 minutes. Strain the milk before you use it. The first two soufflés use this method.

Curried mushroom soufflé

½ pint (275 ml) milk, *infused with:*
   1 bayleaf
   small slice of onion
   1 blade mace
   few black peppercorns
8 oz (225 g) mushrooms
1½ oz (40 g) butter
2 teaspoons (10 ml) hot Madras curry powder
1 teaspoon (5 ml) ground turmeric
grated rind and juice ½ lemon
2 tablespoons (30 ml) wholemeal flour
2 tablespoons (30 ml) chopped parsley
5 eggs, separated
butter, crumbs and greaseproof for preparing a 6-inch (15 cm)
   diameter soufflé dish
2 tablespoons (30 ml) browned crumbs for the top

Preheat the oven to Reg 6/400°F/200°C.

Infuse the milk with the flavourings.

Thinly slice the mushrooms. Melt the butter in a saucepan on a low heat. Mix in the mushrooms, curry powder and turmeric, cover them and cook them gently for 5 minutes. Remove half of them, put them into a bowl and add the lemon juice to them. Raise the heat under those still in the pan to moderate and stir in the flour. Let it cook for 1 minute and stir in the milk. Keep stirring until you have a thick, bubbly sauce. Take the pan from the heat and cool the sauce a little. Beat in the parsley, lemon rind and egg yolks. Stiffly whip the whites and fold them into the yolk mixture with a metal spoon. Pile three-quarters of the mixture into the prepared dish. Put in the reserved mushrooms and lemon juice, in an even layer, and add the rest of the soufflé mixture. Sprinkle the remaining browned crumbs over the top and bake the soufflé for 30 minutes.

N.B. Even though you put the mushrooms fairly near the top they may sink right down. This doesn't matter, as you then have a fluffy yellow top with a base of lemony mushrooms.

Sorrel soufflé

½ pint (275 ml) milk *infused with:*
  1 bayleaf
  1 blade mace
  small slice of onion
  6 black peppercorns
1 oz (25 g) butter
6 large spring onions, finely chopped
20 finely chopped sorrel leaves
1 tablespoon (15 ml) wholemeal flour
½ teaspoon (2.5 ml) ground mace
freshly grated nutmeg
5 eggs, separated
butter and crumbs for preparing 6-inch (15 cm) diameter soufflé
  dish
1 tablespoon (15 ml) browned crumbs for the top

Preheat the oven to Reg 6/400°F/200°C.

Set the milk to infuse with the flavourings.

Melt the butter in a saucepan on a low heat. Stir in the onions and cook them until they are soft. Stir in the sorrel and cook it until it is a dull green and melty. Stir in the flour and cook it for 1 minute. Stir in the milk and add the mace and nutmeg. Cook the sauce, stirring until it is thick and bubbly. Take the pan from the heat and cool the sauce slightly. Beat in the egg yolks. Stiffly whip the whites and fold them into the sauce mixture with a metal spoon. Pile everything into the prepared soufflé dish and scatter the remaining crumbs over the top. Bake the soufflé for 35 minutes.

You can make a lighter soufflé mixture by using puréed vegetables in place of all or part of the milk. This spinach soufflé is light and fluffy and unusually bright green, with a melty layer of cheese in the middle.

Spinach soufflé

1 lb (450 g) spinach
¼ pint (150 ml) milk
1 oz (25 g) butter
1 tablespoon (15 ml) wholemeal flour
5 eggs, separated
2 oz (50 g) grated farmhouse Cheddar cheese
butter and crumbs for preparing 6-inch (15 cm) diameter soufflé
    dish
1 tablespoon (15 ml) browned crumbs for the top

Preheat the oven to Reg 6/400°F/200°C. Break the stalks from the spinach and put the leaves into a saucepan with only the water that clings to them after washing. Cover, and cook on a low heat fo 15 minutes, stirring occasionally. Drain the spinach, pressing down hard to extract as much moisture as possible. Put it into a blender with the milk and work them until you have a smooth purée.

Melt the butter in a saucepan on a moderate heat. Stir in the flour and cook it for ½ minute. Take the pan from the heat and stir in the spinach purée. Bring the resulting sauce to the boil, stirring, and simmer for 2 minutes. Let the sauce cool a little and then beat in the egg yolks. Stiffly whip the whites and fold them into the yolk mixture with a metal spoon. Pile half the soufflé mixture into the prepared dish and quickly sprinkle in all the cheese, not letting it get too close to the edges. Put in the rest of the mixture and scatter the crumbs over the top. Bake the soufflé for 35 minutes.

Here tomatoes make a light summer soufflé.

Tomato soufflé

1 lb (450 g) ripe tomatoes
1 oz (25 g) butter
1 medium onion, finely chopped
2 tablespoons (30 ml) wholemeal flour
2 oz (50 g) grated farmhouse double Gloucester cheese
2 tablespoons (30 ml) chopped fennel
5 eggs, separated
butter and crumbs for preparing 6-inch (15 cm) diameter soufflé
    dish
1 tablespoon (15 ml) browned crumbs for the top

Preheat the oven to Reg 6/400°F/200°C. Scald, skin and roughly chop the tomatoes. Put them into a saucepan, cover them and set them on a low heat. Simmer them gently for 10 minutes; by then they should mostly be reduced to a thick juice. Melt the butter in a saucepan on a low heat. Stir in the onion and cook it until it is soft. Stir in the flour and let the mixture bubble. Stir in the tomatoes. Bring the sauce to the boil and simmer, stirring, until it is thick. Take the pan from the heat and cool the sauce slightly, then beat in the cheese, fennel and egg yolks. Stiffly whip the whites and fold them into the mixture with a metal spoon. Pile everything into the prepared soufflé dish and scatter the crumbs over the top. Bake the soufflé for 30 minutes.

Cottage cheese can also be used instead of milk. You will again get a very light texture, but the soufflé does not rise quite so high. Here, the soft flavour of the cheese is contrasted by the pickled onions.

Pickled onion soufflé

8 oz (225 g) cottage cheese
4 eggs, separated
4 pickled onions, finely chopped
2 teaspoons (10 ml) made English mustard
2 tablespoons (30 ml) chopped parsley
butter and crumbs for preparing 6-inch (15 cm) diameter soufflé
  dish

Preheat the oven to Reg 6/400°F/200°C. Mix the cheese, egg yolks, onions, mustard and parsley together. Stiffly whip the whites and fold them into the rest with a metal spoon. Pile the mixture into a prepared soufflé dish and bake for 30 minutes. You can use a cottage cheese mixture to make tiny individual soufflés which make ideal lunch dishes or first courses. The filling here is cauliflower, but you can also try cooked carrots, leeks, baby onions, asparagus tips, mushrooms, green peas or broad beans. The soufflés rise high and cook a lovely golden brown.

Individual cauliflower soufflés

1 small cauliflower
1 bayleaf
¼ pint (150 ml) stock
3 eggs, separated
3 oz (75 g) cottage cheese
2 teaspoons (10 ml) made English mustard
1 tablespoon (15 ml) browned crumbs
1 tablespoon (15 ml) grated Parmesan cheese
butter, crumbs and greaseproof for preparing 4 individual soufflé
  dishes in the same way as the one large one

Break the cauliflower into small fleurettes. Put them into a saucepan with the bayleaf and stock. Cover, and set on a low heat for 15 minutes (until the fleurettes are just tender). Preheat the oven to Reg 6/400°F/200°C. Lay the cooked cauliflower in the bottom of each prepared soufflé dish. Beat the egg yolks, cottage cheese and mustard together. Whip the whites until they are stiff and fold them into the yolks and cheese. Pile the mixture on top of

the cauliflower and scatter the remaining crumbs and the grated
Parmesan cheese over the top. Bake the soufflés for 20 minutes.

Roulades

To make a roulade a soufflé omelet mixture is spread and cooked
in a Swiss-roll tin, given a savoury filling, and rolled up. Four
eggs will line a normal sized tin, so for a main meal for 4 people,
make the roulade a little more substantial by filling it with
cheese (cream, curd, cottage or a grated hard cheese) or with
2 more eggs which have been hard-boiled, chopped and mixed
with a flavoured bechamel sauce. A cheese sauce is always good
but in the following two recipes I've used mayonnaise to provide
a sharp contrast in flavour. The result is something like a cross
between an omelet and an egg salad. Always use home-made
mayonnaise wherever possible.

Watercress roulade

6 eggs
2 bunches watercress
2 oz (50 g) farmhouse Cheddar cheese
3 tablespoons (45 ml) mayonnaise
1 teaspoon (5 ml) made English mustard
butter for greasing

Preheat the oven to Reg 6/400°F/200°C. Hard-boil two of the
eggs and separate the other 4. Chop the watercress and grate the
cheese. Line a Swiss-roll tin with thickly buttered greaseproof
paper. Mix the egg yolks with half the watercress and half the
cheese. Mix the mustard into the mayonnaise. Stiffly whip the
whites and fold them into the yolk mixture with a metal spoon.
Quickly spread the mixture evenly over the greaseproof and bake
it for 30 minutes. Meanwhile, chop the hard-boiled eggs and
mix them with the remaining cheese and watercress and then the
mayonnaise and mustard. Take the roulade from the oven and
spread the filling all over the top. Gently roll it up, using a flat

knife if necessary to ease it from the paper. Transfer the roulade to a flat, heatproof plate and return it to the oven for 1 minute for the filling to heat through. Serve as soon as you can, preferably with a salad.

Tomato roulade

6 eggs
1 tablespoon (15 ml) tomato purée
1 teaspoon (5 ml) dill seeds
2 boxes mustard and cress
½ oz (15 g) butter
1 medium onion, thinly sliced
1 clove garlic, finely chopped
8 oz (225 g) firm tomatoes
4 tablespoons (60 ml) mayonnaise
butter for greasing

Preheat the oven to Reg 6/400°F/200°C. Hard-boil two of the eggs and separate the other 4. Work the yolks with the tomato purée, ½ the dill seeds and one of the boxes of cress. Melt the butter in a frying pan on a low heat. Stir in the onion and garlic and cook them until the onion is golden. Cool them a little and work them into the yolks. Line a Swiss-roll tin with thickly buttered greaseproof paper. Stiffly whip the egg whites and fold them into the yolk mixture with a metal spoon. Spread the mixture evenly over the greaseproof and bake it for 30 minutes. Meanwhile, scald, skin and chop the tomatoes. Chop the hard-boiled eggs. Mix the tomatoes, eggs, and the remaining cress and dill into the mayonnaise. When the roulade is cooked, spread the filling evenly over the surface and roll it up, using a flat knife to ease it away from the paper if necessary. Transfer it to a flat, heatproof plate and put it back into the oven for 1 minute to heat through.

Bakes and custards

The eggs in bakes can be beaten together, perhaps with a little cream, or they can be separated and the whites stiffly whipped so you get a fluffier texture. Milk is added to eggs for custards to make them creamy.

Egg bakes need to be made with 8 eggs if the vegetable filling is fairly light (for example, French beans, cauliflower or asparagus) or with only 6 if the vegetable is more substantial (for example, parsnips, green peas, potatoes). Beat the eggs with herbs, seasonings and other flavourings such as mustard, and cook your chosen vegetables separately, chopping them either before or after cooking, whichever is most suitable. Mix the vegetables with the eggs and pour the mixture into a buttered, flat, ovenproof dish (an oven-to-table one is best) and bake for 30 minutes in an oven preheated to Reg 6/400°F/200°C.

Here is an example of a simple bake using leeks as the vegetable and olives for flavour.

Leek and olive bake

12 oz (350 g) leeks (both green and white parts)
1 oz (25 g) butter
16 green olives
8 eggs
3 tablespoons (45 ml) double cream
1 tablespoon (15 ml) grated Parmesan cheese
2 tablespoons (30 ml) mixed chopped thyme and marjoram
sea salt
freshly ground black pepper

Preheat the oven to Reg 6/400°F/200°C, and grease a flat ovenproof dish or pie plate with butter. Thinly slice the leeks. Melt the butter in a frying pan on a low heat. Stir in the leeks and cook them until they are soft. Let them cool a little. Stone the olives and quarter them lengthways. Beat the eggs with the cream, cheese, herbs and seasonings and mix in the leeks and olives. Pour the mixture into the prepared dish and bake it for 30 minutes or until it is risen and golden. Serve it hot (it is probably best that way) or you can let it cool completely and have it cold.

Bakes made from separated eggs rise high so it is best to bake them in a pie dish which has been buttered and crumbed like a soufflé dish. You can mix the chopped, cooked vegetables into the yolks before adding the whites, or you can arrange the eggs, vegetables and other ingredients such as cheese, in layers.

This is a really substantial bake, made with artichokes and Edam cheese.

Artichoke and Edam bake

1 lb (450 g) Jerusalem artichokes
6 eggs, separated
1 tablespoon (15 ml) tomato purée
1 teaspoon (5 ml) paprika
2 tablespoons (30 ml) chopped parsley
8 oz (225 g) Edam cheese
butter and crumbs for preparing dish like a soufflé dish

Preheat the oven to Reg 6/400°F/200°C. Boil the artichokes whole in their skins for 20 minutes or steam them for 30 minutes. Peel them while they are still warm and slice them into rounds. Beat the egg yolks with the tomato purée, paprika and parsley. Cut the cheese into very thin slices. Stiffly whip the egg whites and fold them into the yolks with a metal spoon. Put half the egg mixture into the bottom of your prepared pie dish. Lay half the cheese slices on top. Then put in all the artichokes and cover them with the rest of the cheese. Top with the remaining eggs and bake for 25 minutes or until the top is golden.

Here are two savoury custards. The texture of the first is made extra creamy by using 6 yolks but only 3 egg whites. The nutmeg gives it an old English flavour.

Spinach and sorrel custard

1½ lb (675 g) spinach
16 chopped sorrel leaves
2 tablespoons (30 ml) chopped chives
3 egg yolks
3 eggs

¾ pint (425 ml) milk
freshly grated nutmeg

Preheat the oven to Reg 6/400°F/200°C. Grease an 8 in (20 cm) diameter pie plate or flat ovenproof dish with butter. Break the stems from the spinach. Put the leaves into a saucepan with only the water that clings to them after washing, cover them and set them on a low heat for 15 minutes, turning them occasionally. Drain them well, pressing down hard to extract as much water as possible. Turn the spinach onto a board and chop it finely. Beat the eggs, yolks and milk together and stir in the spinach, sorrel and chives. Grate in about one eighth of a nutmeg. Pour the mixture into the prepared dish and distribute the spinach evenly. Bake the custard for 40 minutes and serve it hot or cold with a bright coloured vegetable, such as red peppers or tomatoes, for contrast.

Lay cauliflower fleurettes in a dish, cover them with a flavoured custard and serve them hot or cold.

Savoury cauliflower custard

1 large cauliflower (or 2 small ones)
2 bayleaves
little water
6 eggs
¼ pint (150 ml) milk
½ oz (15 g) butter
1 medium onion, thinly sliced
4 tablespoons (60 ml) chopped parsley
2 teaspoons (10 ml) made English mustard
2 tablespoons (30 ml) tomato purée
2 tablespoons (30 ml) grated Parmesan cheese

Preheat the oven to Reg 6/400°F/200°C. Grease a pie plate or flat ovenproof dish 8 or 9 in (20–25 cm) in diameter with butter. Break the cauliflower into fleurettes. Put it into a saucepan with the bayleaves and about ½ in (1.5 cm) water. Cover the pan and set it on a low heat for 20 minutes, turning the cauliflower once. Beat the eggs with the milk. Melt the butter in a frying pan on a low heat. Mix in the onion and cook it until it is golden. Cool it a little and then mix it into the eggs with the parsley, mustard and tomato purée. Arrange the cauliflower in the buttered dish and pour all the custard mixture over the top. Scatter over the cheese and bake the custard for 30 minutes. It should be risen and golden and reddy-brown with the larger fleurettes just showing through.

ﻬ　　ﻬ　　ﻬ

Puddings

You can make light puddings from beaten eggs, cooked vegetables and granary or wholemeal breadcrumbs. A little wine or wine vinegar just lifts the flavour and prevents it from being too bland. The idea came to me from the eighteenth-century sweet carrot puddings, so I used carrots to make this first savoury one, which retains an old-fashioned flavour.

Baked carrot pudding

12 oz (350 g) carrots
1 medium onion, finely chopped
1 clove garlic, finely chopped
6 eggs
3 oz (75 g) granary or wholemeal breadcrumbs
2 oz (50 g) butter, melted
3 tablespoons (45 ml) dry white wine
2 tablespoons (30 ml) white wine vinegar
freshly grated nutmeg
2 tablespoons (30 ml) chopped parsley

Preheat the oven to Reg 6/400°F/200°C. Grease a pie dish or a fairly deep ovenproof dish with butter. Grate the carrots and put them into a vegetable steamer with the onion and garlic. Steam them for 20 minutes, turning them over several times. Beat the eggs and mix in the crumbs, melted butter, wine and vinegar. Then add the carrot mixture, nutmeg and parsley. Turn the mixture into the buttered pie dish and bake the pudding for 30 minutes.

Leek and cheese pudding

1 lb (450 g) leeks
6 eggs
3 oz (75 g) granary or wholemeal breadcrumbs
2 tablespoons (30 ml) tarragon vinegar
2 tablespoons (30 ml) chopped parsley
4 oz (100 g) grated farmhouse Cheddar cheese

Preheat the oven to Reg 6/400°F/200°C. Grease a pie dish or a
fairly deep ovenproof dish with butter. Thinly slice the leeks and
steam them for 10 minutes, turning them once. Lift them out
as soon as they are done and cool them a little. Beat the eggs and
mix in the crumbs, vinegar, parsley and cheese. Fold in the leeks
and mix everything well. Pour the mixture into the buttered pie
dish and bake it for 30 minutes. The pudding should be risen
and lightly browned.

Scrambled eggs

Scrambled eggs are my good·old stand-by that really can be
prepared in a matter of minutes. They are delicious plain, or with
grated cheese or vegetables mixed in. Serve them piled onto
slices of buttered toast or surrounded by toasted bread fingers or,
if you have more time, with sautéed or baked potatoes.

For plain scrambled eggs for 4 people, beat 8 eggs together
with a little sea salt and freshly ground black pepper. Start to
cook the toast first so it is ready just before the eggs. If you keep
them waiting they will harden slightly.

Melt 1½ oz (40 g) butter in a large heavy saucepan on a low
heat. Stir in the eggs with a metal spoon and keep stirring, lifting
the eggs from the bottom of the pan all the time, until they are
thick and creamy. Keep on making the toast, if you can, at the
same time. With a little practice, you will be able to prepare
both at once in a 'spread-one-slice-and-then-stir' fashion.

When both are done, pile your eggs onto the toast.

For light flavourings add some chopped chervil (the best herb of all for eggs), parsley or chives, or about 2 oz (50 g) grated cheese. Once you can scramble eggs easily, try stirring the eggs into buttery, cooked vegetables to make a more substantial dish. Sautée some mushrooms gently in the butter first and then mix in the eggs. If when you are looking for wild mushrooms you find some yellow, trumpet-like chanterelles, they are the best of all for scrambles. But if your search is unsuccessful, or you don't trust your powers of recognition, use delicate flavoured button mushrooms.

Creamy mushroom and egg scramble

8 oz (225 g) button mushrooms
8 eggs
6 tablespoons (90 ml) double cream
4 tablespoons (60 ml) chopped chervil (or parsley)
2 oz (50 g) butter
for serving:
as much buttered brown toast as you need

Thinly slice the mushrooms. Beat the eggs with the cream and chervil. Melt the butter in a heavy saucepan on a low heat. Stir in the mushrooms, cover them and cook them gently for 5 minutes. Stir in the eggs and cream and keep stirring until the mixture sets. Pile it onto the waiting toast and serve as soon as you can.

Leeks and a spicy granular mustard make a more robust-flavoured scramble.

Leek and egg scramble

1½ lb (675 g) leeks
1½ oz (40 g) butter
8 eggs, beaten
1 tablespoon (15 ml) English Vineyard mustard
for serving:
as much brown toast as you need

Cut the leeks in half lengthways and if they are fat cut them lengthways again. Slice them thinly. Melt the butter in a saucepan on a low heat, stir in the leeks, cover them and let them sweat for 10 minutes. Stir in the eggs and mustard and keep stirring until the eggs are set. Pile them on top of the buttered toast.

Brussels tops go really well with eggs so mix them together in a scramble. This one is best served with potatoes.

Scrambled Brussels tops

1½ lb (675 g) Brussels tops
1½ oz (40 g) butter
1 large onion, thinly sliced
4 tablespoons (60 ml) water
8 eggs, beaten
6 oz (175 g) grated farmhouse Cheddar cheese
2 tablespoons (30 ml) chopped parsley

Wash and finely chop the Brussels tops. Melt the butter in a large, heavy saucepan on a low heat. Mix in the Brussels tops and onion and add the water. Cover the pan and keep it on the low heat for 20 minutes, stirring the tops occasionally. Stir in the eggs, cheese and parsley and keep stirring until the eggs are set and creamy textured.

Red peppers and tomatoes give the eggs a South American touch. Use coriander, if you can get it (or grow it) for its pungent, almost sweet flavour. If you have none try chervil or the more readily available parsley.

Red pepper and tomato scramble

8 eggs
2 tablespoons (30 ml) chopped coriander (or chervil or parsley)
1 teaspoon (5 ml) Tabasco sauce
2 medium-sized red peppers
1 lb (450 g) tomatoes
1½ oz (40 g) butter
1 medium onion, thinly sliced
1 large clove garlic, finely chopped

Beat the eggs with the coriander and Tabasco. Core, de-seed and dice the peppers. Scald, skin and roughly chop the tomatoes. Melt the butter in a heavy saucepan on a low heat. Mix in the onion and garlic and cook them until the onion is just beginning to soften. Stir in the peppers, cover the pan and simmer everything gently for 5 minutes. Stir in the eggs and tomatoes and keep stirring on the low heat until the eggs are set. Either pile the scramble onto buttered toast or serve it with Tomato rice (*see* rice section).

Spinach has a high water content, so to prevent it from spoiling your eggs in a scramble, cook it first and drain it well.

Spinach scramble

1 lb (450 g) spinach
8 eggs
4 oz (125 g) grated farmhouse Cheddar cheese
12 oz (350 g) firm tomatoes
1½ oz (40 g) butter
1 large onion, thinly sliced
2 teaspoons (10 ml) chopped rosemary

Wash the spinach and break off the stems. Put the leaves into a saucepan with only the water that clings to them after washing, cover them and set them on a low heat for 10 minutes, stirring occasionally. Drain the spinach well, pressing down to get as much water out as possible. Turn it onto a board and chop it finely. Beat the eggs with the cheese. Scald, skin and roughly chop the tomatoes. Melt the butter in a heavy saucepan on a low heat. Add the onion and rosemary and cook them until the onion is golden. Stir in the spinach, egg and cheese mixture, and tomatoes. Keep stirring until the eggs are set. Either pile the scramble onto buttered toast or serve with sautéed potatoes.

Baked eggs

To serve as a first course eggs can be baked singly with herbs and cream in small, buttered cocottes. Make sure the cream covers the yolk and bake them uncovered for 30 minutes. Tarragon, chervil, marjoram and rosemary are the best herbs for this, and you will need 2 tablespoons (30 ml, double cream per egg.

For a main course, eggs can be baked on a bed of vegetables. If you cover this type of dish with foil before putting it in the oven the eggs will keep their soft texture, even when set completely, and you will cut down on the cooking time. Here we have a winter dish of Savoy cabbage and eggs, brought together in flavour and texture with caraway seeds and cream.

Eggs baked with Savoy cabbage and caraway

1 medium-sized Savoy cabbage
2 tablespoons (30 ml) olive oil
1 medium onion, thinly sliced
1 clove garlic, finely chopped
1 lb (450 g) ripe tomatoes, scalded, skinned and chopped
1 tablespoon (15 ml) caraway seeds
1 carton sour cream
8 eggs
little butter or oil for greasing foil

Preheat the oven to Reg 6/400°F/200°C. Discard the tough outer leaves of the cabbage and shred the rest. Put it into a saucepan with the oil, onion, garlic, tomatoes and half the caraway seeds. Cover the pan and set it on a moderate heat for 20 minutes, stirring occasionally. Take the pan from the heat, cool the cabbage a little and stir in half the sour cream. Put the cabbage into a large flat, ovenproof dish and make 8 indentations in it. Break the eggs into these. Mix the remaining sour cream and caraway seeds together and spoon them over the eggs, covering the yolks if possible. (If the cream is thick it may slip off but this won't matter as you have the foil covering.) Cover the dish completely with buttered or oiled foil and put it into the oven for 20 minutes.

In the summer, use French beans, spring onions and tomatoes for a lighter texture, and flavour them with fennel.

Eggs baked with French beans

1 lb (450 g) French beans
12 medium-sized spring onions
1 lb (450 g) ripe tomatoes
3 tablespoons (45 ml) chopped fennel
½ oz (15 g) butter
8 eggs
1 tablespoon (15 ml) grated Parmesan cheese
oil or butter for greasing foil

Preheat the oven to Reg 6/400°F/200°C. Top and tail the beans and chop them into ¾ in (2 cm) lengths. Chop the onions into pieces the same size. Scald, skin and chop the tomatoes. Put the beans, onions and tomatoes into a saucepan with half the fennel and the butter. Cover them and set them on a low heat for 20 minutes. Put all the contents of the saucepan into a large, flat ovenproof dish and make 8 indentations in it. Break in the eggs and scatter the Parmesan cheese and remaining fennel over the top. Cover the dish with buttered or oiled foil and put it into the oven for 20 minutes.

And now for an autumn dish of corn and peppers, spiced with chillis.

Eggs baked with corn and peppers

4 corn cobs
1 red pepper
1 green pepper
4 green chillis (or ¼ teaspoon (½ a 2.5 ml spoon) cayenne pepper)
3 tablespoons (45 ml) olive oil
1 large onion, finely chopped
1 large clove garlic, finely chopped
½ pint (275 ml) stock
3 tablespoons (45 ml) chopped coriander (or chervil or parsley)
1 teaspoon (5 ml) paprika
8 eggs
little oil for greasing foil

Preheat the oven to Reg 6/400°F/200°C. Cut the corn from the

cobs. Core, de-seed and dice the peppers. Core and very finely
chop the chillis. Heat the oil in a frying pan or shallow saucepan
on a low heat. Stir in the onion and garlic and cook them until
the onion is soft. Stir in the corn, peppers and chillis. Pour in
the stock and bring it to the boil. Mix in the coriander and
paprika and, if you are using it, the cayenne pepper. Cover the
pan and simmer everything gently for 15 minutes, by which time
most of the stock should be absorbed. Transfer all the contents
of the pan to a large, flat, ovenproof dish. Make 8 indentations
in it and break in the eggs. Cover the dish with oiled foil and put
it into the oven for 20 minutes.

꽃   꽃   꽃

Poached eggs

Poached eggs are light and good for those on diets, but although
they are simple on the plate, they are perhaps the trickiest of all
egg dishes to prepare. You need a shallow, wide-based saucepan
and a perforated spoon. Put about 2 in (6 cm) of water into
the saucepan together with a squeeze of lemon juice or 1 teaspoon
(5 ml) white wine vinegar.

Set the pan on a low heat and just bring the water to simmering point. Stir the water round in a clockwise direction and,
while the current is still quite fast, break in your egg (or 2 eggs
if the saucepan is a large one). Let the eggs cook very gently,
keeping the water at a bare tremble, until the white is set over
the yolk. They will now be soft poached. If you want the yolk
completely set, leave them in the water for 2 minutes more. Lift
the eggs out with the perforated spoon and let them drain well;
if you are going to serve them cold in a salad lay them on
absorbent kitchen paper to cool.

Soft-poached eggs, either hot or cold, are good served with a
sharp sauce or dressing; when you cut into them the creamy yolk
oozes out and blends with it. Serve them cold on top of a crisp
salad or hot on a bed of cooked vegetables; the eggs and sauce
together will form the dressing.

Here, spinach is used as both sauce and vegetable. The dish is made into a complete meal by serving it on a bed of cooked rice or pasta, but if you would rather serve potatoes or have no accompaniment these can easily be omitted.

Poached eggs with spinach sauce

2 lb (900 g) spinach
2 oz (50 g) butter
1 large onion, thinly sliced
2 teaspoons (10 ml) chopped rosemary
½ pint (275 ml) stock
1 tablespoon (15 ml) wholemeal flour
1 tablespoon (15 ml) chopped capers
1 tablespoon (15 ml) chopped parsley
juice ½ lemon
8 eggs
water to poach with a dash of wine vinegar
if required, enough cooked brown rice or wholemeal pasta for 4, hot and buttered

Break the stems from the spinach and wash the leaves. Melt 1 oz (25 g) of the butter in a saucepan on a low heat. Stir in the onion and cook it until it is soft. Fold in the spinach and rosemary, cover them and cook for 10 minutes, stirring occasionally.

Put a quarter of the spinach into a blender with the stock and work until you have a smooth liquid. (Or rub it through the fine blade of a mouli.) Melt the second ounce (25 g) butter in a saucepan on a moderate heat. Stir in the flour and let the mixture bubble. Stir in the spinach purée and bring it to the boil. Simmer the sauce for 2 minutes and stir in the capers, parsley and lemon juice. Soft-poach the eggs in the water and vinegar, and drain them well. Put the rice or pasta into the bottom of a large flat serving dish. Add the cooked spinach in an even layer and set the eggs on top. Spoon over the sauce.

Boiled eggs

When you are boiling eggs add a dash of malt vinegar to the

water (or any kind really – malt is just cheaper). Then, if the
eggs crack, the whites won't seep out, giving you hollow eggs
and white, scummy water.

For hard-boiled eggs, put them into a saucepan of hot water,
bring them to the boil and simmer them gently for 10 minutes.

If you want them soft-boiled, bring the water to the boil first,
carefully lower in the eggs with a spoon and simmer them for
3–4 minutes, depending on the size of the egg.

Hard-boiled eggs are excellent for salads, but you can also
make them into hot dishes. Here are three, using different
vegetables and cheese.

Eggs and squeak (or bubble and eggs!)

6–8 eggs (depending on your appetite – it works well with either)
1 lb (450 g) Brussels sprouts
$\frac{1}{4}$ pint (150 ml) stock
1 oz (25 g) butter
4 tablespoons (60 ml) chopped parsley
grated rind and juice 1 lemon
2 oz (50 g) grated farmhouse Cheddar cheese

Hard boil and chop the eggs. Trim the sprouts and put them into
a saucepan with the stock. Cover and set on a moderate heat for
15 minutes so all the liquid is absorbed and the sprouts just
tender. Heat the butter in a frying pan on a high heat. Put in the
sprouts and brown them quickly, moving them around all the
time. Mix in the eggs, parsley and lemon rind and just heat them
through. Transfer everything to a heatproof serving dish. Set
the frying pan back on the heat and pour in the lemon juice. Let
it bubble and pour it over the sprouts and eggs. Scatter the cheese
over the top and put the dish under a moderate grill so the cheese
just melts.

Boiled eggs and kale

1 lb (450 g) curly kale
6 or 8 hard-boiled eggs (depending on your appetite)
1 oz (25 g) butter
1 large onion, finely chopped

4 tablespoons (60 ml) chopped parsley
2 teaspoons (10 ml) paprika
4 oz (125 g) Edam cheese, diced

Remove the stalks from the kale and break the leaves into small pieces about 1 in (3 cm) square. Put them into a saucepan with about ½ in (1.5 cm) water. Cover the pan and set it on a low heat for 20 minutes, stirring occasionally. Drain the kale if necessary. Chop the eggs. Melt the butter in a large frying pan on a low heat. Mix in the onion and cook it until it is soft. Raise the heat to moderate and mix in the kale. Move it around on the heat for 1 minute and mix in the eggs, parsley, paprika and cheese. Let them all heat through but don't let the cheese melt. Pile everything into a warm serving dish and serve as soon as possible.

Boiled eggs and leeks

1 lb (450 g) leeks
8 hard-boiled eggs
4 oz (125 g) farmhouse Cheddar cheese
1 oz (25 g) butter
2 teaspoons (10 ml) made English mustard

Cut the leeks in half lengthways, wash them well and slice them thinly. Chop the eggs. Cut the cheese into ½ in (1.5 cm) dice. Melt the butter in a saucepan on a low heat. Stir in the leeks, cover them and let them sweat for 5 minutes. Mix the mustard in well and then add the eggs and cheese. Heat them through quickly without letting the cheese melt, and serve as soon as you can.

In this recipe, the eggs are kept whole. In the following proportions it makes a first course or a light lunch or supper. To make a main meal for four, double all the ingredients.

Boiled eggs with sorrel

4 eggs
1 oz (25 g) butter
20 chopped sorrel leaves

2 teaspoons (10 ml) English Vineyard mustard
juice 1 lemon
shredded lettuce for serving

Hard-boil the eggs. Melt the butter in a saucepan on a low heat. Stir in the sorrel and let it wilt. Mix in the mustard and lemon juice. Put in the eggs and turn them over in the sorrel. Cover and simmer very gently for 5 minutes so the eggs heat through and pick up the flavour of the sauce. Lift out the eggs and cut them in half lengthways. Put them cut-side down on a bed of shredded lettuce and spoon all the sauce over the top.

Boiled egg salads

Eggs go very well with lettuce, particularly with the more substantial varieties, and although lettuce is one of the most common of salad ingredients it is rarely given priority treatment and made the most of. Here, then, is a simple lettuce and egg salad with a creamy dressing that brings out the best in both of them. If they are available in your area, use a Density lettuce. If not, then a Webb's is the next best thing.

Egg and lettuce salad

9 eggs
1 large Density or Webb's lettuce
4 fl oz (125 ml) olive oil
2 teaspoons (10 ml) white wine vinegar
1 tablespoon (15 ml) chopped capers
2 tablespoons (30 ml) chopped chervil (or parsley)

Soft-boil one of the eggs and hard-boil the rest. Wash the lettuce leaves and drain them well. Tear them into small pieces and put in a bowl. Carefully cut open the soft-boiled egg and let the yolk fall into a bowl. Reserve and finely chop the white. Gradually work the olive oil into the yolk, drop by drop as if you were making mayonnaise. Beat in the vinegar, capers, chervil (or parsley) and finely chopped white. Mix this dressing into the lettuce. Cut the hard-boiled eggs in halves or quarters lengthways and arrange them on the top.

This is another simple salad. The main feature here is the lemony sorrel mayonnaise.

Mixed sorrel and lemon salad with eggs

for the dressing:
8 large chopped sorrel leaves
2 egg yolks
freshly ground black pepper
1 teaspoon (5 ml) mustard powder
grated rind 1 lemon
8 fl oz (250 ml) olive oil
juice 1 large lemon
for the salad:
16 chopped sorrel leaves
1 small Webb's lettuce, shredded
½ medium cucumber, chopped but not peeled
2 medium-sized carrots, grated
2 oz (50 g) currants
2 oz (50 g) peanuts
8 hard-boiled eggs

Put the sorrel for the dressing into a bowl with the egg yolks, pepper, mustard powder and grated lemon rind. Work them together with a wooden spoon, pounding the sorrel to release its flavour. Gradually add 2 tablespoons (30 ml) of the oil, drop by drop. Mix in 2 teaspoons (10 ml) of the lemon juice. Beat in the rest of the oil and then the remaining lemon juice. Combine all the ingredients for the salad and arrange them in a large fairly flat serving dish. Cut the eggs in half lengthways and arrange them on the salad, cut-side down. Spoon the dressing evenly over the eggs and the top of the salad.

You can nearly always buy sweet ridge cucumbers at the main salad time of the year. Here are two different ways of using them with boiled eggs.

Egg and ridge cucumber salad

8 hard-boiled eggs
2 medium-sized ridge cucumbers each about 6–8 in (20 cm) long
4 oz (125 g) chopped walnuts
1 carton natural yoghurt
2 teaspoons (10 ml) dill seeds
1 Webb's lettuce
lemon slices for garnish

Chop the eggs. Cut the cucumbers into lengthways quarters and cut away and discard the seeds. Try a piece and if you find the skins very bitter then peel the quarters as well. Dice the flesh. Mix the eggs, cucumber, walnuts, yoghurt and dill together. Line a salad bowl with separated lettuce leaves and pile the egg mixture inside. Chill the salad very slightly and garnish it with thin slices of lemon.

Ridge cucumbers stuffed with eggs

2 ridge cucumbers each about 6–8 in (20 cm) long
8 hard-boiled eggs
4 tablespoons (60 ml) natural yoghurt
2 tablespoons (30 ml) chopped mint
2 teaspoons (10 ml) ground cumin
mint leaves for garnish

Cut the cucumbers in half lengthways. Remove the seeds and peel each half. Scoop out the flesh of the cucumbers leaving 4 shells $\frac{1}{8}$ to $\frac{1}{4}$ in (0.5 cm) thick. Chop the scooped-out flesh and put it in a bowl. Chop the eggs and mix them into the cucumber with the yoghurt, mint and cumin. Pile the mixture back into the cucumber shells and garnish the top with mint leaves.

The yolks of hard-boiled eggs can be scooped out, sieved and creamed with other ingredients to make a tasty stuffing for the whites. The eggs can then be pieced together again or served still in halves as a first or a main course.

With French beans, olives and mayonnaise they make a substantial main course.

Egg, French bean and olive salad

8 eggs
1½ lb (675 g) French beans
2 tablespoons (30 ml) chopped thyme
¼ pint (150 ml) water
4 tablespoons (60 ml) olive oil
2 tablespoons (30 ml) white wine vinegar
1 clove garlic, crushed with a pinch sea salt
16 black olives
8 green olives
6 tablespoons (90 ml) mayonnaise
8 teaspoons (40 ml) grated Parmesan cheese
1 lb (450 g) tomatoes

Hard boil the eggs. Top and tail the beans. Put them into a saucepan with the thyme and water and set them on a moderate heat for 15 minutes. Drain them if necessary.

While the beans are cooking, make a dressing with the oil, vinegar and garlic. Stone and quarter the black olives. Stone and chop the green olives. When the beans are done mix them into the dressing with the black olives while they are still warm. Leave until quite cool.

Cut each egg in half lengthways. Scoop out the yolks, rub them through a sieve and cream them. Pound the green olives to a paste and work them into the egg yolks with half the mayonnaise and half the Parmesan cheese. Fill the eggs with the mixture and sandwich them back together. Scald, skin and slice the tomatoes and mix them into the cooled beans. Arrange the salad in a flat serving dish and set the eggs on top. Just before serving, spoon the remaining mayonnaise over the eggs and sprinkle them with the rest of the cheese.

Only six eggs are used in the next recipe as the broad beans make the eggs into quite a filling meal and three halves per person will be quite enough. For a first course, use three eggs, and cut each half into two lengths after they have been stuffed. This allows three quarters for each person.

Eggs filled with broad beans

6 hard-boiled eggs
1½ lb (675 g) broad beans (weighed before shelling)
3 tablespoons (45 ml) mayonnaise
grated rind and juice 1½ lemons
3 tablespoons (45 ml) chopped savory

Shell the beans and cook them in lightly salted simmering water
for 20 minutes. Drain them and skin them as soon as they are
cool enough to handle. Mash them to a purée (or rub them
through a sieve or *mouli*). Cut the eggs in half lengthways and
scoop out the yolks. Sieve the yolks and cream them into the
beans. Mix in the mayonnaise, lemon rind and juice and half
the chopped savory. Pile the mixture back into the egg whites
and sprinkle the remaining savory over the top.

Buttered eggs

Hard-boiled eggs can be chopped, mixed with melted butter and
flavourings, and then chilled to make a buttery sort of egg pâté.
The proportions given here are enough to be pressed into a
1 lb (450 g) loaf tin to make a main course for 4 people.

To serve the recipes as a first course, halve all the ingredients
(unless otherwise stated) and press the mixture into 1 fairly large
earthenware bowl or into 4 small soufflé dishes or ramekins.
Serve them with hot brown toast.

Light, savoury lettuce and nutty chervil make a perfect summer
loaf.

Buttered egg and lettuce loaf

8 eggs
1 small cabbage lettuce
2 oz (50 g) butter
grated rind and juice 1 lemon
¼ teaspoon (½ a 2.5 ml spoon) ground mace

4 tablespoons (60 ml) chopped chervil (or parsley if none is available)

Hard boil and chop the eggs. Finely chop the lettuce. Melt the butter in a frying pan on a low heat. Stir in the lettuce and just let it wilt. With the pan still on the heat, thoroughly mix in the eggs. Take the pan from the heat and mix in the lemon rind and juice, mace and chervil. Press the mixture into a 1 lb (450 g) loaf tin and chill it until it is firm. Turn out to serve.

Spring onions and a mild granular mustard make a very simple loaf that is ideal for both first and main courses.

Buttered egg and spring onion loaf

8 eggs
24 medium-sized spring onions
2 oz (50 g) butter
4 tablespoons (60 ml) chopped parsley
1 tablespoon (15 ml) Urchfont honey mild mustard

Hard boil and chop the eggs. Chop the spring onions. Melt the butter in a frying pan on a low heat. Mix in the onions and cook them until they are soft. With the pan still on the heat, thoroughly mix in the eggs and parsley. Take the pan from the heat and mix in the mustard. Press the mixture into a 1 lb (450 g) loaf tin and chill it until it is firm. Turn out to serve.

Flavour leeks with savory and a different kind of mustard.

Buttered eggs and leeks

8 eggs
12 oz (350 g) leeks
3 oz (75 g) butter
2 tablespoons (30 ml) chopped savory
1 tablespoon (15 ml) English Vineyard mustard
1 tablespoon (15 ml) grated Parmesan cheese

Hard boil and chop the eggs. Thinly slice the leeks. Melt half the butter in a frying pan on a low heat. Mix in the leeks and cook them until they are soft. Put in the remaining butter and let it melt. With the pan still on the heat, thoroughly mix in the eggs and savory. Take the pan from the heat and work in the mustard and cheese. Press the mixture into a 1 lb (450 g) loaf tin and chill it until it is firm. Turn out the loaf to serve.

(N.B. For a first course, when you are halving the other ingredients, use 2 teaspoons (10 ml) each mustard and Parmesan cheese.)

In this one, mustard and cress is used like a herb while the savoury English mustard brings out the flavour of the mushrooms.

Buttered egg and mushroom loaf

6 eggs
6 oz (175 g) open mushrooms
2 oz (50 g) butter
2 teaspoons (10 ml) made English mustard
1 box mustard and cress
2 tablespoons (30 ml) chopped chives, Welsh onions, scallions or
    the green part of spring onions
for garnish:
another box mustard and cress if desired

Hard boil and chop the eggs. Melt 1 oz (25 g) of the butter in a frying pan on a moderate heat. Put in the mushrooms and cook them for 2 minutes, stirring frequently. Put in the rest of the butter and let it melt. With the pan still on the heat, thoroughly mix in the eggs. Remove the pan from the heat and mix in the mustard and cress and chives. Press the mixture into a 1 lb (450 g) loaf tin and chill it until it is firm. Turn it out to serve and garnish if wished with the other box of cress.

(N.B. To serve as a first course use the same amount of butter and 4 oz (125 g) mushrooms; halve everything else.)

This spicy tomato loaf is best served as a main course.

Buttered egg and tomato loaf

6 eggs

1 lb (450 g) firm tomatoes
2 oz (50 g) butter
2 teaspoons (10 ml) whole coriander seeds
1 tablespoon (15 ml) tomato purée
1 teaspoon (5 ml) paprika
2 tablespoons (30 ml) chopped parsley
juice ½ lemon

Hard boil and chop the eggs. Oil a 1 lb (450 g) loaf tin. Scald and skin the tomatoes; slice one of them into 4 rings and de-seed and roughly chop the rest. Melt the butter in a frying pan on a very low heat. Put in the coriander seeds and cook them gently for 2 minutes. Mix in the eggs, tomato purée, paprika, parsley and lemon juice. Remove the pan from the heat and mix in the chopped tomatoes. Arrange the 4 tomato slices in the bottom of the oiled loaf tin and press in the egg mixture. Smooth the top and chill the loaf until it is firm. Turn it out to serve so the tomato slices are on top.

Pulses

'Pulses' is the extraordinary word used collectively for all the different types of dried beans and lentils that play such a large part in vegetarian (and in particular vegan) diets, supplying B group vitamins, essential minerals and, most importantly, protein. Only the soya bean contains all the essential amino acids that you need in a balanced diet, but if you eat the other pulses alongside whole grains (rice, wholemeal pasta or wholemeal bread) or with a miso or tamari sauce your protein needs will be supplied.

In most grocers and supermarkets there are usually only two types of beans available, haricot and butter or Lima beans, with red lentils and split peas, so to discover the real meaning of 'bean' go to your favourite wholefood shop.

Before I started looking around, I hadn't realised quite how many varieties of pulses you can buy. I should think that if you put them all together in different coloured heaps, you could find 30 or even more in shops up and down the country. Added to that the names vary from shop to shop and the terms 'bean' or 'pea' sometimes seem interchangeable. Even so you should be able to identify the various kinds from my brief description at the head of each section.

In my local bulk shop they are packed in biodegradable cellophane bags so you can see the musty browns, deep reds, moss greens and pale ivories and creams. There are round beans, flat beans, oval and kidney shaped ones. Beside the beans there are the usual red lentils and two others, a larger, whole, dull-green variety and a very tiny type which is a deep, soft greyish brown. There are also crinkly, whole marrow-fat peas and green and yellow split peas.

These, then, are pulses. How are we to cook them? They are so cheap that it's quite possible to buy some of each and take them home and experiment. First of all find the quickest and most effective way of cooking each one plainly. Then taste them to discover which accompaniments and flavourings can be used to complement and blend with their individual qualities. Gradually, you really will begin to 'feel your pulses'. Here are some tips to help you on your way.

Quantities

8 oz (225 g) dry weight of any of the beans will be just right for a main dish for 4 people. When they have been soaked and cooked they will more or less double in weight so that, depending on the variety, you will get 1 lb 15 oz to 2 lb 1 oz (875–925 g) of cooked beans from 8 oz (225 g) dried. To serve beans as a first course, halve the amounts of all the ingredients in the recipe, unless otherwise stated.

Lentils and split peas tend to be so appetising that you will probably find that 12 oz (350 g) is a more satisfactory amount to make up into a main dish. Really the best thing to do is to experiment a little to find the amount that is best for your family. All the ingredients in the lentil recipes can easily be adjusted up or down in proportion.

Basic cooking

Each type of bean varies as to the amount of cooking it needs and the exact times are given in the appropriate sections. Here, though, are a few points that apply to all types. (There is general advice for handling lentils and split peas in their respective sections.)

It is often very difficult to remember in the evening to put something to soak for the next day, so I was pleased to find that with most beans this isn't necessary. The one real exception is soya beans; and butter beans do benefit from long soaking if you remember.

Unless you have an oven that is permanently hot, such as one in an Aga cooker, using the oven for just one dish of beans is not really economical as they do take a long time. Probably the best way of initially softening them is to simmer them gently on top of the stove. If you are used to cooking beans and have your own favourite way then use this and follow only the next stages of the recipes. If you are new to beans, and use an ordinary gas or electric stove, try this way. The exact amounts and times are given in the individual sections.

Put the beans into a saucepan with the required amount of water, cover them, bring them gently to the boil and simmer them for 2 minutes. Turn off the heat and soak them (*see* under the individual beans for how long). Bring them to the boil again and simmer them until they are tender.

The amount of water recommended for each type of bean is for 8 oz (225 g), and by the end of the cooking time it should either be completely absorbed or there should only be a little left over. The idea is not to have too much liquid goodness wasted. If you halve or quarter the amount of beans you are cooking, then do the same with the water, but check regularly as, with some saucepans, smaller amounts dry up much quicker. If you find this to be the case, add a little more water to the pan as it is needed.

Most of the recipes I have given for beans use this basic cooking method, but a few use the oven for finishing off and some are cooked completely in the oven. In other recipes, the beans are simmered alone for a short time and then mixed with rice or other fresh vegetables. When in doubt, simmer them first. You can do virtually anything with them then and slightly overcooked beans are far preferable to undercooked.

Seasonings and flavourings
It is best not to season any of the beans during the initial cooking as this makes the skins tough. A bayleaf or bouquet garni can be added to the pan if you like, but I usually prefer to leave all the flavouring until later. However split peas and lentils can be seasoned as they cook.

Although the combinations of beans, herbs, spices and other vegetables are seemingly endless, try not to mix a dash of this and a pinch of that or half a pound of something else indiscriminately into the pan. Each bean has its individual flavour, and sometimes this is so delicate that a strong addition could clash or mask it completely. Taste the beans first and then think of an addition that will either complement or blend with them. Try to match the colours of the ingredients, too, to make a good-looking dish. Choose either similar colours or contrasting ones.

The addition of salt in the latter stages of cooking is a matter of taste. Try the beans first and add it only if you think it necessary.

Serving

Bean dishes make excellent main courses. Accompany them with brown rice, wholemeal pasta, brown toast or baked jacket potatoes and a green vegetable or salad. Serve them either alone in one large or four separate serving bowls, or arranged on a large dish with the other parts of the meal. Garnish them with parsley sprigs or other herbs, lemon slices or tomato rings, or whatever else goes best in flavour and appearance with the beans themselves and with the additional ingredients. For the first courses, the same dishes can be halved in quantity, garnished and served with fingers of toast or brown bread and butter.

Serve bean salads on beds of lettuce, watercress, mustard and cress or curly endive. Garnish them with sliced hard-boiled eggs, wedges or slices of lemon and tomatoes or radishes. Scatter chopped nuts, sesame seeds or chopped herbs over the top. Serve one salad as a main dish or a selection of different kinds for salad buffets, parties or sit-down meals. Again, halve the amounts for a first course.

Pies, quiches and pasties

I have given some definite recipes for shepherd's pies and scone-topped dishes to suggest what can be done with basic bean ideas. These toppings can be used for many of the other more substantial bean recipes, especially those that have a fairly rich sauce. Other types of beans can be put into a pie dish and covered with pastry, made into flatter plate-pies and quiches, or baked in Cornish pasty shapes. Even the salads can be made into a simple flan by putting them into a pre-cooked pastry case and topping them with the appropriate garnish.

As accompanying dishes

Any of the simpler, more gently flavoured bean dishes (except those made from rich soya beans) can also be served as an accompaniment to a main dish to replace potatoes, rice or pasta. They are particularly good with egg dishes and quiches.

Leftovers

First, a tip not strictly related just to leftovers: it is a good idea to cook twice the amount of beans that you will need for one meal. It saves time and gas or electricity later on and ensures that you have some ready-cooked ingredients in the refrigerator for emergency and spur-of-the-moment meals. Put the beans into a covered container and store them in the middle or bottom of the refrigerator for up to 5 days. You can make them up into hot dishes, salads or spreads whenever convenient.

Leftovers from hot dishes can always be gently reheated and served again in the same form. Or you can rub them through the fine blade of a *mouli* or work them in a blender with stock to make soup. Mash them up and mix them with fresh breadcrumbs or mashed potatoes to make savoury cakes, coated in flour and fried. Mash or *mouli* them with a little lemon juice or vinegar, olive oil and some finely chopped pickles to make a sandwich spread. This is the best way of using up leftover bean salads.

Lentils and split peas can also be made into soups. Gradually stir stock into the smooth purées and rub whole lentils through a *mouli* or put them into a blender with the stock. Add herbs and flavourings to taste if you need them. Lentils can also be made into savoury cakes or croquettes with mashed potatoes. The purées can be mixed with leftover cooked brown rice to make patties.

All the recipes below work well for their own particular type of bean, but you don't by any means have to stick to them. Start first with the suggested ingredients and the next time you cook the dish make changes and additions to suit your own particular taste and storecupboard. Make the mixtures into pies and quiches, serve some of the hot ones cold and the cold ones hot; surround them with rice or scatter them with herbs; accompany them with salads or with cooked vegetables; or cook them plainly and coat them with one of the savoury sauces that are given in a later chapter. Discover how versatile pulses can be.

☙   ☙   ☙

Soya beans

Soya beans have the highest nutritional value of all the pulses. They are the only ones that contain fats and the essential amino acids necessary to make a complete protein. Dried Soya beans are round and about the same size as a large pea. They can be yellow, green, brown or black, but the ones most readily available in this country are ivory coloured (and are usually called white).

When you put these hard, round little pellets into water one evening for the first time, and then look at them the following morning, you get quite a surprise. Instead of just expanding, they elongate to about the size and shape of large peanuts and their colour changes to that of yellow cream.

After this initial soaking, you can eat them as they are by adding a few to crunchy salads. They have the flavour and texture of raw green peas that are very young and fresh. An even better way of using them as a salad ingredient is to salt them, when they are rather like salted peanuts or almonds. Use them up quickly though. After about 6 hours they tend to go slightly soggy, although the flavour stays the same. Salted soya beans can also be handed round with pre-dinner drinks or used as party snacks.

Salted soya beans

4 oz (125 g) soya beans
1 tablespoon (15 ml) fine sea salt
3 tablespoons (45 ml) olive oil

Soak the soya beans in cold water for at least 12 hours. Drain them and squeeze as many as possible from their fine, outer skins. (This isn't absolutely essential if the skins are still fairly firmly stuck, but do it if they are loose or you will get a pan full of cooked skins.) Scatter the salt over a piece of absorbent kitchen paper. Heat the oil in a frying pan on a moderate heat. Put in the beans and cook them until they are a golden brown, moving them around constantly. Transfer them to the kitchen paper and coat them with the salt. Let them cool and pick out any pieces of skin. Eat them as soon as you can.

But soya beans are far more commonly cooked and served in casserole-type dishes. Here is the initial soaking and cooking process.

Basic method for soya beans

8 oz (225 g) soya beans
2 pints (1.125 l) water

Put the beans into a saucepan with the water, cover them and soak them for at least 12 hours. Bring them to the boil and simmer them on top of the stove (or in the oven if you have it on in any case for something else) for 3 hours. Drain them if necessary. They will be ready now for further cooking, with other ingredients, for 1½–2 hours in the oven. But if the beans are to be used in a salad or for a final dish that requires only quick cooking, simmer them for 4 hours instead of 3 at this stage.

Cooked soya beans are quite different from all the other types of beans in both flavour and texture. In all my experiments with beans, I liked them the best of all. They are firm and slightly oily, rather like a cross between the other types of white beans and roasted peanuts. They are so substantial and full of goodness that they should always be served as the main dish and not as an accompaniment. Cooked like meat and with similar flavourings they are absolutely delicious and far better (and cheaper!)

in their natural state than after they have been 'spun' into grey lumps of TVP.

First of all, here is a very simple dish with the traditional flavour of a Lancashire hot-pot.

Soya bean hot-pot

8 oz (225 g) soya beans
2 pints (1.125 l) water
1 oz (25 g) butter or vegetable margarine
2 medium onions, thinly sliced
1 lb (450 g) carrots, thinly sliced
¾ pint (425 ml) stock
2 tablespoons (30 ml) Worcestershire sauce or Yorkshire Relish
4 tablespoons (60 ml) chopped parsley
sea salt
freshly ground black pepper

Soak the beans and cook them for 3 hours. Drain them if necesssary.

Preheat the oven to Reg 4/350°F/180°C. Melt the butter or margarine in a flameproof casserole on a low heat. Mix in the onions and cook them until they are soft. Pour in the stock and bring it to the boil. Add the beans, carrots, Worcester sauce and parsley and season. Cover the casserole and put it into the oven for 1½ hours. Serve with jacket-baked potatoes.

I intended this soya bean recipe to have a thick, creamy sauce like that of a veal blanquette. It came out with a translucent glaze and the flavour of a rich stew. 'Soya Bean Stew' doesn't sound too good, so the original name was kept.

Soya bean blanquette

8 oz (225 g) soya beans
2 pints (1.125 l) water
1 small head celery
8 oz (225 g) carrots
8 oz (225 g) mushrooms
4 tablespoons (60 ml) olive oil
2 medium onions, thinly sliced

2 tablespoons (30 ml) soya flour
1 pint (575 ml) stock
4 tablespoons (60 ml) chopped parsley
2 bayleaves
large bouquet garni

Soak the beans and simmer them for 3 hours. Drain them if
necessary. Preheat the oven to Reg 4/350°F/180°C. Chop the
celery. Thinly slice the carrots and mushrooms. Heat the oil in
a flameproof casserole on a low heat. Stir in the celery, carrots
and onions, cover them and let them sweat for 10 minutes. Stir
in the soya flour and cook it for 1 minute. Stir in the stock and
bring it to the boil. Mix in the mushrooms and bring the stock
to the boil again. Mix in the beans and parsley and tuck in the
bayleaves and bouquet garni. Cover the casserole and put it into
the oven for 1½ hours. Serve with plainly boiled rice or one of
the milder flavoured savoury rice dishes.

Here the beans are cooked with the vegetables and spices of a
Hungarian goulash.

Soya bean goulash

8 oz (225 g) soya beans
2 pints (1.125 l) water
8 oz (225 g) mushrooms
4 tablespoons (60 ml) olive oil
2 medium onions, thinly sliced
1 large clove garlic, finely chopped
1 tablespoon (15 ml) paprika
2 teaspoons (10 ml) caraway seeds
1 tablespoon (15 ml) tomato purée
¾ pint (425 ml) stock
2 tablespoons (30 ml) chopped parsley
1 bayleaf
2 large, pickled Hungarian gherkins

Soak the soya beans and simmer them for 3 hours. Drain them
if necessary. Preheat the oven to Reg 3/325°F/160°C. Thinly
slice the mushrooms. Heat the oil in a flameproof casserole on a

low heat. Stir in the onions and garlic and cook them until the onions are beginning to soften. Stir in the paprika and caraway. Keep cooking until the onions are completely soft. Mix in the tomato purée and then the stock. Bring the stock to the boil, add the beans and mushrooms and tuck in the bayleaf. Cover the casserole and put it into the oven for 2 hours. Finely chop the gherkins and add them to the casserole for the final 10 minutes of cooking time.

Cook the beans in the natural juices of tomatoes; they turn out a rich red colour and slightly nutty in flavour.

Soya bean and tomato casserole

8 oz (225 g) soya beans
2 pints (1.125 l) water
1½ lb (675 g) ripe tomatoes (use so-called 'frying' ones for cheapness)
2 medium onions, thinly sliced
1 large clove garlic, finely chopped
4 tablespoons (60 ml) chopped parsley
2 tablespoons (30 ml) chopped thyme
2 teaspoons (10 ml) paprika
2 pinches cayenne pepper
4 oz (125 g) grated farmhouse double Gloucester cheese (optional)

Soak the beans and simmer them for 3 hours. Drain them if necessary. Preheat the oven to Reg 4/350°F/180°C. Scald and skin the tomatoes and slice them into rings. Arrange half of them in the bottom of a casserole (an oven-to-table one if you have it). Lay on one of the sliced onions and on top of these put half the garlic, herbs, paprika and cayenne pepper. Put in all the beans, then the rest of the flavourings, the remaining onion and, lastly, the rest of the tomatoes. Cover the casserole and put it into the oven. If you are not using the cheese leave the casserole in the oven for 1½ hours, then serve. If you are using it, remove the casserole after 1¼ hours, scatter the cheese on top of the tomatoes and put the casserole back, uncovered, for 15 minutes. In either case serve straight from the dish with wholemeal pasta.

The lemon juices and spices in the following recipe are often used to flavour chicken, but with soya beans they work superbly well. The final dish is a musty-brown colour, refreshingly but not heavily spiced. It is flecked with darker brown pieces of slightly sticky spices from the sides of the casserole.

Spiced lemon soya beans

8 oz (225 g) soya beans
2 pints (1.125 l) water
4 tablespoons (60 ml) olive oil
2 medium onions, thinly sliced
1 large clove garlic, finely chopped
2 teaspoons (10 ml) ground cumin
2 teaspoons (10 ml) ground coriander
4 tablespoons (60 ml) soya flour
1 pint (575 ml) stock
2 bayleaves
grated rind and juice 1 lemon

Soak the beans and simmer them for three hours. Drain them if necessary. Preheat the oven to Reg 4/350°F/180°C. Heat the oil in a flameproof casserole on a low heat. Stir in the onions, garlic, cumin, coriander and soya flour. Cook them gently, stirring frequently, until the onions are soft. Stir in the stock, bring it to the boil and let it simmer for one minute. Mix in the beans, bayleaves and lemon rind. Cover the casserole and put it into the oven for 1½ hours. Remove the bayleaves and stir in the lemon juice, bringing in all the tasty spicy brown pieces that will be clinging round the edges of the pot. Cover again, and return the casserole to the oven for a further 10 minutes. Serve the beans with brown rice fried with turmeric.

The barbecue sauce used here is similar to Chinese marinades for pork. It is red and gently sweet and sour.

Barbecued soya beans

8 oz (225 g) soya beans
2 pints (1.125 l) water

¾ pint (425 ml) stock
2 tablespoons (30 ml) tomato purée
2 tablespoons (30 ml) tamari sauce
2 teaspoons (10 ml) clear honey
1 tablespoon (15 ml) white wine vinegar
2 teaspoons (10 ml) chopped rosemary
1 clove garlic, crushed without salt
freshly ground black pepper

Soak the beans and simmer them for 3 hours. Drain them if necessary. Preheat the oven to Reg 4/350°F/180°C. Put the beans into a casserole. Mix all the other ingredients together and pour them into the casserole. Cover the beans and put them into the oven for 2 hours. Serve them with Chinese egg-fried rice or rice fried with turmeric.

In this recipe, the beans are completely cooked in the initial simmering. It is another Chinese-style dish, delicate in both appearance and flavour. If you are serving it with a selection of other Chinese dishes, halve all the ingredients.

Soya beans with cucumber—Chinese style

8 oz (225 g) soya beans
2 pints (1.125 l) water
1 medium-sized cucumber
12 medium-sized spring onions
2 tablespoons (30 ml) cornflour
8 tablespoons (120 ml) dry sherry
½ pint (275 ml) stock
1 tablespoon (15 ml) tamari sauce
4 tablespoons (60 ml) olive oil
1 large clove garlic, finely chopped
½ oz (15 g) fresh ginger root, peeled and grated
or 2 teaspoons (10 ml) ground ginger

Soak the soya beans and simmer them for 4 hours. Drain them if necessary. Cut the cucumber into eighths lengthways and cut away and discard the seeds. Chop the remaining parts into 1½ in (4 cm) lengths. Chop the white and green parts of the onions into pieces the same length. Put the cornflour into a bowl and blend in the sherry, stock and tamari sauce. Heat the oil in a frying pan on a high heat. Put in the cucumber, onions, and garlic and move them around on the heat until the garlic browns. Mix in the beans and ginger. Stir in the cornflour mixture and keep stirring until it thickens to make a pale brown, translucent sauce.

Haricot beans

The common baked bean is a kind of haricot or kidney bean, and haricots are probably the most widely used of all the bean varieties. They are small, white and oval and when they are cooked expand slightly and turn even whiter and almost translucent. This gives them a delicate appearance to match a fine, delicate flavour that should not be masked by too many strong spices or herbs.

Basic method for haricot beans

8 oz (225 g) haricot beans
1½ pints (850 ml) water

Put the beans into a saucepan with the water. Cover them and bring them gently to the boil. Simmer them for 2 minutes. Turn off the heat and let the beans soak for 2–3 hours. Bring them to the boil again and simmer for 2 hours. Drain them if necessary.

Carrots, nutmeg and parsley are superb mild-flavoured accompaniments for haricot beans.

Haricot beans with carrots and onions

8 oz (225 g) haricot beans
1½ pints (850 ml) water
1 lb (450 g) carrots
2 medium onions
4 tablespoons (60 ml) olive oil
¼ pint (150 ml) dry white wine

1 pint (575 ml) stock
4 tablespoons (60 ml) chopped parsley
freshly grated nutmeg (about one-eighth of a nut)

Soak the beans and cook them for only 1½ hours. Drain them if necessary. Preheat the oven to Reg 3/325°F/160°C. Dice the carrots finely. Quarter the onions lengthways and thinly slice them. Heat the oil in a flameproof casserole on a low heat. Stir in the onions and cook them until they are soft. Stir in the beans and carrots. Pour in the wine and stock and bring them to the boil. Add the parsley and nutmeg. Cover the casserole and put it into the oven for 2 hours. Serve with potato cakes or sautéed potatoes.

Leeks are another not-too-strong accompaniment for haricot beans, and the cider and mild mustard that always go with them so well complement the beans beautifully.

Haricot beans and leeks

8 oz (225 g) haricot beans
1½ pints (850 ml) water
1 lb (450 g) leeks
½ pint (275 ml) stock
¼ pint (150 ml) dry cider
2 teaspoons (10 ml) Dijon mustard
2 tablespoons (30 ml) chopped parsley

Soak the beans and simmer them for 2 hours. Drain them if necessary. Wash and thinly slice the leeks. Put the beans and leeks into a saucepan and add the stock, cider, mustard and parsley. Cover the pan and set it on a moderate heat for 20 minutes. The liquid should be just absorbed and the beans and leeks completely tender and flavoured gently with cider and mustard.

This recipe has a similar flavour to baked beans but it still allows the delicate haricot bean taste to come through. You don't have

to serve them as I have suggested, but it really does complete
the meal.

Savoury haricot beans on toast

8 oz (225 g) haricot beans
1½ pints (850 ml) water
4 tablespoons (60 ml) olive oil
1 large onion, finely chopped
2 tablespoons (30 ml) tomato purée
1 tablespoon (15 ml) Worcestershire sauce or Yorkshire Relish
1 teaspoon (5 ml) mustard powder
for serving:
wholemeal toast
butter or vegetable margarine
little made English mustard
1 thin slice farmhouse Cheddar cheese per slice toast

Soak the beans and simmer them for 2 hours. Drain them if
necessary. Heat the oil in a saucepan on a low heat. Stir in the
onion and cook it until it is soft. Stir in the beans, tomato purée,
Worcester sauce and mustard powder. Cover the pan and keep
it on a very low heat for 10 minutes. Toast the bread, butter it
and spread it with a thin layer of made mustard. Lay all the
slices on a large, flat heatproof serving dish and pile the beans
on top. Put a slice of cheese over each piece of toast and put the
dish under a high grill until the cheese melts.

Here the beans are cooked in less water because more liquid is
obtained from the pumpkin and, towards the end of cooking,
from the juices of the tomatoes.

Haricot beans in spiced pumpkin sauce

8 oz (225 g) haricot beans
1 pint (575 ml) water
2 lb (900 g) chopped raw pumpkin
1 large onion, finely chopped
1 clove garlic, finely chopped
1 tablespoon (15 ml) chopped savory
2 tablespoons (30 ml) tomato purée
½ lb (225 g) tomatoes

Soak the beans, bring them to the boil and simmer them for 15 minutes. Mix in the pumpkin, onion, garlic, savory and tomato purée. Cover and simmer very gently for 1½ hours. While the beans are cooking, scald and skin the tomatoes. Squeeze the seeds into a sieve placed over a bowl and rub them with a wooden spoon to extract the juices. After the 1½ hours, add these juices to the beans and cook for a further 30 minutes, still covered. Slice the tomato shells and add them to the pan just before serving so they heat through but stay firm. Serve the beans with wholemeal pasta.

This recipe is finished off in the oven. The beans are enlivened by the slightly sharp flavour of cider and Bramley apples.

Haricot beans with apples

8 oz (225 g) haricot beans
1½ pints (850 ml) water
4 tablespoons (60 ml) olive oil
1 large onion, thinly sliced
1 large Bramley apple, peeled, quartered, cored and sliced
½ pint (275 ml) dry cider
½ pint (275 ml) stock
2 tablespoons (30 ml) chopped parsley
sea salt
freshly ground black pepper

Soak the beans and simmer them for 1 hour. Preheat the oven to Reg 4/350°F/180°C. Heat the oil in a flameproof casserole on a low heat. Put in the onion and cook it until it is soft. Mix in the beans and apple. Pour in the cider and stock and bring them to the boil. Add the parsley and seasonings. Cover the casserole and put it into the oven for 1 hour. Serve with a savoury rice. N.B. This bean dish makes a good accompaniment to a light main course.

Use the beans for a salad made green with parsley and green olives, its dressing thickened with breadcrumbs. The amounts given here make a really substantial main course. To serve it as one of a selection of salads or as a first course, halve the amounts.

Green haricot bean salad

8 oz (225 g) haricot beans
1½ pints (850 ml) water
3 oz (75 g) wholemeal breadcrumbs
6 tablespoons (90 ml) olive oil
3 tablespoons (45 ml) white wine vinegar
1 clove garlic, crushed with a pinch sea salt
freshly ground black pepper
6 tablespoons (90 ml) chopped parsley
12 green olives

Soak the beans and cook them for 2 hours. Drain them if necessary. Pound the breadcrumbs with the oil and gradually work in the vinegar. Mix in the garlic, pepper and chopped parsley. Fold the dressing into the beans while they are still warm. Stone the olives and quarter them lengthways. Mix them into the salad and let it get quite cold. The longer you leave this salad the better it becomes as the beans gradually soak up the dressing.

Black olives are used here rather than green. All you need with this salad is a crisp lettuce and some firm, sweet tomatoes.

Haricot bean and black olive salad

8 oz (225 g) haricot beans
1½ pints (850 ml) water
4 tablespoons (60 ml) olive oil
1 large onion, thinly sliced
1 large clove garlic, finely chopped
12 black olives, stoned and quartered
2 tablespoons (30 ml) white wine vinegar
1 tablespoon (15 ml) tomato purée
2 tablespoons (30 ml) chopped parsley

Soak the beans and simmer them for 2 hours. Drain them if necessary. Heat the oil in a saucepan on a low heat. Stir in the onion and garlic, cover them and cook them gently for 10 minutes. Stir in the beans, olives, vinegar and tomato purée. Cover and cook for a further 10 minutes. Mix in the parsley and let the salad get quite cold.

Butter beans

Butter beans are sometimes also called Lima beans. They are large, flat and white and are one of the most readily available beans. They go a pinky, ivory colour when cooked and have a strong, savoury flavour that is good with thick brown sauces. Next to soya beans, they need the longest cooking.

Basic method for butter beans

8 oz (225 g) butter beans
2 pints (1.125 l) water

Put the beans into a saucepan with the water. Cover and either soak them overnight or bring them to the boil, simmer for two minutes and soak for 4 hours. Bring them to the boil again and simmer for 3 hours. Drain them if necessary.

This first recipe, with only beer and pickled onions for flavouring, makes an excellent accompaniment. Serve it with a rich dish such as the root vegetable crumble and you have a perfect winter meal.

Butter beans in beer

8 oz (225 g) butter beans
2 pints (1.125 l) water
½ pint (275 ml) bitter beer
4 pickled onions, finely chopped
1 bayleaf
sea salt
freshly ground black pepper

Soak the beans and cook them for 2½ hours only. Drain them if necessary. Preheat the oven to Reg 4/350°F/180°C. Put the beans into a casserole with the beer, onions and bayleaf and season. Cover the casserole and put it into the oven for 1 hour.

Use pickled walnuts with the butter beans this time, to make a rich, savoury, dark brown dish that is excellent with jacket potatoes and a green vegetable. You can also serve it as a side dish with egg dishes and quiches.

Butter beans and pickled walnuts

8 oz (225 g) butter beans
2 pints (1.125 l) water
1 oz (25 g) butter *or* vegetable margarine
2 medium onions, thinly sliced
4 pickled walnuts, finely chopped
4 tablespoons (60 ml) chopped parsley
½ teaspoon (2.5 ml) ground mace
1½ pints (850 ml) stock
sea salt
freshly ground black pepper

Soak the beans and simmer them for 2 hours. Drain them and reserve any liquid. Preheat the oven to Reg 3/325°F/160°C. Melt the butter or margarine in a flameproof casserole on a low heat. Mix in the onions and cook them until they are golden. Stir in the beans, walnuts, parsley and mace. Make the reserved cooking liquid up to 1½ pints (850 ml) with the stock, pour it into the casserole and bring it to the boil. Cover the casserole and put it into the oven for 2 hours.

Miso is added to the sauce in the next two recipes, to make the dishes dark and tasty. The first is excellent on toast or with jacket-baked potatoes. The second needs only a salad to accompany it.

Butter beans in brown onion sauce

8 oz (225 g) butter beans
2 pints (1.125 l) water
1 oz (25 g) butter *or* 4 tablespoons (60 ml) olive oil
1 medium onion, finely chopped

1 tablespoon (15 ml) wholemeal flour
2 teaspoons (10 ml) miso
¾ pint (425 ml) stock

Soak the beans and simmer them for three hours. Drain them if necessary. Melt the butter or heat the oil in a saucepan on a low heat. Stir in the onion and cook it until it is a good brown. Stir in the flour and cook it, stirring, until it turns russet brown. Take the pan from the heat and stir in the miso and the stock. Bring the sauce to the boil, stirring. Mix in the cooked beans, cover, and simmer gently for 20 minutes.

Butter beans and potatoes in miso gravy

8 oz (225 g) butter beans
2 pints (1.125 l) water
2 lb (900 g) potatoes
4 tablespoons (60 ml) olive oil
2 large onions, thinly sliced
2 tablespoons (30 ml) miso
1½ pints (850 ml) stock
4 tablespoons (60 ml) chopped parsley
8 chopped sage leaves

Soak the butter beans and cook them for 2 hours only. Drain them if necessary. Preheat the oven to Reg 3/325°F/160°C. Scrub the potatoes and chop them into ¾ in (2 cm) dice. Heat the oil in a large flameproof casserole on a low heat. Put in the onions and cook them until they are soft. Remove the pan from the heat and mix in the miso. Gradually stir in the stock. Put the pan back on the heat and bring the stock to the boil. Add the parsley and sage and mix in the beans and potatoes. Cover the casserole and put it into the oven for 2 hours.

This dish of butter beans and Brussels sprouts is lighter but still has a strong individual flavour. It is smooth-textured and nutty.

Butter beans and Brussels sprouts

8 oz (225 g) butter beans

2 pints (1.125 l) water
1 lb (450 g) Brussels sprouts
up to ½ pint (275 ml) stock (approx.)
1 tablespoon (15 ml) Dijon mustard
2 tablespoons (30 ml) chopped parsley

Soak the beans and cook them for 3 hours. Drain them and
reserve any liquid. Trim and thinly slice the sprouts. Put the
beans and sprouts into a saucepan. Make the bean liquid up to
½ pint (275 ml) with the stock and add it to the saucepan with
the mustard and parsley. Cover the saucepan and set it on a
moderate heat for 20 minutes.

Chick Peas

Chick peas are round and creamy coloured, with a lengthways
groove and a small pointed top. They expand slightly all round
when they are cooked and their colour is slightly deepened. They
have a nutty flavour and are often used in spreads and pâtés,
such as the Greek *hummus*, and also in Indian curries. Cooked
fairly plainly, they are perhaps best served as an accompaniment
rather than as a main dish.

Basic method for chick peas

8 oz (225 g) chick peas
2 pints (1.125 l) water

Put the chick peas into a saucepan with the water. Cover them,
set them on a low heat and bring them to the boil. Simmer them
for 2 minutes, then turn off the heat and let them soak for 3 hours.
Bring them to the boil again and simmer for a further 3 hours, by
which time they will be tender and most of the water will be
absorbed. Drain them if necessary.

The first two recipes make excellent accompanying dishes. In the
first, the rich nutty flavour is sharpened a little with lemon juice.

Chick peas with green peppers and chillis

8 oz (225 g) chick peas
2 pints (1.125 l) water
2 medium-sized green peppers
4 green chillis (or, if not available, ½ teaspoon (2.5 ml) Tabasco sauce
3 tablespoons (45 ml) olive oil
1 large clove garlic, finely chopped
juice 1 lemon

Soak the chick peas and simmer them for 3 hours. Drain them if necessary. Core and dice the peppers. Core the chillis and chop them finely. Heat the oil in a frying pan on a low heat. Stir in the peppers, chillis and garlic and cook them for 5 minutes. Add the chick peas and cook them until they are just showing signs of browning. Pour in the lemon juice (and the Tabasco sauce if you are using it), and let it bubble. Serve as soon as you can.

This simple, nutty purée goes excellently with all kinds of vegetable main course dishes, and with those based on cheese.

Chick pea purée

8 oz (225 g) chick peas
2 pints (1.125 l) water
4 tablespoons (60 ml) olive oil
juice 1 lemon
1 clove garlic, crushed with a pinch sea salt
4 tablespoons (60 ml) chopped parsley

Soak the chick peas and simmer them for 3 hours. Drain them if necessary. Put them through the fine blade of a *mouli*, work them in a blender or pound them well with a potato masher. Heat the oil in a saucepan on a low heat and gradually work in the chick peas, lemon juice, garlic and parsley. Let the purée heat through completely and serve.

Serve this salad as a main course, on a bed of crisp lettuce, endive or mustard and cress. If you halve the amounts it makes an excellent first course.

Chick pea and cider salad

8 oz (225 g) chick peas
2 pints (1.125 l) water
2 tablespoons (30 ml) soya flour
½ pint (275 ml) dry cider
4 tablespoons (60 ml) olive oil
4 tablespoons (60 ml) cider vinegar
8 sticks celery
2 large, sharp eating apples
4 oz (125 g) seedless raisins
freshly grated nutmeg (about one-eighth of a nut)

Soak, simmer and drain the chick peas. Let them cool. Put the
soya flour into a small saucepan and stir in the cider with a
wooden spoon. Set the pan on a low heat and bring the contents
to the boil. Simmer, uncovered, for 20 minutes, stirring occasionally. Take the pan from the heat and let the sauce cool. Gradually
beat in the oil and vinegar. Chop the celery and quarter, core and
chop the apples. Put them into a bowl with the chick peas and
raisins. Grate in the nutmeg and fold in the dressing.

꽃   꽃   꽃

Black-eyed beans

Black-eyed beans look just as you would expect – small, cream,
rough-skinned and kidney shaped, with a black mark around the
tiny cream sprouting part that makes them look as if they have
one black eye. They cook quickly, keep the same shape but
expand a little and turn a very faint pinky colour. Because they
swell, their skin becomes smooth. Their flavour is musty and
very savoury.

They have become a great favourite amongst the many beans
I have tried, and I can't resist calling them 'Black-Eyed Susies' as
they seem such an amenable and easily-cooked bean.

Basic method for black-eyed beans

8 oz (225 g) black-eyed beans
1 pint (575 ml) water

Put the beans into a saucepan with the water. Cover them, bring them gently to the boil and simmer them for 2 minutes. Turn off the heat and let them stand for 2 hours. Bring them to the boil again and simmer for 30 minutes if there is going to be a further cooking process and 45 minutes if they are to be mixed into a salad or coated with a simple savoury sauce.

The musty flavour of cinnamon goes well with the musty flavour of the black-eyed beans, especially if they both can be lightened with tomatoes.

Black-eyed beans with cinnamon and tomatoes

8 oz (225 g) black-eyed beans
1 pint (575 ml) water
12 oz (350 g) firm tomatoes
4 tablespoons (60 ml) olive oil
2 medium onions, thinly sliced
1 large clove garlic, finely chopped
2 teaspoons (10 ml) ground cinnamon
½ pint (275 ml) stock
2 teaspoons (10 ml) tomato purée

Soak the beans and simmer them for 30 minutes. Drain them if necessary. Scald, skin and de-seed the tomatoes and cut them into strips. Heat the oil in a saucepan on a low heat. Stir in the onions and garlic and cook until the onions are soft. Stir in the beans and cinnamon, cover them and cook them gently for 2 minutes. Pour in the stock and bring it to the boil. Mix in the tomato purée, cover and simmer for 20 minutes so the beans pick up the cinnamony flavour. Mix in the tomatoes just before serving, so they heat through but stay firm.

Mushrooms, allspice and cloves here provide the blending flavours, while savory gives lightness.

Black-eyed beans and mushrooms

8 oz (225 g) black-eyed beans
1 pint (575 ml) water

12 oz (350 g) open mushrooms
1 oz (25 g) butter *or* vegetable margarine *or* 4 tablespoons (60 ml)
  olive oil
2 medium onions, thinly sliced
½ pint (275 ml) stock
6 allspice berries
6 black peppercorns
4 cloves
2 tablespoons (30 ml) chopped savory

Soak the beans and simmer them for 30 minutes. Drain them if
necessary. Thinly slice the mushrooms. Melt the butter or
margarine or heat the oil in a saucepan on a low heat. Stir in the
onions and cook them until they are soft. Stir in the mushrooms
and the beans and let them get well coated with the butter or oil.
Pour in the stock and bring it to the boil. Crush the spices
together with a small pestle and mortar, and add the spices and
savory to the pan. Cover and set on a very low heat for 20
minutes.

Put musty beans with earthy turnips and sharpen them up with
spicy pickled onions.

Black-eyed beans and turnips

8 oz (225 g) black-eyed beans
1 pint (575 ml) water
12 oz (350 g) white turnips
3 tablespoons (45 ml) olive oil
1 medium onion, finely chopped
4 large, pickled onions, finely chopped
1 tablespoon (15 ml) grated horseradish
¾ pint (425 ml) stock
2 tablespoons (30 ml) chopped parsley

Soak the beans and simmer them for 30 minutes. Drain them if
necessary. Preheat the oven to Reg 4/350°F/180°C. Scrub and
finely dice the turnips. Heat the oil in a flameproof casserole on
a low heat. Stir in the turnips and onion, cover them and let them
sweat for 10 minutes. Mix in the beans, pickled onions and horse-

radish. Pour in the stock and bring it to the boil. Mix in the parsley. Cover the casserole and put it into the oven for 30 minutes.

Here is another dish of beans and vegetables together. This time, the cabbage provides the lighter side while the sherry enhances the beans.

Black-eyed beans and Savoy cabbage

8 oz (225 g) black-eyed beans
1 pint (575 ml) water
up to ¼ pint (150 ml) stock
1 small Savoy cabbage
6 tablespoons (90 ml) sherry
2 teaspoons (10 ml) dill seeds
freshly ground black pepper
1 clove garlic, finely chopped

Soak the beans and simmer them for 45 minutes. Drain them if necessary, reserving the liquid. Make the liquid up to ¼ pint (150 ml) with stock. Shred the cabbage. Put it into a saucepan with the beans, stock, sherry, dill, pepper and garlic. Cover the pan and set it on a moderate heat for 20 minutes, stirring once or twice.

Red kidney beans

Red kidney beans are about ½ in (1.5 cm) long, kidney shaped (obviously!) and have a deep red, glossy skin. They cook quite quickly and swell slightly, turning a rich maroon colour. They have a rather floury texture and a savoury but fairly light flavour that can be turned in any direction with a subtle change of spice or herb.

Basic method for red kidney beans

8 oz (225 g) red kidney beans
1 pint (575 ml) water

Put the beans into a saucepan with the water. Cover them, bring them gently to the boil and simmer them for 2 minutes. Let them stand for 2 to 3 hours. Bring them to the boil again and simmer them for 1 hour. Drain them if necessary.

These kidney beans are often flavoured with hot, red peppers and spices and used in the beef dish called chilli con carne. Without the beef it is just as good. After the initial cooking the beans are cooked slowly in the oven so they absorb all the sauce's spicy flavour.

Red-hot bean casserole

8 oz (225 g) red kidney beans
1 pint (575 ml) water
1 lb (450 g) tomatoes
2 large red peppers
2 fresh red chillis (if you can only buy green, use these; if you can't find either, use ¼ teaspoon (½ a 2.5 ml spoon) cayenne pepper
2 medium onions, thinly sliced
1 large or 2 small cloves garlic, finely chopped
2 teaspoons (10 ml) paprika

Soak the beans and simmer them for 1 hour. Drain them if necessary. Preheat the oven to Reg 3/325°F/160°C. Scald, skin and slice the tomatoes. Core and de-seed the peppers and cut them into strips about 1 in by ¼ in (3 cm by 0.75 cm). Core the chillis and chop them very finely. Put half the tomatoes in the bottom of a casserole. Add half the onions and garlic, one of the peppers, half the chopped chillis and half the paprika. (If you are using cayenne pepper instead of chillis put in half of that as well.) Put in all the beans and follow with the other layers in reverse order, topping with the onion and, finally, the tomatoes. Cover the casserole and put it into the oven for 1½ hours. Mix everything together before serving.

Savoury brown rice is almost essential with this one.

Cinnamon and celery give a milder flavour to a dish that is cooked completely in the oven.

Middle-Eastern red beans

8 oz (225 g) red kidney beans
1 pint (575 ml) water
1½ pints (850 ml) stock
2 teaspoons (10 ml) ground cinnamon
2 teaspoons (10 ml) paprika
1 large clove garlic, crushed with a pinch sea salt
2 large or 4 small sticks celery, chopped
2 medium onions, thinly sliced
2 tablespoons (30 ml) chopped celery leaves
2 tablespoons (30 ml) chopped parsley
2 oz (50 g) currants
2 oz (50 g) almonds

Put the beans into a saucepan with the water and simmer and soak them as usual. Then drain them without the long simmering, reserving the water. Preheat the oven to Reg 3/325°F/160°C. Put the beans into a casserole with their soaking water and 1 pint (575 ml) of the stock. Mix in the cinnamon, paprika, garlic, celery, onions, celery leaves, parsley and currants. Cover the casserole and put it into the oven for 3 hours. Check after the first two hours and if the beans look like drying up, add a little more stock. Blanch and slice the almonds, and stir them into the beans just before serving.

This is another dish best served with brown rice.

In complete contrast, here is a lovely bright red, glossy dish with a Chinese flavour. In these quantities it will provide a main course for 4 people. Halve the amounts if you are serving the beans in a selection of Chinese dishes.

Sweet and sour red beans with red peppers

8 oz (225 g) red kidney beans
1 pint (575 ml) water
2 medium-sized red peppers
2 tablespoons (30 ml) cornflour
1 tablespoon (15 ml) tamari sauce
½ pint (275 ml) stock
2 tablespoons (30 ml) tomato purée

1 tablespoon (15 ml) soft brown sugar
4 tablespoons (60 ml) cider vinegar
4 tablespoons (60 ml) olive oil
2 medium onions, thinly sliced
1 large clove garlic, finely chopped

Soak the beans and simmer them for 1 hour. Drain them if necessary. Core the peppers and cut them into strips about 1 in by ¼ in (3 cm by 0.75 cm). Put the cornflour into a bowl and gradually mix in the tamari sauce, stock, tomato purée, sugar and vinegar. Heat the oil in a frying pan on a low heat. Put in the onions and garlic and cook them until the onions are soft. Mix in the peppers and carry on cooking until the onions are golden. Mix in the beans. Pour in the cornflour mixture, bring it to the boil and simmer everything for two minutes, stirring frequently.

This salad uses tomatoes and paprika again; they seem to be perfect additions to the red bean pot. The coriander gives the final special touch, but don't be deterred if you have none. Use parsley or chervil instead.

Red bean and tomato salad

8 oz (225 g) red kidney beans
1 pint (575 ml) water
4 tablespoons (60 ml) olive oil
1 medium onion, thinly sliced
1 clove garlic, finely chopped
2 tablespoons (30 ml) red wine vinegar
2 teaspoons (10 ml) paprika
1 teaspoon (5 ml) Tabasco sauce
8 oz (225 g) firm tomatoes
2 tablespoons (30 ml) chopped fresh coriander (use parsley or
  chervil if none is available)

Soak the beans as usual then bring to the boil again and simmer for 1 hour. Drain them if necessary. Heat the oil in a saucepan on a low heat. Stir in the onion and garlic, cover them and cook gently for 5 minutes. Stir in the beans and add the vinegar, paprika and Tabasco sauce. Cover the pan again and simmer everything for 2 minutes. Transfer the salad to a bowl and let it get completely cold. Scald, skin, de-seed and slice the tomatoes. Add them to the salad with the coriander just before serving.

ᘜ　　ᘜ　　ᘜ

Brown kidney beans

Brown kidney beans, or brown beans, are the same size and shape as the red ones and have a dull, nut brown skin. When cooked, they swell slightly and go a slightly darker brown. They have a musty, almost bitter flavour.

Basic method for brown beans

8 oz (225 g) brown beans
1 pint (575 ml) water

Put the beans into a saucepan with the water. Cover them, bring them gently to the boil and simmer them for 2 minutes. Turn off the heat and let them stand for 2 to 3 hours. Bring them to the boil again and simmer for 1 hour. Drain them if necessary.

A chasseur sauce of white wine, tomato purée and mushrooms makes brown beans into a rich, glossy dish with a dark, mushroomy flavour.

Brown bean chasseur

8 oz (225 g) brown beans
1 pint (575 ml) water
8 oz (225 g) button mushrooms
4 tablespoons (60 ml) olive oil
2 medium onions, thinly sliced
1 large clove garlic, finely chopped
¼ pint (150 ml) dry white wine
¼ pint (150 ml) stock
2 tablespoons (30 ml) tomato purée
for serving:
4 tablespoons (60 ml) chopped parsley
sautéed potatoes

Soak, simmer and drain the beans. Quarter the mushrooms. Heat the oil in a large frying pan on a low heat. Put in the onions and garlic and cook until they are golden. Raise the heat to moderate and add the mushrooms. Cook them, moving them around constantly, for 2 minutes. Pour in the wine and stock and stir in the tomato purée. Bring the mixture to the boil and mix in the beans. Simmer, uncovered, for 10 minutes.

Serve the beans strewn with chopped parsley and accompanied by sautéed potatoes.

After initial cooking the beans can be finished off in a casserole. Carrots and apples make a dish lighter in texture, colour and flavour than brown bean chasseur.

Baked brown beans with carrots and apples

8 oz (225 g) brown beans
1 pint (575 ml) water
up to ¾ pint (425 ml) stock
8 oz (225 g) carrots
2 medium-sized cooking apples
3 tablespoons (45 ml) olive oil
1 medium onion, thinly sliced
1 clove garlic, finely chopped
2 teaspoons (10 ml) mustard powder
10 chopped sage leaves
2 tablespoons (30 ml) tomato purée
sea salt and freshly ground black pepper

Soak the beans, simmer them for one hour and drain them, reserving the liquid. Make the liquid up to ¾ pint (425 ml) with the stock. Preheat the oven to Reg 4/350°F/180°C. Grate the carrots. Peel, core and finely chop the apples. Heat the oil in a flameproof casserole on a low heat. Mix in the onion and garlic and cook them until the onion is soft. Stir in the mustard and let it bubble and thicken for ½ minute. Stir in the stock and bring it to the boil. Mix in the beans, carrots, apples, sage and tomato purée and season. Cover the casserole and put it into the oven for 45 minutes.

'Cobbler' is a name given to dishes with a scone topping. In this spicy bean cobbler the scones are gently flavoured with the same spices as the beans. As they cook they form a firm, crispy top and underneath soak up a little of the chutney sauce from the beans, while the inside becomes light and fluffy.

Spiced brown bean cobbler

8 oz (225 g) brown beans
1 pint (575 ml) water
up to ¾ pint (425 ml) stock
4 tablespoons (60 ml) olive oil
2 medium onions, thinly sliced
2 teaspoons (10 ml) ground cumin
2 teaspoons (10 ml) ground coriander
3 tablespoons (45 ml) mango chutney (or a home-made, fairly rich, sweet chutney)
for the topping:
8 oz (225 g) wholemeal self-raising flour
1 teaspoon (5 ml) sea salt
1 teaspoon (5 ml) ground cumin
1 teaspoon (5 ml) ground coriander
2 oz (50 g) vegetable margarine or butter
2 tablespoons (30 ml) chopped parsley
8–10 tablespoons (120–150 ml) cold water to mix

Soak the beans, simmer them for 1 hour, drain them and reserve the liquid. Make the liquid up to ¾ pint (425 ml) with the stock. Preheat the oven to Reg 6/400°F/200°C.

Put the flour, salt and spices for the topping into a bowl and rub in the butter. Toss in the parsley and mix everything to a pastry-like dough with the water. Divide the dough into 8 pieces and form them into round scones ¾ to 1 in (2–3 cm) thick.

Heat the oil in a saucepan on a low heat. Stir in the onions, cumin and coriander and cook them until the onions are soft. Pour in the stock and bring it to the boil. Stir in the beans and mango chutney. Take the pan from the heat and transfer all the contents to a large pie dish. Set the scones on top and bake the cobbler for 30 minutes.

This salad is a shiny brown and lemon flavoured. Adding the

mushrooms after cooking but while the beans are still hot means they remain firm but succulent.

Brown bean, cress and mushroom salad

8 oz (225 g) mushrooms
8 oz (225 g) brown kidney beans
1 pint (575 ml) water
4 tablespoons (60 ml) olive oil
2 medium onions, thinly sliced
1 large clove garlic, finely chopped
2 tablespoons (30 ml) Worcestershire sauce or Yorkshire Relish
juice 1 lemon
2 boxes mustard and cress

Soak the beans, simmer them for 1 hour and drain them. Thinly slice the mushrooms. Heat the oil in a saucepan on a low heat. Stir in the onions and garlic, cover them and cook gently for 5 minutes. Stir in the beans, Worcester sauce and lemon juice, cover again and cook for 5 minutes more. Take the pan from the heat and stir in the mushrooms. Let the salad cool completely and mix in the mustard and cress just before serving.

To serve, pile the salad onto lettuce leaves or more mustard and cress and garnish with lemon slices.

Black beans

Black beans are also ½ in (1.5 cm) long and kidney shaped. They are quite spectacular in appearance with a shiny, jet black skin that stays the same when they are cooked. Their flavour is musty, with a slight sweetness. They take a little longer to cook than the other kidney beans and are also a little harder to find in the shops.

Basic method for black beans

8 oz (225 g) black beans
1½ pints (850 ml) water

Put the beans into a saucepan with the water. Cover them, bring them gently to the boil and simmer for 2 minutes. Turn off the heat and let them stand for 3 hours. Bring them to the boil again and simmer gently for 2 hours. Drain if necessary.

Oranges, green cress, shiny black beans and olives make a dish of jewel-like colours that is rich yet refreshing.

Black beans with orange

8 oz (225 g) black beans
1½ pints (850 ml) water
2 large Spanish oranges (or others if not available)
8 black olives
4 tablespoons (60 ml) olive oil
2 medium onions, thinly sliced
1 large clove garlic, finely chopped
2 tablespoons (30 ml) chopped thyme
1 box mustard and cress

Soak the beans, simmer them for 2 hours and drain if necessary. Squeeze the juice from one of the oranges. Cut the rind and pith from the other, cut it into quarters lengthways and thinly slice them. Stone and chop the olives. Heat the oil in a saucepan on a low heat. Stir in the onions and garlic and cook them until the onions are soft. Mix in the beans, olives and thyme, cover them and simmer gently for 5 minutes. Mix in the sliced orange and cut in the cress. Just heat through, and serve as soon as you can.

Tamari sauce gives a rich, caramelly flavour and the lemon juice provides a contrast in another very simple, but no less delicious, dish of black beans.

Black beans with tamari and lemon

8 oz (225 g) black beans
1½ pints (850 ml) water
4 tablespoons (60 ml) olive oil
2 medium onions, thinly sliced

1 large clove garlic, finely chopped
4 tablespoons (60 ml) tamari sauce
grated rind and juice 1 lemon
2 teaspoons (10 ml) chopped rosemary

Soak the beans, simmer them for 2 hours and drain if necessary. Heat the oil in a saucepan on a low heat. Stir in the onions and garlic, cover them and cook gently for 10 minutes. Stir in the beans, tamari sauce, lemon rind and juice and rosemary. Cover them and keep them on the lowest heat possible for 10 minutes.

Olives are used again in this salad. It looks rich, black and shiny and tastes that way too. Serve it with a salad of Florence fennel for an absolutely perfect combination of flavours.

Black bean and black olive salad

8 oz (225 g) black beans
1½ pints (850 ml) water
4 tablespoons (60 ml) olive oil
1 medium onion, thinly sliced
1 clove garlic, finely chopped
2 tablespoons (30 ml) red wine vinegar
8 black olives, stoned and chopped
1 tablespoon (15 ml) thyme, chopped

Soak the beans, simmer them for 2 hours and drain them. Heat the oil in a saucepan on a low heat. Stir in the onion and garlic, cover them and cook them gently for 5 minutes. Stir in the beans, vinegar, olives and thyme. Cover and simmer gently for 2 minutes. Turn the salad into a bowl and cool it completely before serving.

Aduki beans

Aduki (or adzuki or azuki) beans are tiny, round and maroon red with a soft, sweet flavour as delicate as their appearance. You need to be especially careful not to over-spice them.

Basic method for aduki beans

8 oz (225 g) aduki beans
1 pint (575 ml) water

Put the beans into a saucepan with the water. Cover them, bring them gently to the boil and simmer for 2 minutes. Turn off the heat and let them stand for 1 hour. Bring them to the boil again and simmer for 1 hour. Drain them if necessary.

Aduki beans are most often cooked in 'one-pot' dishes with rice. In the following two dishes, they are cooked alone for a short time first and then the rice and other flavourings are added. The first is a plainer, more everyday combination, that turns out a rich, reddy brown.

Aduki beans with rice

8 oz (225 g) aduki beans
1½ pints (850 ml) water
½ pint (275 ml) stock
8 oz (225 g) brown rice
1 large onion, finely chopped
1 large clove garlic, finely chopped
2 tablespoons (30 ml) tomato purée
2 teaspoons (10 ml) paprika
2 teaspoons (10 ml) cinnamon
1 tablespoon (15 ml) white wine vinegar
2 tablespoons (30 ml) chopped parsley

Give the beans the initial short simmer and soak. Bring them to the boil again and simmer them very gently, covered, for 30 minutes. Stir in the stock, rice, onion, garlic, tomato purée, paprika and cinnamon. Simmer, covered and undisturbed for 45 minutes. Turn off the heat, quickly stir in the vinegar and parsley and cover again. Let the dish stand in a warm place for 10 minutes. All you need to accompany this is a salad.

Aduki beans and rice with tomatoes and white wine

8 oz (225 g) aduki beans

1 pint (575 ml) water
1 lb (450 g) tomatoes
4 tablespoons (60 ml) olive oil
1 large onion, thinly sliced
1 large or 2 small cloves garlic, finely chopped
8 oz (225 g) brown rice
¼ pint (150 ml) dry white wine
2 teaspoons (10 ml) Tabasco sauce
¾ pint (450 ml) water

Soak the beans in 1 pint (575 ml) water and simmer them for 30 minutes only. Drain them. Scald, skin and chop the tomatoes. Heat the oil in a saucepan on a low heat. Stir in the onions and garlic and cook them gently until they are soft. Mix in the rice and cook it for 1 minute. Mix in the beans, Tabasco sauce, ¾ pint (450 ml) water and tomatoes. Bring everything to the boil and cover. Set the pan on a very low heat for 45 minutes. Turn off the heat and let the dish rest for 10 minutes. Serve with a salad or a green vegetable such as spinach, kale or spring greens.

Dark beans and pale celery complement each other in colour and their delicate flavours are blended with mild herbs and spices.

Aduki beans braised with celery

8 oz (225 g) aduki beans
1 pint (575 ml) water
up to ½ pint (275 ml) stock
1 small head celery
3 tablespoons (45 ml) olive oil
2 medium onions, thinly sliced
10 chopped sage leaves
2 tablespoons (30 ml) chopped parsley
¼ teaspoon (½ a 2.5 ml spoon) ground mace
freshly grated nutmeg

Soak the beans and simmer them again for only 30 minutes. Drain them and reserve the liquid. Make the liquid up to ½ pint (275 ml) with stock. Preheat the oven to Reg 6/400°F/200°C. Chop the celery. Heat the oil in a flameproof casserole on a low heat. Stir in the celery and onions, cover them and cook them gently for 10 minutes. Pour in the liquid and bring it to the boil. Add the beans, sage, parsley, mace and nutmeg. Cover the casserole and put it into the oven for 40 minutes. Serve with a savoury rice or wholemeal or buckwheat spaghetti.

Dill and dill cucumbers have a soft, subtle flavour that goes beautifully in an aduki bean salad.

Aduki bean and dill salad

8 oz (225 g) aduki beans
1 pint (575 ml) water
4 tablespoons (60 ml) olive oil
1 medium onion, thinly sliced
1 clove garlic, finely chopped
2 tablespoons (30 ml) red wine vinegar
2 teaspoons (10 ml) dill seeds
2 large pickled dill cucumbers, very finely chopped

Soak the beans, simmer them for 1 hour and drain them if necessary. Heat the oil in a saucepan on a low heat. Stir in the onion and garlic, cover them and cook them gently for 5 minutes. Mix in the beans, vinegar and dill seeds. Cover again and cook for a further 5 minutes. Turn the salad into a bowl and mix in the chopped dill cucumbers. Cool the salad completely before serving.

Mung (or Moong) beans

Mung beans are also round and even tinier than aduki beans. They are a deep moss-green colour, even after cooking. Their savoury flavour is midway between that of the blander beans and green vegetables, and they have a slightly creamy texture.

Basic method for Mung beans

8 oz (225 g) Mung beans
1 pint (575 ml) water

Put the beans into a saucepan with the water. Cover them, bring them gently to the boil and simmer for 2 minutes. Turn off the heat and let them stand for 1 hour. Bring them to the boil again and simmer for 40 minutes. Drain if necessary.

Here are two recipes for Mung beans, each flavoured with other green or fresh-tasting ingredients.

Mung beans with capers and lemon

8 oz (225 g) Mung beans
1 pint (575 ml) water
4 tablespoons (60 ml) olive oil
2 medium onions, finely chopped
2 tablespoons (30 ml) chopped capers
grated rind and juice 1 large lemon
4 tablespoons (60 ml) chopped parsley

Soak the beans, simmer them for 40 minutes and drain them if necessary. Heat the oil in a saucepan on a low heat. Mix in the onions and garlic and cook them until they are soft. Stir in the beans, capers and lemon rind and juice. Cover them and simmer for 2 minutes. Mix in the parsley just before serving.

Mung beans with mustard and cress

8 oz (225 g) Mung beans
1 pint (575 ml) water
4 tablespoons (60 ml) olive oil
2 medium onions, thinly sliced
1 large clove garlic, finely chopped
2 teaspoons (10 ml) mustard seeds
1 tablespoon (15 ml) Dijon mustard
2 boxes mustard and cress

Soak the beans, simmer them for 40 minutes and drain them if necessary. Heat the oil in a saucepan on a low heat. Stir in the onion, garlic and mustard seed. Cover and cook them gently for 10 minutes. Stir in the Dijon mustard and let it bubble for 1 minute, still stirring. Mix in the beans, cover the pan and heat through for 1 minute. Cut in the cress and just let it wilt before taking the pan from the heat.

Give Mung beans an appropriately Chinese flavour with green peppers and a translucent tamari sauce. If you are serving them as part of a complete Chinese meal with several small dishes, halve all the ingredients.

Mung beans and green peppers, Chinese style

8 oz (225 g) Mung beans
1 pint (575 ml) water
2 medium-sized green peppers
2 medium onions
1 tablespoon (15 ml) cornflour
1 tablespoon (15 ml) tamari sauce
½ pint (150 ml) stock
4 tablespoons (60 ml) olive oil
1 large clove garlic, finely chopped
1 oz (25 g) fresh ginger root, peeled and grated *or*, if this isn't available, 2 teaspoons (10 ml) ground ginger

Soak the beans, simmer them for 40 minutes and drain them if necessary. Core and de-seed the peppers and dice them. Chop the onions. Put the cornflour in a bowl and gradually mix in the tamari sauce and stock. Heat the oil in a large frying pan on a moderate heat. Stir in the onions, garlic and peppers and cook them for 3 minutes, moving them around frequently. Mix in the beans. Pour in the cornflour mixture and bring it to the boil. Stir in the ginger and simmer, uncovered, for 3 minutes, stirring frequently.

Pigeon peas

Pigeon peas are about ¼ in (0.75 cm) long, round and slightly flattened. They are light grey in colour, speckled with rich brown. (The colour of pigeons' eggs – hence the name!) As they are soaking, they smell like raisins and they go a dark, reddy brown when they are cooked. Their flavour is slightly bitter-sweet.

Basic method for pigeon peas

8 oz (225 g) pigeon peas
1½ pints (850 ml) water

Put the pigeon peas into a saucepan with the water. Cover them, bring them to the boil and simmer for 2 minutes. Turn off the heat and let them stand for 2 to 3 hours. Bring them to the boil again and simmer for 1½ hours. Drain them if necessary.

As pigeon peas smell like raisins, that particular dried fruit is excellent added to the final dish. Freshen the flavours with apples and chopped coriander leaves.

Pigeon peas, apples and raisins

8 oz (225 g) pigeon peas
1½ pints (850 ml) water
up to ¼ pint (150 ml) stock
1 large Bramley apple
4 tablespoons (60 ml) olive oil
2 medium onions, thinly sliced
2 oz (50 g) raisins
1 teaspoon (5 ml) ground cinnamon
1 teaspoon (5 ml) ground coriander
2 tablespoons (30 ml) chopped coriander leaves (*or* parsley if none
   is available)

Soak the peas, simmer them for 1½ hours, drain them and reserve any liquid. Make the liquid up to ¼ pint (150 ml), if necessary, with stock. Peel, quarter, core and slice the apple. Heat the oil in a saucepan on a low heat. Stir in the onions and apple and cook them until they are soft. Mix in the beans, raisins, cinnamon and ground and fresh coriander. Pour in the liquid and bring it to the boil. Cover and simmer gently for 10 minutes.

With mushrooms, red wine and miso pigeon peas make a rich, dark casserole.

Pigeon peas with mushrooms and red wine

8 oz (225 g) pigeon peas
1½ pints (850 ml) water
4 tablespoons (60 ml) olive oil
2 medium onions, thinly sliced
1 large clove garlic, finely chopped
8 oz (225 g) flat mushrooms, thinly sliced
¼ pint (150 ml) dry red wine
up to ¾ pint (425 ml) water (if you are not using the miso, use stock instead)
2 tablespoons (30 ml) chopped parsley
1 tablespoon (15 ml) chopped thyme
1 tablespoon (15 ml) miso (not absolutely essential but it enriches the sauce)

Soak the peas and simmer them for 1 hour only. Drain them and reserve any liquid. Preheat the oven to Reg 4/350°F/180°C. Heat the oil in a flameproof casserole on a low heat. Stir in the onions and garlic, cover them and cook them gently for 10 minutes. Mix in the mushrooms. Pour in the wine and the cooking liquid made up to ¾ pint (425 ml) with water (or stock if you are not using miso). Bring the liquids to the boil. Mix in the parsley, thyme, miso and, finally, the peas. Cover the casserole and put it into the oven for 1 hour.

Field beans

Field beans are round, very slightly flattened and ¼–½ in (0.75–1 cm) in diameter. Their skins are a rich, shiny brown like the skin of a sweet chestnut. They go a darker brown when cooked and have a slightly bitter flavour which is mostly contained in the skin. They have a tendency to split just as they get tender.

Basic method for field beans

8 oz (225 g) field beans
1½ pints (850 ml) water

Put the beans into a saucepan with the water. Cover them, bring them to the boil and simmer for 2 minutes. Turn off the heat and let them stand for 2 to 3 hours. Bring them to the boil again and simmer for 1½ hours. Drain them if necessary.

The strong, slightly bitter flavour of field beans makes them more suitable for serving in the winter, and they go particularly well with root vegetables.

Field beans and grated carrots

8 oz (225 g) field beans
1½ pints (850 ml) water
up to 1 pint (575 ml) stock
1 lb (450 g) carrots
4 tablespoons (60 ml) olive oil
2 medium onions, finely chopped
1 large clove garlic, finely chopped
1 tablespoon (15 ml) chopped thyme
lots of freshly grated nutmeg
sea salt
freshly ground black pepper

Soak the beans, simmer them for 1½ hours and drain if necessary. Reserve the liquid and make it up to 1 pint (575 ml) with stock. Preheat the oven to Reg 3/325°F/160°C. Grate the carrots. Heat the oil in a flameproof casserole on a low heat. Stir in the onions and garlic and cook them until the onions are soft. Mix in the carrots and beans. Pour in the stock and bring it to the boil. Add the nutmeg, thyme and seasoning. Cover the casserole and put it into the oven for 1 hour.

Field beans and swede in beer

8 oz (225 g) field beans
1½ pints (850 ml) water
12 oz (350 g) swede
1 oz (25 g) butter or vegetable margarine
2 medium onions, thinly sliced
1 pint (575 ml) draught bitter
1 tablespoon (15 ml) grated horseradish

1 tablespoon (15 ml) tomato purée
1 bayleaf

Soak the beans, simmer them for 1½ hours and drain them if
necessary. Preheat the oven to Reg 4/350°F/180°C. Scrub the
swede and cut it into ½ in (1.5 cm) dice. Melt the butter or
margarine in a flameproof casserole on a low heat. Stir in the
onions and swede, cover them and let them sweat for 10 minutes.
Pour in the beer and bring it to the boil. Mix in the beans, horseradish and tomato purée and tuck in the bayleaf. Cover the
casserole and put it into the oven for 45 minutes.

Field beans and parsnips

8 oz (225 g) field beans
1½ pints (850 ml) water
1 lb (450 g) parsnips
1 oz (25 g) butter *or* 4 tablespoons (60 ml) olive oil
2 medium onions, thinly sliced
1 pint (575 ml) stock
¼ pint (150 ml) dry cider
12 chopped sage leaves
sea salt
freshly ground black pepper
1 tablespoon (15 ml) tomato purée

Soak the beans, simmer them for 1½ hours and drain them if
necessary. Preheat the oven to Reg 4/350°F/180°C. Remove
the woody cores from the parsnips and chop the rest into small,
thin slices. Melt the butter or heat the oil in a flameproof casserole
on a low heat. Stir in the parsnips and onions, cover them and let
them sweat for 7 minutes. Stir in the beans. Pour in the stock
and cider and bring them to the boil. Add the sage, season and
stir in the tomato purée. Cover the casserole and put it into the
oven for 45 minutes.

The robust flavour of field beans combines very well with the
basic ingredients that are often put into the traditional shepherd's
pie.

Field bean shepherd's pie

8 oz (225 g) field beans
1½ pints (850 ml) water
1½ lb (675 g) potatoes
1½ oz (40 g) butter *or* vegetable margarine
4 tablespoons (60 ml) chopped parsley
4 tablespoons (60 ml) olive oil
2 medium onions, thinly sliced
1 clove garlic, finely chopped
12 oz (350 g) carrots, finely chopped
4 oz (125 g) mushrooms, thinly sliced
1 lb (450 g) tomatoes, scalded, skinned and chopped
1 tablespoon (15 ml) miso (optional but it makes a richer dish)
½ pint (275 ml) stock
1 tablespoon (15 ml) chopped thyme

Soak the beans, simmer them for 1½ hours and drain them if necessary. Boil the potatoes in their skins until they are tender. Drain them and peel them while they are still warm. Mash them with the butter or margarine and mix in 2 tablespoons (30 ml) of the chopped parsley.

Preheat the oven to Reg 6/400°F/200°C. Heat the oil in a saucepan on a low heat. Stir in the onions, garlic and carrots, cover them and let them sweat for 10 minutes. Stir in the mushrooms and tomatoes. Mix the miso with the stock and pour them into the saucepan. Bring everything to the boil and mix in the beans, remaining parsley and thyme. Transfer everything to a large pie dish. Cover the bean mixture with the mashed potatoes and make patterns in the top with a fork. Bake the pie for 30 minutes, so the ridges in the topping brown very slightly.

❧   ❧   ❧

Split peas

Both green and yellow split peas are readily available in most supermarkets and wholefood shops. They are usually cooked to a purée and then either served as they are or made into croquettes, loaves or pease puddings. The recipes below include a quiche and a crumble, and any of the other purées or croquette mixtures can also be used in these ways.

In flavour, green split peas are usually lighter and fresher than the slightly musty yellow ones. But both types are thick and quite rich and often need a lighter, sharper ingredient for contrast.

Lighten the green ones with lemon and mace to give them an almost summery flavour of fresh peas, available, this way, all the year round.

Green split-pea and lemon croquettes

12 oz (350 g) green split peas
1½ pints (850 ml) water
2 bayleaves
sea salt and freshly ground black pepper
4 tablespoons (60 ml) olive oil
1 large onion, finely chopped
juice 1 lemon
½ teaspoon (2.5 ml) ground mace
4 tablespoons (60 ml) chopped parsley
6 tablespoons (90 ml) browned crumbs
oil or vegetable margarine for frying

Put the split peas into a saucepan with the bayleaves and water and season them well. Bring them to the boil, cover and simmer them very gently for 1 hour, beating occasionally with a wooden spoon towards the end so they cook to a thick purée without sticking to the bottom of the pan. Remove the bayleaves. Heat the oil in a frying pan on a low heat. Put in the onion and cook it until it is soft. Beat the onion and the oil into the peas and then add the lemon juice, mace and parsley. Form the mixture into 12 long sausage shapes and coat them in the breadcrumbs. Fry them in shallow fat on a moderate heat until they are golden brown.

Alternative: if eggs are allowed in your diet, coat the croquettes first in wholemeal flour, dip them in beaten egg, roll them in the crumbs and deep fry them.

These croquettes are given a sharp sauce of tarragon vinegar for contrast.

Green split-pea and tarragon croquettes

12 oz (350 g) green split peas
1½ pints (850 ml) water
2 bayleaves
sea salt and freshly ground black pepper
3 tablespoons (45 ml) olive oil
1 large onion, finely chopped
1 large clove garlic, finely chopped
4 tablespoons (60 ml) chopped fresh tarragon *or* 1 tablespoon
(15 ml) dried
approx. 6 tablespoons (90 ml) seasoned wholemeal flour
2 oz (50 g) butter *or* vegetable margarine
3 tablespoons (45 ml) tarragon vinegar

Put the peas into a saucepan with the water and bayleaves and
season them well. Cover them and bring them gently to the boil.
Simmer them for 1 hour, beating them occasionally towards the
end so they cook to a thick purée and do not stick to the bottom
of the pan. Remove the bayleaves. Heat the oil in a frying pan
on a low heat. Put in the onion and garlic and cook them until
the onion is soft. Beat the onion, garlic and oil into the peas.
Mix in half the tarragon. Form the mixture into 16 small balls
and coat them in the seasoned flour. Melt half the butter or
margarine in a frying pan on a moderate heat. Fry the croquettes
until they are golden brown all over. Remove them and put
them into a warm serving dish. Put the remaining butter into
the frying pan and let it melt. Swirl in the vinegar and the
remaining tarragon. Let the sauce bubble and pour it immediately
over the croquettes.

Green split peas and leeks make a substantial and very attractive
quiche.

Green split-pea and leek quiche

for the pastry:
6 oz (175 g) wholemeal flour
3 oz (100 g) vegetable margarine
pinch sea salt

cold water to mix
little oil for brushing
for the filling:
8 oz (225 g) green split peas
1 pint (575 ml) water
2 bayleaves
sea salt and freshly ground black pepper
8 oz (225 g) leeks, both white and green parts
2 tablespoons (30 ml) olive oil
2 tablespoons (30 ml) chopped parsley
1 tablespoon (15 ml) chopped savory
½ teaspoon (2.5 ml) ground mace
freshly grated nutmeg
grated rind and juice 1 lemon

Make the pastry and set it aside to chill.

Put the peas into a saucepan with the water and bayleaves and season them well. Cover them, bring them to the boil and simmer for 1 hour, beating them to a thick purée towards the end. Preheat the oven to Reg 6/400°F/200°C. Wash and thinly slice the leeks. Heat the oil in a saucepan on a low heat. Stir in the leeks, cover them and cook them gently for 10 minutes. Mix them into the peas with the herbs, spices and lemon juice and rind. Set aside a quarter of the pastry. Roll out the rest and use it to line a flan ring 8 in (20 cm) in diameter. Put in the pea and leek filling and spread it evenly. Roll out the remaining pastry and cut it into strips about ½ in (1.5 cm) wide. Lay them in a lattice pattern over the leeks. Trim the edges of the flan pastry evenly and bend them over the leeks to cover the ends of the lattice. Brush the pastry with a little oil and bake the quiche for 30 minutes. The quiche is best served hot with a tomato salad.

When Seville oranges are available, make a light, puffy dish of peas with a crumble top.

Green split-pea and Seville crumble

12 oz (350 g) green split peas
1½ pints (850 ml) water
2 bayleaves

sea salt and freshly ground black pepper
2 oz (50 g) butter *or* vegetable margarine
2 medium onions, finely chopped
1 large or 2 small cloves garlic, finely chopped
1 teaspoon (5 ml) ground coriander
1 tablespoon (15 ml) chopped thyme
grated rind and juice 1 large Seville orange
8 tablespoons (120 ml) browned crumbs
for serving:
large square croutons of granary or wholemeal bread

Put the peas into a saucepan with the water and bayleaves and season them well. Cover them, bring them to the boil and simmer them gently for 1 hour, beating them to a thick purée towards the end. Remove the bayleaves. Preheat the oven to Reg 4/ 350°F/180°C. Melt 1 oz (25 g) of the butter or margarine in a frying pan on a low heat. Stir in the onion and garlic and cook them until they are just beginning to brown. Beat all the contents of the pan into the peas together with the coriander, thyme and orange rind and juice. Put the mixture into a pie dish or other fairly deep oven-proof dish and smooth the top. Press the bread-crumbs evenly into the surface and dot them with the remaining butter or margarine. Bake the crumble for 30 minutes. Serve it with crispy hot croutons and with baked or grilled tomatoes or a tomato salad for contrast.

This yellow split-pea purée has an eighteenth-century flavour. Serve it as a main dish with a green vegetable or a salad or as an accompaniment to another dish.

Spiced yellow pea purée

8 oz (225 g) yellow split peas
1 pint (575 ml) water
2 bayleaves
sea salt and freshly ground black pepper
12 black peppercorns
6 cloves
4 tablespoons (60 ml) olive oil *or* 1 oz (25 g) butter
1 medium onion, thinly sliced
4 tablespoons (60 ml) dry white wine

Put the split peas into a saucepan with the water and bayleaves and season them well. Bring them to the boil and simmer them, covered, for 1 hour, beating them to a thick purée towards the end. Remove the bayleaves. Crush the peppercorns and cloves together with a pestle and mortar. Heat the oil or melt the butter in a saucepan on a low heat. Mix in the onion and spices and cook them until the onion is soft. Pour in the wine and let it bubble. Mix in the pea purée, cover the pan and simmer gently for 2 minutes.

Flavour yellow pea croquettes with lemon and lemon thyme and give them a sharp buttery caper sauce.

Lemon yellow pea balls

12 oz (350 g) yellow split peas
1½ pints (850 ml) water
bouquet of parsley and thyme tied with 2 thinly pared strips lemon rind
sea salt and freshly ground black pepper
4 tablespoons (60 ml) chopped parsley
3 tablespoons (45 ml) chopped lemon thyme
the rest of the lemon rind, grated
approx. 6 tablespoons (90 ml) browned crumbs
2 oz (50 g) butter or margarine
1 tablespoon (15 ml) chopped capers
juice 2 lemons

Put the peas into a saucepan with the water, parsley, thyme and pared lemon rind. Season them well and simmer them, covered, for 1 hour, beating them to a thick purée towards the end. Beat in half the herbs and all the grated lemon rind. Form the mixture into 16 small balls and roll them in the crumbs. Melt half the butter or margarine in a frying pan on a low heat. Put in the balls and cook them till they are golden brown all over. Remove them and put them in a warm serving dish. Melt the remaining butter or margarine in the pan. Put in the remaining herbs and the capers and pour in the lemon juice. Let it bubble and pour the resulting sauce over the pea balls.

With potatoes, yellow split-peas make an excellent accompaniment to all kinds of main vegetable, cheese and egg dishes.

Yellow pea and potato layers

4 oz (125 g) yellow split peas
¾ pint (400 ml) stock
2 small onions, thinly sliced
1 bayleaf
sea salt and freshly ground black pepper
1 lb (450 g) potatoes
2 oz (50 g) butter or vegetable margarine

Put the peas into a saucepan with the stock, 1 of the sliced onions, the bayleaf and plenty of seasonings. Bring them to the boil and simmer them for 1 hour, beating them to a thick purée towards the end.

While they are cooking, scrub the potatoes and boil them in their skins in lightly salted water with the remaining onion. Drain them, peel them while they are still warm and mash them with 1 oz (25 g) of the butter and some pepper.

Preheat the oven to Reg 6/400°F/200°C. Use some of the remaining butter or margarine to thickly grease a deep, oven-proof dish such as a large pie dish or soufflé dish. Put half the potato into the bottom of the dish and smooth over evenly. Then put in all the pea purée and cover this with the remaining potato. Make patterns in the top with a fork and dot with the remaining butter or margarine. Bake for 30 minutes until the edges are crispy golden and the top brown.

Alternative: Mix 2 tablespoons (30 ml) chopped parsley, or a mixture of parsley and sage or spring onions, into one or both of the layers.

꙳   ꙳   ꙳

Lentils

Lentils have a very distinct, savoury flavour; they are far less bland than many of the beans. The most readily available are

the small, split, bright orange ones that are usually referred to
as red lentils. You can buy them in both supermarkets and whole-
food shops. They quickly cook to a purée and so are best used for
soups, croquettes, quiches and loaves; and if you beat in a little
oil and vinegar they make excellent salads.

To make a good thick purée, use 1 pint of liquid (stock or
water) to 8 oz (225 g) uncooked lentils. Season them well and
simmer them gently for 45 minutes, beating them quite frequently with a wooden spoon towards the end to blend them
together and prevent them from sticking.

If you want to leave the cooked purée standing for a time
before going on to complete the recipe, either leave it in the
saucepan with the lid on or turn it into a bowl and cover it with
a damp cloth. Otherwise, the top will dry.

Whenever I cook red lentils I always get a slight surprise at the
way they always blend in so well with the flavours, colours and
textures of the other ingredients. With curry and apples they go
bright yellow and taste almost creamy.

Red lentil, curry and apple purée

12 oz (350 g) red lentils
1½ pints (850 ml) stock
2 bayleaves
sea salt and freshly ground black pepper
2 large cooking apples
4 tablespoons (60 ml) olive oil
1 large onion, thinly sliced
1 tablespoon (15 ml) hot Madras curry powder

Put the lentils into a saucepan with the stock and bayleaves and
season them well. Cover them, bring them to the boil and simmer
them gently for 45 minutes, beating them to a thick purée
towards the end. Remove the bayleaves. Peel, quarter, core and
thinly slice the apples. Heat the oil in a saucepan on a low heat.
Stir in the apples, onion and curry powder. Cover them and cook
them gently for 10 minutes (or until you can beat the apples to
a purée). Mix in the lentils, cover them and keep everything on

the lowest heat possible for 1 minute. Serve with a savoury rice or as an accompanying dish.

With paprika and tomato purée the lentils can be made a deep orangey red that reflects the hot flavour of the chillis and looks really good with a spicy tomato sauce.

Lentil, pepper and chilli croquettes

12 oz (350 g) red lentils
1½ pints (850 ml) water
1 medium-sized red or green pepper
3 green chillis (or, if not available, 1 teaspoon (5 ml) Tabasco sauce)
3 tablespoons (45 ml) olive oil
1 medium onion, finely chopped
1 large clove garlic, finely chopped
2 tablespoons (30 ml) tomato purée
2 teaspoons (10 ml) paprika
3 tablespoons (45 ml) chopped coriander or parsley
1 egg, beaten (optional)
8 tablespoons (120 ml) browned granary or wholemeal breadcrumbs
up to 6 tablespoons (90 ml) olive oil for frying

Put the lentils into a saucepan with the water and season them well. Bring them to the boil and simmer them, covered, for 45 minutes, beating them to a thick purée towards the end. Core and finely chop the pepper and the chillis. Heat 3 tablespoons (45 ml) oil in a frying pan on a low heat, put in the onion and garlic and cook them until the onion is soft. Mix in the pepper and chillis and keep cooking until the onion browns. Beat the onion, pepper, chillis and any oil in the pan into the lentils together with the tomato purée, paprika and coriander or parsley. If you are using Tabasco sauce instead of the chillis add this now.

Form the mixture into 16 croquette shapes, dip them in the beaten egg and then coat them in crumbs. (If you are not using the egg then just roll them in the crumbs.) Heat 4 tablespoons (60 ml) of the frying oil in a frying pan on a moderate heat and cook the croquettes until they are golden brown all over. Do this in two batches if necessary, adding more oil as and when you need it. Serve with spicy tomato sauce handed separately or with the tomato rice.

A red lentil and pumpkin purée makes a savoury, moist filling for an open pie. Self raising flour is used for the pastry to make it rich and crumbly like the American pastry used for the sweet pumpkin pies.

Pumpkin and lentil pie

a slice of pumpkin weighing 1½ lb (675 g) *or* about 14 oz (400 g) when peeled, de-seeded and diced
2 tablespoons (30 ml) water
8 oz (225 g) red lentils
1 pint (575 ml) stock
1 bayleaf
sea salt and freshly ground black pepper
1 oz (25 g) butter *or* vegetable margarine
1 medium onion, finely chopped
4 tablespoons (60 ml) chopped mixed herbs
2 tablespoons (30 ml) tomato purée
for shortcrust pastry:
6 oz (175 g) wholemeal self-raising flour
4 oz (100 g) vegetable margarine
pinch fine sea salt
cold water to mix

Make the pastry and set it aside to chill.

Chop the pumpkin into small, thin slices and put it into a saucepan with the water. Set it on a low heat for 20 minutes, beating it occasionally to reduce it to a thick purée. Put the lentils into a saucepan with the stock, bayleaf and seasoning. Bring them to the boil and simmer them gently for only 30 minutes so you have a purée that isn't too dry.

Preheat the oven to Reg 5/375°F/190°C. Line an 8 in (20 cm) flan ring with the pastry. (It will be very short so don't worry if you have to do a bit of patching up!) Melt the butter or margarine in a small frying pan on a low heat. Stir in the onion and cook it until it is golden. Mix together the pumpkin, lentils, onion and any of the margarine or butter still in the pan. Beat in the herbs

and tomato purée. Spoon the mixture into the pastry case and
bake the pie for 40 minutes. Serve it hot.

This savoury bake looks as though it is made only of lentils, but
when you taste it you realise there is something more – the
delicate flavour of grated swede and nutmeg which blend in
beautifully in colour as well as taste.

Lentil and swede bake

12 oz (350 g) red lentils
1½ pints (850 ml) water
2 bayleaves
sea salt and freshly ground black pepper
8 oz (225 g) swede
4 tablespoons (60 ml) olive oil
1 medium onion, finely chopped
2 large sticks celery, finely chopped
freshly grated nutmeg
2 tablespoons (30 ml) chopped parsley
4 tablespoons (60 ml) browned crumbs
for serving:
celery and white wine sauce (see under sauces)

Put the lentils into a saucepan with the water, bayleaves and
seasonings. Cover them, bring them to the boil and simmer them
gently for 45 minutes, beating to a thick purée towards the end.
Grate the swede during the first stage of cooking the lentils and
mix them into the purée for the last 10 minutes of cooking time.
Take the pan from the heat.
   Preheat the oven to Reg 6/400°F/200°C and oil a deep pie
dish or large soufflé dish. Heat the oil in a frying pan on a low
heat. Mix in the onion and celery and cook them until they are
soft. Mix them into the lentils with lots of nutmeg and the parsley.
Put the mixture into your oiled dish and smooth over the top.
Press the crumbs into the surface and put the dish into the oven
for 30 minutes.

To make really attractive lentil salads, chill the flavoured purée
in a ring mould and fill the centre with a fresh, contrasting mix-

ture of fruit and salad vegetables. This apple salad once again demonstrates the chameleon-like qualities of red lentil purées: it comes out a soft, greeny colour.

Red lentil, celery and apple salad

8 oz (225 g) red lentils
1 pint (575 ml) water
sea salt and freshly ground black pepper
6 tablespoons (90 ml) olive oil
1 medium onion, thinly sliced
2 teaspoons (10 ml) caraway seeds
4 tablespoons (60 ml) cider vinegar
1 clove garlic, crushed with a pinch sea salt
4 sticks celery
1 large russet or other smooth-textured eating apple

Put the lentils into a saucepan with the water and season them well. Simmer them for 45 minutes, beating them to a thick purée towards the end. Remove them from the heat.

Heat 2 tablespoons (30 ml) of the oil in a frying pan on a low heat. Mix in the onion and cook until it is soft. Mix this into the lentils with 2 tablespoons (30 ml) more oil, half the caraway seeds, half the vinegar and half the garlic. Finely chop 2 of the celery sticks and mix these in as well. Put the mixture into a 7 in (18–20 cm) oiled ring mould and smooth over the top. Chill it until it is quite cold and firm.

Make a dressing with the remaining 2 tablespoons (30 ml) oil, 2 tablespoons (30 ml) vinegar and the remaining caraway seeds and garlic. Chop the remaining celery and quarter, core and chop the apple and coat these with the dressing. Turn out the lentil mould and put the salad in the middle.

The sharp lemon and pineapple in this salad contrast with the creamy lentil purée while the watercress provides an added touch of colour.

Lentil and pineapple salaa

8 oz (225 g) red lentils

8 tablespoons (120 ml) olive oil
2 medium onions, thinly sliced
1 large clove garlic, finely chopped
¼ pint (150 ml) dry white wine
¾ pint (425 ml) water
sea salt and freshly ground black pepper
juice 1 lemon
1 medium-sized pineapple
2 bunches watercress
1 clove garlic crushed with a pinch sea salt
freshly ground black pepper

Put 4 tablespoons (60 ml) of the oil into a saucepan and set it on
a low heat. Mix in the onions and chopped garlic and cook them
until the onion is golden. Stir in the lentils and cook them for
1 minute. Pour in the wine and water, season and bring them
gently to the boil. Cover the pan and simmer gently for 45
minutes, beating the lentils to a thick purée towards the end.
Take the pan from the heat, beat in half the lemon juice and let
the lentils cool completely, keeping them covered.

Cut the husk from the pineapple. Cut the flesh into slices and
stamp out the cores. Chop the pineapple into ½ in (1.5 cm) pieces.
Chop the watercress. Mix half the pineapple and watercress into
the lentils. Put the mixture into a 7 in (18–20 cm) oiled ring
mould and chill it until it is firm.

Put the rest of the pineapple and watercress into a bowl. Beat
together the remaining lemon juice and oil, the garlic and pepper
and fold the resulting dressing into the salad. Turn the lentil
mould onto a flat plate and fill the centre with the salad.

❧   ❧   ❧

Brown, or Chinese, lentils look like tiny, flattened, greyish-brown
flying saucers. Simmer them with seasonings and 1 pint (575 ml)
liquid to every 8 oz (225 g) lentils. In an hour all the liquid will
be absorbed and they will be tender but will not readily break up
into a purée, so you can serve them whole in sauces and with
other vegetables. You can also mash them to a purée with a

potato masher or a large pestle and mortar to make them into savoury cakes and pâtés.

Brown lentils make an excellent substitute for minced beef, far better in flavour and texture than TVP. When cooked, they are a rich dark brown with a flavour to match.

Instead of beefburgers, have brown-lentil burgers and serve them with jacket potatoes, a salad and horseradish sauce.

Brown lentil burgers

8 oz (225 g) brown lentils
1 pint (575 ml) stock
2 bayleaves
sea salt and freshly ground black pepper
6 tablespoons (90 ml) olive oil
1 medium onion, finely chopped
1 large clove garlic, finely chopped
4 oz (125 g) mushrooms, finely chopped
12 chopped sage leaves
2 tablespoons (30 ml) tomato purée
approx. 4 tablespoons (60 ml) seasoned wholemeal flour

Put the lentils into a saucepan with the stock, bayleaves and seasonings. Cover them, bring them to the boil and simmer them for 1 hour. Mash them well with a potato masher.

Heat 2 tablespoons (30 ml) of the oil in a frying pan on a low heat. Put in the onion and garlic and cook them until they are just beginning to brown. Raise the heat to moderate, mix in the mushrooms and cook them, stirring, for 2 minutes. Remove the pan from the heat and mix in the lentils, sage and tomato purée. Form the mixture into 12 small, flat cakes and put them in a cool place for about 30 minutes to set into shape.

Coat the burgers with the seasoned flour. Heat 2 tablespoons (30 ml) more oil in a frying pan on a moderate heat. Put in the lentil burgers (in 2 batches if necessary) and fry them until they are really brown on both sides, adding more oil as and when you need it. Turn and lift the burgers very carefully with a fish slice or wide palette knife so they don't break in the pan.

Cook brown lentils with dark mushrooms and give them a hint
of spicy pickles. Serve them with a savoury rice.

Brown lentils with mushrooms and onions

12 oz (350 g) brown lentils
1½ pints (850 ml) stock
sea salt and freshly ground black pepper
4 tablespoons (60 ml) olive oil
2 medium onions, thinly sliced
8 oz (225 g) dark, flat mushrooms, thinly sliced
4 large pickled onions, finely chopped
2 tablespoons (30 ml) chopped parsley

Put the lentils into a saucepan with the stock and season them
well. Cover them, bring them to the boil and simmer for 1 hour.
Heat the oil in another saucepan on a low heat. Stir in the onions
and mushrooms, cover them and cook them gently for 10 minutes.
Mix in the lentils, pickled onions and parsley. Cover and cook
gently for 2 minutes.

ℱ   ℱ   ℱ

Green, or Egyptian, lentils are larger than the brown, but the
same flying saucer shape and a pale, dull green, occasionally
greeny brown, colour. They stay whole when they are cooked and
have an almost peppery flavour, fresher than the other types.

For a main dish you will need 12 oz (350 g) for 4 people.
Simmer them with seasonings in 1½ pints (850 ml) water or
stock for 1 hour. They will be tender but still whole and the
liquid will be absorbed.

For this recipe, use whatever herbs are in season. Serve the
lentils with wholemeal or buckwheat pasta.

Herbed green lentils

12 oz (350 g) green lentils
1½ pints (850 ml) stock
2 bayleaves
sea salt and freshly ground black pepper

4 tablespoons (60 ml) olive oil
16 medium-sized spring onions, chopped
6 tablespoons (90 ml) mixed chopped fresh herbs

Put the lentils into a saucepan with the stock and bayleaves and season them well. Cover them, bring them to the boil and simmer for 1 hour. Make sure all the liquid is absorbed and keep the pan on the heat. Stir in the oil, onions, herbs and more pepper. Cover and simmer for 2 minutes more.

This is another simple recipe in which the lentils are made to taste very nutty with the browned garlic and tamari sauce. Serve with a savoury rice.

Green lentils and celery

12 oz (350 g) green lentils
1½ pints (850 ml) stock
2 bayleaves
sea salt and freshly ground black pepper
4 large sticks celery
4 tablespoons (60 ml) olive oil
1 large clove garlic, finely chopped
2 tablespoons (30 ml) tamari sauce

Put the lentils into a saucepan with the stock and bayleaves and season them well. Cover them, bring them to the boil and simmer for 1 hour. Finely chop the celery. Heat the oil in a saucepan on a moderate heat. Stir in the celery and garlic and let them brown. Mix in the lentils and tamari sauce. Heat them through and serve.

Green lentils make a pleasantly different kind of green salad that can be served hot or cold.

Green lentil and caper salad

12 oz (350 g) green lentils
1½ pints (850 ml) water
2 bayleaves
sea salt and freshly ground black pepper

4 tablespoons (60 ml) olive oil
1 large onion, thinly sliced
2 tablespoons (30 ml) chopped capers
4 tablespoons (60 ml) chopped parsley
3 tablespoons (45 ml) white wine vinegar

Put the lentils into a saucepan with the water and bayleaves and season them well. Cover them and simmer for 1 hour. Heat the oil in a frying pan on a low heat. Stir in the onion and cook it until it is soft. Raise the heat to moderate and quickly mix in the lentils, capers and parsley. Pour in the vinegar, let it bubble and take the pan from the heat immediately. Either serve the salad hot or let it get completely cold.

Spread them thick

Mixed with other ingredients to moisten and flavour them, many of the cooked pulses can be made into savoury spreads for bread, toast, scones or plain biscuits. In a way, they are a more sophisticated form of beans on toast! As many of the spreads contain oil to make them smooth you will probably find they do not need butter or margarine on the bread, but this is very much a matter of taste.

Left-over bean dishes can be worked in a blender, rubbed through the fine blade of a *mouli* sieve, or simply mashed to a purée to make spreads. Very often they will need to be moistened and sharpened a little with lemon juice or vinegar. Taste your purée first to find out which will go best, or whether it needs any additions at all. Small amounts of finely chopped pickles, such as capers, dill cucumbers or large gherkins, are excellent mixed into the blander purées. Beat your flavourings in gradually, tasting as you go to get the right balance.

To make a spread for one light meal for four people you only need about 4 oz (125 g) of cooked beans or 2 oz (50 g) of dried. So for both economy and convenience it is best to either make up enough spread for several meals or, when you are preparing beans for another recipe, to cook more than you need so you will have some for a spread as well.

Store spreads in the refrigerator and they will keep for up to a week. The best containers are plastic yoghurt pots or cottage cheese containers with fitted lids. If you use a glass jar, cover it with a plastic lid or put a piece of polythene or waxed grease-proof paper over the mouth of the jar before screwing on the metal lid. This will stop it going rusty and contaminating the spread.

This first recipe is an example of how you can use cooked beans from another dish as a base. The original ingredients, puréed, are too stiff, so they are lightened in flavour and texture with tomatoes and a little more wine vinegar.

Barbecued soya bean and tomato spread

Cook more barbecued soya beans than you require for 1 meal. For every 4 oz (125 g) that you have left over you will need:

4 medium-sized ripe tomatoes
2 tablespoons (30 ml) olive oil
1 small onion, very finely chopped
1 clove garlic, very finely chopped
1 tablespoon (15 ml) white wine vinegar

Either rub the beans through the fine blade of a *mouli* sieve or mash them well and pound them with a wooden spoon or large pestle and mortar. Scald, skin, de-seed and chop the tomatoes. Heat the oil in a small saucepan on a low heat. Mix in the onion and garlic and cook them until they are soft. Stir in the tomatoes and cook them to a thick pulp. Mix in the mashed or puréed beans and the vinegar and simmer everything for 2 minutes, stirring. Transfer the spread to a bowl and let it cool completely.

You can hardly distinguish this soya bean spread from one made with eggs and mayonnaise. Serve it in wholemeal or granary bread sandwiches. The amounts given will more or less fill 2 half-pint yoghurt or cottage cheese pots or 4 quarter-pint ones. It seems a lot but the spread is so good it will rapidly disappear.

Crunchy soya bean sandwich spread

4 oz (125 g) dried soya beans
soya bechamel sauce made with ½ pint (275 ml) water (*see* under
sauces)
4 tablespoons (60 ml) white wine vinegar
1 tablespoon (15 ml) chopped capers
2 large pickled dill cucumbers *or* 2 large pickled Hungarian
gherkins, whichever you prefer, very finely chopped

Soak the soya beans in water for 24 hours. Drain them and
squeeze off as many of the thin outer skins as possible. Put them
into a blender or grinder or press them through a nut mill so
they are about the same size as the pieces in crunchy peanut
butter. Mix the vinegar and soya bechamel together and fold
them into the beans. Mix in the capers and pickles.

Sieved butter beans make a creamy coloured, smooth basic
purée which is lightened in flavour and given a more interesting
texture by adding finely chopped celery. The flavour of the garlic
also comes through quite strongly.

Butter bean and celery spread

4 oz (125 g) dried butter beans
2 tablespoons (30 ml) olive oil
1 small onion, finely chopped
1 clove garlic, finely chopped
1 large stick celery, finely chopped
2 tablespoons (30 ml) crunchy peanut butter
2 tablespoons (30 ml) cider vinegar

Cook the butter beans until they are quite tender. Rub them
through a sieve or pass them through the fine blade of a *mouli*.
Heat the oil in a frying pan on a low heat. Mix in the onion,
garlic and celery and cook them until they are soft and transparent but not coloured. Beat them into the butter-bean
purée, together with any oil still in the pan, the peanut butter and
the vinegar. Leave the spread until it is quite cold and firm.

Aduki beans make a dark, pinky-red spread with a delicate, almost sweet flavour. It is good on open pumpernickel sandwiches or on crisp wholemeal biscuits or oatcakes.

Aduki bean and apple spread

2 oz (50 g) dried aduki beans
1 medium-sized cooking apple
8 black peppercorns
4 cloves
4 tablespoons (60 ml) olive oil
1 small onion, finely chopped
1 clove garlic, finely chopped
6 chopped sage leaves
2 tablespoons (30 ml) cider vinegar

Cook the beans until they are completely soft, and then pound them to a paste with a heavy wooden spoon or with a large pestle and mortar. Peel, quarter, core and finely chop the apple. Crush the peppercorns and cloves together. Heat the oil in a small saucepan on a low heat. Stir in the apple, onion and garlic. Cover them and cook them for 10 minutes, then beat them to a purée. Stir in the beans, ground spices, sage and vinegar. Simmer everything, uncovered, for 5 minutes, stirring frequently. Turn the spread into a bowl and let it cool completely.

Chick peas are used to make the Greek spread called *hummus*, the other ingredients of which are tahini and lemon juice. This one has toasted sesame seeds for a crunchy texture and toasty flavour. Since it is really more than just a spread the amounts given are larger. It can be served as a snack with bread or it can make a first course or even a salad for a main meal if it is piled onto lettuce leaves and garnished with slices or wedges of lemon.

Toasty hummus

8 oz (225 g) dried chick peas
8 tablespoons (120 ml) sesame seeds
2 cloves garlic, crushed with a pinch sea salt
juice 2 lemons

4 tablespoons (60 ml) tahini
8 tablespoons (120 ml) olive oil
6 tablespoons (90 ml) chopped parsley
freshly ground black pepper

Cook the chick peas until they are quite tender and rub them
through a sieve or pass them through the fine blade of a *mouli*.
Put the sesame seeds into a heavy frying pan and set them on a
low heat. Stir them around until they brown and start to pop and
jump about. Mix them into the chick-pea purée. Beat in the
garlic, lemon juice and tahini and then gradually add the oil. Mix
in the parsley and season with the pepper.

To serve the dish as the main feature of a meal you can press
it into a lightly oiled pudding basin and then turn it out onto
a bed of lettuce.

Curries

Indian restaurants are ideal eating places for vegetarians as there is always a really comprehensive selection of dishes that contain only fresh vegetables and pulses (usually lentils) on the menu.

Curries are full of goodness; the very spices themselves contain vitamins and minerals. Spices can be expensive, particularly if they are sold in elaborate jars, but if you live near a Pakistani or Indian community you will be able to benefit from a cultural exchange of ingredients, and some of the new whole-food shops now stock a good range as well. I heard recently that there was an Indian shop somewhere in the vicinity of a local station. Half an hour's searching found it: up and down a rabbit-warren of narrow, terraced streets. It was just a house with an ordinary front door, but with the window crammed full of jars of different coloured ingredients. From outside it looked dull and dark and almost deserted, but inside was Aladdin's Cave! The smell was sweet and pungent, there were open sacks of spices and pulses all different colours and all higgledy-piggledy. Bags of wholemeal chapatti flour were stacked high and, as a contrast to all the warm colours, there were bright green peppers, sour mangoes, green chillis, okra and bunches of fresh coriander. There were purple aubergines, pink sweet potatoes, white mooli and grey ginger root. The proprietor was helpful and jovial and slightly amused at my wide-eyed appreciation. I came away with whole spices and ground spices, some dried tamarind, almonds, a bunch of coriander and a big selection of vegetables.

You can make two kinds of curries – the very simple, quickly prepared ones in which you just use curry powder and one or two easily obtainable spices; and the more complex ones containing unusual ingredients such as coconut, fresh chillis, ginger root and dried tamarind. These are really worthwhile if you want to serve a special Indian meal with several different curries, rice, a refreshing yoghurt raïta and perhaps some sauces and chutneys. The recipes below include both types; but first, if you are new to the different curry ingredients, here is a short description of those most widely used.

Cumin: a dry-flavoured, musty spice. In most delicatessens you can buy it ground, but Indian shops sell whole seeds, which make interesting additions to some curries.

Coriander: (seed) a light coloured, light-flavoured spice, sweeter than cumin. Ground coriander can be bought in most delicatessens. Indian shops also sell the whole seeds, which can be added to dishes as they are or crushed at the last minute to get the maximum flavour.

Cardamom: this spice is very expensive now wherever you buy it, so use it sparingly. It has a light, sherberty flavour.

Turmeric: a bright yellow spice with a dry to sweet flavour. It is a relative of the ginger family and you can sometimes buy the whole roots, but usually it comes ground and is quite widely available. It colours and gently flavours rice and curry dishes and can often be used as a cheaper substitute for saffron. You need very little in most dishes. If you spill any on a white work surface, wipe it up as soon as you can or it will stain.

Garam masala: this is a mixture of different spices ground together. If you would like to mix your own there are many formulas in Indian recipe books, but you can buy excellent ones, ready mixed, in Indian shops.

Fresh coriander: a very pungent herb that is a member of the parsley family. You can grow it yourself from seed and it thrives in hot, damp conditions. Most Indian shops and some markets sell it in large bunches all the year round.

Green chillis: these are fairly common nowadays in green-grocers and markets all over the country. If you have any difficulty, they are always available in Indian shops. To prepare them for cooking, cut off the stalk end and cut each chilli in half length-ways. Remove all the core and seeds with a small, sharp, pointed knife. If you don't your curry will be so hot you won't be able to taste it! Chop the chillis very finely. Wash your hands after preparing them and don't lick your fingers or rub your eyes for a time.

Ginger root: fresh ginger root is similar in appearance to Jerusalem artichokes and is sold by the quarter pound. Weigh as much as you need, peel or scrape it and then grate it straight into the dish you are making, whether hot or cold. Its flavour is like that of ground ginger but sharper and more citrus-like. A combination of a little ground ginger and lemon juice could be used instead. Cooked dishes containing fresh ginger can easily be kept and reheated if necessary, but chutneys and raïtas containing raw ginger such as the cucumber one below will not keep very long as the ginger, once grated, deteriorates fairly quickly. Always make this sort of dish as near to serving as you can.

Tamarind: this is a fruit that comes dried in 14 oz or pound packets wrapped in cellophane. It is a dark, reddy brown and contains seeds. You can buy it in most delicatessens and in Indian shops. It has to be soaked before use and then rubbed through a sieve to remove the seeds and fibres. It has a sharp, citrusy flavour that is much fuller and rounder than lemon. If you can't find any, try using a mixture of lemon and fresh orange juice with a little lemon rind. Once you have opened the packet store it in a dark cupboard in a polythene bag and it should last for about six months.

꙳   ꙳   ꙳

Pulses provide the main ingredient for many vegetarian curries and they are widely sold in oriental shops. Unless otherwise stated, the amounts given below make a main meal for four. Halve or even quarter them if you are serving a selection of curry dishes.

This brown bean curry is a very dusky one – in flavour as well as colour.

Brown bean curry

8 oz (225 g) brown beans
1½ pints (850 ml) water
4 tablespoons (60 ml) olive oil
2 medium onions, thinly sliced
1 large clove garlic, finely chopped
¼ teaspoon (half a 2.5 ml spoon) cayenne pepper
2 teaspoons (10 ml) ground cumin
1 teaspoon (5 ml) garam masala
½ pint (275 ml) stock

Cook the beans as described in the pulses section (p. 185).

Heat the oil in a saucepan on a low heat. Stir in the onions and garlic and cook them until the onions are just beginning to soften. Stir in the cayenne pepper and spices and carry on cooking until the onions are completely soft. Stir in the beans and coat them well with the onion mixture. Pour in the stock and bring it to the boil. Cover and simmer for 30 minutes. The stock will reduce a little and thicken slightly, picking up the flavours of both the spices and the beans to make a sauce.

Red kidney beans make a hot, dark maroon curry.

Red kidney bean curry

8 oz (225 g) red kidney beans
1½ pints (850 ml) water
1 oz (25 g) tamarind
8 tablespoons (120 ml) boiling water
1 oz (25 g) butter *or* vegetable margarine *or* 4 tablespoons (60 ml) olive oil
1 large onion, thinly sliced
½ teaspoon (2.5 ml) cayenne pepper
2 teaspoons (10 ml) garam masala

2 teaspoons (10 ml) ground cumin
up to ½ pint (275 ml) stock

Cook the beans as directed in the pulses section (p. 185). Drain and save the liquid.

Soak the tamarind in the boiling water for 20 minutes and rub it through a sieve. Heat the butter, margarine or oil in a saucepan on a low heat. Stir in the onion and cook until it is soft. Stir in the cayenne pepper and spices and cook them for ½ minute. Stir in the bean liquid, made up to ½ pint (275 ml) with stock, and the sieved tamarind and mix in the beans. Bring everything to the boil, cover and simmer for 20 minutes.

Green Mung beans and fresh chillis provide an unusual fresh taste.

Mung bean curry

8 oz (225 g) Mung beans
1 pint (575 ml) water
3 green chillis
4 tablespoons (60 ml) olive oil
1 large onion, thinly sliced
1 clove garlic, finely chopped
2 teaspoons (10 ml) ground coriander
½ pint (275 ml) stock
2 oz (50 g) fresh ginger root
2 boxes mustard and cress

Cook the beans as directed in the pulses section (p.185).

De-seed and finely chop the chillis. Heat the oil in a saucepan on a low heat. Stir in the onion and garlic and cook them until the onion is soft. Stir in the coriander and chillis and cook for 1 minute more. Pour in the stock, grate in the ginger root, and mix in the beans. Bring everything to the boil, cover and simmer for 20 minutes. Turn the beans into a warm serving dish and scatter the cress over the top.

Chillis are used again in this one, which is nutty and golden-coloured.

Chick-pea curry

½ lb (225 g) chick peas
2 pints (1.150 l) water
1 oz (25 g) butter *or* vegetable margarine
2 medium onions, thinly sliced
1 large clove garlic, finely chopped
1 teaspoon (5 ml) cumin seeds
2 green chillis, de-seeded and finely chopped
½ teaspoon (2.5 ml) ground turmeric
½ teaspoon (2.5 ml) ground cumin
½ teaspoon (2.5 ml) ground coriander
½ teaspoon (2.5 ml) paprika
½ pint (275 ml) stock
1 oz (25 g) fresh ginger root, scraped or peeled

Cook the chick peas as directed in the pulses section (p. 185).

Melt the butter in a saucepan on a low heat. Stir in the onions, garlic and cumin seeds and cook them until the onions are golden. Stir in the prepared chillis and the spices and cook for 1 minute more. Mix in the cooked chick peas and pour in the stock. Grate in the ginger root. Bring the stock to the boil, cover and simmer for 30 minutes.

Gram beans are similar in size and shape to chick-peas and are a dull, brown colour. If you can't find any, chick peas work equally well.

Curried gram beans

8 oz (225 g) gram beans
1½ pints (850 ml) water
1 oz (25 g) dried tamarind
¼ pint (150 ml) boiling water
4 tablespoons (60 ml) olive oil
2 medium onions, finely chopped
1 teaspoon (5 ml) ground coriander
1 teaspoon (5 ml) garam masala
¼ teaspoon (half a 2.5 ml spoon) cayenne pepper
½ pint (275 ml) stock
2 tablespoons (30 ml) chopped fresh coriander *or* 1 box mustard and
  cress

Cook the gram beans as for chick peas only simmer them for the shorter time of 1¼ hours. Soak the tamarind in the boiling water for 20 minutes and rub it through a sieve. Heat the oil in a saucepan on a low heat. Stir in the onions, coriander, garam masala and cayenne pepper and simmer them gently until the onions are soft. Stir in the beans and the tamarind. Pour in the stock and bring it to the boil. Cover and simmer for 15 minutes. Turn the curry into a warm serving dish and strew the chopped fresh coriander or the mustard and cress over the top.

The soft, mustiness of black-eyed beans blends well with curry flavours. Stir in some yoghurt at the end for a light contrast.

Curried black-eyed beans and green peppers

8 oz (225 g) black-eyed beans
1 pint (575 ml) water
2 medium-sized green peppers
1 oz (25 g) butter *or* vegetable margarine
2 medium onions, finely chopped
1 large (or 2 small) cloves garlic, finely chopped
1 tablespoon (15 ml) hot Madras curry powder
1 tablespoon (15 ml) ground cumin
1 tablespoon (15 ml) ground coriander
up to ½ pint (275 ml) stock
1 carton natural yoghurt

Cook the beans as directed in the pulses section (p. 185), reserving any liquid to be made up to ½ pint (275 ml) with the stock.

Core and de-seed the peppers and chop them into small dice. Melt the butter in a saucepan on a low heat. Stir in the onions and garlic, cover and cook gently for 10 minutes. Stir in the peppers and spices, cover again and cook for a further 5 minutes. Mix in the beans and pour in the stock. Bring everything to the boil and simmer, uncovered for 5 minutes. Turn off the heat and stir in the yoghurt. Cover the pan and let the dish rest for 1 minute.

Yellow split peas can be made into a base for a mixed vegetable curry. More water is used here for cooking than in the other split pea recipes to make a slightly softer purée.

Yellow pea and vegetable curry

½ lb (225 g) yellow split peas
1½ pints (850 ml) water
1 bayleaf
sea salt and freshly ground black pepper for seasoning
1 large aubergine
2 teaspoons (10 ml) fine sea salt
1 oz (25 g) dried tamarind
6 tablespoons (90 ml) boiling water
1 large green pepper
¼ lb (125 g) mushrooms
4 tablespoons (60 ml) olive oil
1 large onion, thinly sliced
1 large clove garlic, finely chopped
2 teaspoons (10 ml) ground cumin
2 teaspoons (10 ml) garam masala
½ teaspoon (2.5 ml) cayenne pepper
3 tablespoons (45 ml) chopped fresh coriander

Put the split peas into a saucepan with the water and bayleaf and season them. Bring them to the boil, cover them and simmer for 1 hour until they are reduced to a soft purée. Remove them from the heat and keep them covered.

Meanwhile cut the aubergine into ½ in (1.5 cm) dice. Put them into a colander, scatter them with the 2 teaspoons (10 ml) sea salt and leave them to drain for 30 minutes. Soak the tamarind in the boiling water for 20 minutes and rub it through a sieve. Cut the pepper into strips about 1 in by ¼ in (3 cm by 0.75 cm). Thinly slice the mushrooms.

Rinse the aubergine in cold water and dry it on absorbent kitchen paper. Heat the oil in a large saucepan on a low heat. Stir in the onion and garlic and cook them until the onion is soft. Stir in the spices, mushrooms, aubergine and green pepper, cover them and cook them gently for 10 minutes. Stir in the cooked split peas and sieved tamarind. Bring the mixture to the boil, cover and cook on the lowest heat possible for

20 minutes. Turn the curry into a warm serving dish and scatter the chopped fresh coriander over the top.

Dal, or dhal, is the Hindi name for all the pulses, but in most Indian restaurants it refers to a spiced purée of red lentils that is served as an accompanying dish, usually to moisten and enrich plainly cooked rice. In texture, a dhal should be thicker than a soup but not as stiff as the lentil purées given in the pulses section, so again a little more liquid is used for cooking.

Red lentil dhal

4 tablespoons (60 ml) olive oil
2 medium onions, thinly sliced
1 large clove garlic, finely chopped
2 teaspoons (10 ml) cumin seeds
2 teaspoons (10 ml) hot Madras curry powder
2 teaspoons (10 ml) ground coriander
1 piece cinnamon stick about 3 inches (10 cm) long
8 cloves
8 oz (225 g) red lentils
1¼ pints (725 ml) stock
2 bayleaves

Heat the oil in a wide-based, fairly shallow saucepan on a low heat. Stir in the onions, garlic and cumin seeds and cook them until the onion is soft. Stir in the curry powder and ground coriander and carry on cooking until the onions are brown. Stir in the lentils, cinnamon stick and cloves and cook them for 1 minute, stirring all the time. Pour in the stock and bring it to the boil. Add the bayleaves, cover and simmer for 45 minutes, stirring occasionally.

To serve: leave the cloves, cinnamon stick and bayleaves in the purée and bring them to the top of the serving dish for an authentic-looking peasant dhal.

In this recipe, a thick purée of red lentils is flavoured with curry spices and made into croquettes. Use fresh ginger if you can, but ground ginger and lemon make a good substitute. The croquettes taste spicy and fresh at the same time. Serve them with rice moistened with a curry sauce.

Curried lentil balls

12 oz (350 g) red lentils
1½ pints (850 ml) water
2 bayleaves
sea salt and freshly ground black pepper
4 tablespoons (60 ml) olive oil
2 medium onions, finely chopped
1 large clove garlic, finely chopped
1 teaspoon (5 ml) ground cumin
1 teaspoon (5 ml) ground coriander
1 tablespoon (15 ml) hot Madras curry powder
1 oz (25 g) fresh ginger root, scraped or peeled (or ½ teaspoon (2.5 ml) ground ginger and the juice of half a lemon)
approx. 6 tablespoons (90 ml) browned crumbs
oil for frying

Put the lentils into a saucepan with the water and bayleaves and season them well. Cover them, bring them to the boil and simmer them for 45 minutes, beating them to a thick purée towards the end. Discard the bayleaves. Heat the oil in a frying pan on a low heat. Put in the onions and garlic and cook them until the onions are soft. Stir in the cumin, coriander and curry powder. (If you are using ground ginger add this now.) Keep cooking until the onions are golden. Mix all the contents of the pan into the lentils and grate in the fresh ginger (or add the lemon juice). Make the mixture into 12 small balls and coat them in browned crumbs. Fry them in shallow oil on a moderate heat until they are well-browned and crisp.

If you are making curries from fresh vegetables have several lighter dishes, with cauliflower or spinach for example, and one good filling one made from root vegetables or potatoes.

Mixed root vegetable curry

8 oz (225 g) white turnips
8 oz (225 g) potatoes
8 oz (225 g) parsnips
8 oz (225 g) carrots
1½ oz (40 g) butter
1 teaspoon (5 ml) ground turmeric
1 teaspoon (5 ml) ground cumin
1 teaspoon (5 ml) ground coriander
2 teaspoons (10 ml) garam masala
½ teaspoon (2.5 ml) cayenne pepper
1 pint (575 ml) stock
2 bayleaves
2 large cloves garlic, crushed with ½ teaspoon (2.5 ml) sea salt
3 tablespoons (45 ml) chopped fresh coriander or parsley

Scrub and dice the vegetables, having removed the woody cores from the parsnips. Melt the butter in a large saucepan on a low heat. Stir in the spices and let them cook for ½ minute. Stir in the vegetables and coat them well, then cover them and let them sweat for 10 minutes. Pour in the stock and bring it to the boil. Tuck in the bayleaves and mix in the crushed garlic. Cover and simmer for 30 minutes. Serve in a warm serving dish with the coriander or parsley scattered over the top.

Simple curried potatoes

1½ lb (675 g) small old potatoes
1 oz (25 g) butter or 4 tablespoons (60 ml) olive oil
1 medium onion, thinly sliced
1 clove garlic, finely chopped
2 teaspoons (10 ml) hot Madras curry powder
1 teaspoon (5 ml) ground turmeric
½ pint (275 ml) stock
1 bayleaf
1 box mustard and cress

Preheat the oven to Reg 4/350°F/180°C. Scrub the potatoes and cut them into ¼ in (0.75 cm) slices. Melt the butter or heat the oil in a flameproof casserole on a low heat. Stir in the onion, garlic, curry powder and turmeric and cook them until the onion is golden. Mix in the potatoes and let them get well-coated with the onion and spices. Pour in the stock and bring it to the boil. Tuck in the bayleaf. Cover the casserole and put it into the oven for 1¼ hours so the potatoes are soft and yellow and all the liquid absorbed. Discard the bayleaf. Mix in the mustard and cress just before serving.

Lighter vegetable curries are excellent served with the more filling pulses. Here are two cauliflower curries, both with refreshing flavours. The first uses coconut and is a little more complicated.

Cauliflower, green pepper and coconut curry

4 oz (100 g) fresh coconut
½ pint (275 ml) stock
1 medium-sized cauliflower
2 large green peppers
4 tablespoons (60 ml) olive oil
1 large onion, thinly sliced
½ teaspoon (2.5 ml) cayenne pepper
1 teaspoon (5 ml) paprika
½ teaspoon (2.5 ml) ground ginger
1 teaspoon (5 ml) garam masala

Grate the coconut and soak it in the stock for 30 minutes. Break the cauliflower into small fleurettes. Cut the peppers into strips about 1 in by ¼ in (3 cm by 0.75 cm). Heat the oil in a saucepan on a low heat. Stir in the onion and cook it until it is soft. Add the spices and continue cooking until the onion begins to brown. Fold the cauliflower and the peppers. Pour in the coconut and stock mixture and bring it the boil. Cover the pan and cook on a moderate heat for 20 minutes.

Apart from the cumin seeds, this second cauliflower curry recipe has simple, readily available ingredients. It is still good even without the seeds, so don't let it deter you if you can't find any.

Cauliflower curry with tomatoes

1 large cauliflower
3 tablespoons (45 ml) olive oil
1 large onion, thinly sliced
1 clove garlic, finely chopped
1 teaspoon (5 ml) cumin seeds, if available
2 teaspoons (10 ml) hot Madras curry powder
1 teaspoon (5 ml) ground turmeric
¼ pint (150 ml) stock
1 tablespoon (15 ml) tomato purée
½ lb (225 g) firm tomatoes

Break the cauliflower into small fleurettes and use some of the inner leaves as well, breaking the longer ones in half. Heat the oil in a saucepan on a low heat. Stir in the cauliflower, onion, garlic, cumin seeds, curry powder and turmeric. Cover the pan and let everything cook gently for 5 minutes, stirring once. Mix the stock and tomato purée together and pour them into the pan. Bring them to the boil, cover again and simmer for 15 minutes. Scald, skin and roughly chop the tomatoes and fold them into the cauliflower just before serving so the pieces heat through but stay firm.

Make a green curry, light and pleasantly bitter with the strong flavours of spinach and green peppers.

Spinach and green pepper curry

2 lb (900 g) spinach
2 medium-sized green peppers
3 tablespoons (45 ml) olive oil
1 large onion, thinly sliced
1 clove garlic, finely chopped
2 teaspoons (10 ml) ground coriander
2 teaspoons (10 ml) ground cumin
¼ teaspoon (half a 2.5 ml spoon) cayenne pepper
1 tablespoon (15 ml) tomato purée

Break the stems from the spinach. Put the leaves into a saucepan with only the water that clings to them after washing. Cover them and set them on a low heat for 15 minutes, stirring once or twice. Drain the spinach well, pressing down hard to extract as much moisture as possible. Turn it onto a board and chop it fairly coarsely. Core and de-seed the peppers and cut them into strips about 1 in by $\frac{1}{4}$ in (3 cm by 0.75 cm). Heat the oil in a large frying pan or paella pan on a low heat. Mix in the peppers, onion and garlic and cook them until the onion is soft. Stir in the spices and cook for 1 minute more. Raise the heat to moderate. Mix in the spinach and the tomato purée and stir everything around on the heat for 2 minutes.

Both courgettes and mushrooms make very simple but delicious curry dishes.

Curried courgettes

1 lb (450 g) fairly small courgettes (the size that gives roughly 6 to the pound)
4 tablespoons (60 ml) olive oil
1 large onion, thinly sliced
1 clove garlic
1 teaspoon (5 ml) ground cumin
1 teaspoon (5 ml) hot Madras curry powder
juice 1 lemon
1 bayleaf

Wipe the courgettes and cut them into $\frac{1}{2}$ in (1.5 cm) diagonal slices. Heat the oil in a frying pan on a low heat. Mix in the onion and garlic, cover them and cook for 5 minutes. Stir in the cumin and curry powder and then the courgettes, making sure they are well-coated with oil and spices. Pour in the lemon juice and tuck in the bayleaf. Cover and cook gently for 10 minutes.

Simple curried mushrooms

1 lb (450 g) dark flat mushrooms
$1\frac{1}{2}$ oz (40 g) butter
2 teaspoons (10 ml) ground turmeric
$\frac{1}{4}$ teaspoon (half a 2.5 ml spoon) cayenne pepper

juice 1 lemon
2 boxes mustard and cress

Thinly slice the mushrooms. Melt the butter in a saucepan on a low heat. Stir in the turmeric and cayenne and let them cook gently for 2 minutes. Stir in the mushrooms and lemon juice. Cover the pan and simmer gently for 10 minutes. Just before serving mix in the mustard and cress for a light contrast.

The next two recipes can be used in the same way as the red lentil dhal. Pumpkin makes a golden, thick, sweet-and-sour purée.

Pumpkin curry

2 lb (900 g) chopped raw pumpkin
6 tablespoons (90 ml) water
4 tablespoons (60 ml) olive oil
2 medium onions, thinly sliced
1 large clove garlic, finely chopped
2 teaspoons (10 ml) ground cumin
2 teaspoons (10 ml) hot Madras curry powder
2 oz (50 g) sultanas

Put the pumpkin into a saucepan with the water. Cover it and set it on a moderate heat for 20 minutes, mashing it down from time to time to reduce it to a thick purée. Remove it from the stove. Heat the oil in a large frying pan on a low heat. Put in the onions and garlic and cook them until the onions are soft. Stir in the cumin and curry powder and carry on cooking until the onions are brown. Stir in the pumpkin purée and the sultanas and simmer gently, uncovered, for 5 minutes.

This is an excellent way of using up large, tough old broad beans at the end of their season. Don't use young beans. They are really too good for this sort of dish, and in any case would not give the right texture.

Broad bean dhal

2 lb (900 g) old broad beans, weighed before shelling

1 oz (25 g) butter
1 medium onion, finely chopped
1 mint sprig
1 tablespoon (15 ml) hot Madras curry powder
1 teaspoon (5 ml) ground turmeric
1½ pints (850 ml) stock
2 thinly pared strips lemon rind
juice 1 lemon

Shell and chop the beans and reserve 4 of the best pods. Melt the butter in a saucepan on a low heat. Stir in the beans, onion, mint sprig, curry powder, turmeric and pods. Cover them and set them on a low heat for 10 minutes. Pour in the stock and bring it to the boil. Add the lemon rind and juice and simmer, uncovered, for 15 minutes. Remove the pods, mint sprig and lemon rind and work the bean mixture in a blender until it is smooth. Return to the pan and reheat before serving.

You will find a curry and lemon sauce in the sauces chapter but this sauce is a little more special with slightly more authentic curry ingredients. It is excellent spooned over a savoury rice when the other dishes have only a small amount of sauce.

Tamarind and coconut sauce

1 oz (25 g) tamarind
¼ pint (150 ml) boiling water
4 oz (125 g) fresh coconut
¼ pint (150 ml) stock
2 tablespoons (30 ml) olive oil
1 small onion, finely chopped
1 teaspoon (5 ml) ground cumin
1 teaspoon (5 ml) garam masala

Soak the tamarind in the boiling water and the coconut in the stock, both for 30 minutes. Rub the tamarind through a sieve. Heat the oil in a small saucepan on a low heat. Stir in the onion and cook it until it is soft. Stir in the spices and let them cook for 1 minute. Stir in the coconut and stock and the strained tamarind liquid. Bring the sauce to the boil, cover it and simmer gently for 30 minutes.

Whenever I eat in Indian restaurants, the only thing I miss, whether or not the meal is a vegetarian one, is a fresh salad to contrast with all the dark, rich spices. Some places serve a natural yoghurt, but very few provide the refreshing raïtas (or rayitas) that are really the Indian equivalent of our salads. They consist of yoghurt mixed with grated, puréed or chopped fresh vegetables. You can spoon them over rice and over other curries or just have them on the side to refresh you between the hot mouthfuls of the main curry dishes.

Cucumber and ginger raïta

1 carton natural yoghurt
½ a small cucumber
1 oz (25 g) fresh ginger root
3 tablespoons (45 ml) chopped fresh coriander
1 tablespoon (15 ml) chopped mint, if available

Put the yoghurt into a bowl. Wipe but don't peel the cucumber and grate it into the yoghurt. Scrape the ginger and grate it into the bowl. Mix in the coriander and mint and serve, just slightly chilled, as soon as possible.

Carrot and apple raïta

1 carton natural yoghurt
2 tablespoons (30 ml) cider vinegar
1 clove garlic, crushed with a pinch sea salt
freshly ground black pepper
1 teaspoon (5 ml) ground cumin
1 teaspoon (5 ml) ground coriander
1 large Bramley apple
4 large carrots

Mix the yoghurt, vinegar, garlic, pepper and spices in a bowl.

Quarter and core the apple but don't peel it; grate it into the yoghurt, stirring as you go to prevent it from turning brown. Grate in the carrots and mix everything together well. Chill very slightly before serving.

𝔂   𝔂   𝔂

Vegetable curries should always be served with rice and brown rice is far the best. You will find plainer rice dishes in the next chapter, but biriani (or biryani) dishes are so typical of Indian food that I have included one here. There are many different ways of making these dishes, in which the rice and other main ingredients (meat or vegetables) are all eventually mixed together. This fairly simple one uses the basic method of steaming rice.

Special vegetable biriani

a good selection of vegetables in season, such as:
carrots, new or old, thinly sliced
potatoes, diced (not too many of these)
fresh green peas
spring greens, Brussels tops or curly kale, all finely chopped
mushrooms, thinly sliced
okra, left whole
courgettes, thinly sliced
aubergines, diced and salted for 30 minutes
green peppers, diced
tomatoes, scalded, de-seeded and sliced
for the basic rice:
10 oz (275 g) brown rice
4 tablespoons (60 ml) olive oil
1 large onion, thinly sliced
2 teaspoons (10 ml) ground turmeric
1 teaspoon (5 ml) garam masala
1¼ pints (725 ml) stock
optional extras:
4 hard-boiled eggs
1 box mustard and cress
2 tablespoons (30 ml) chopped fresh coriander

Heat the oil in a saucepan on a low heat. Stir in the onion and cook it until it is soft. Stir in the spices and cook them for 1 minute. Mix in any of the following: carrots, potatoes, peas, greens, okra, mushrooms. Mix in the rice. Cook everything for 1 minute, stirring. Pour in the stock and bring it to the boil. Cover, and keep the pan on a very low heat for 45 minutes.

During cooking add any of these:

courgettes, after the first 15 minutes.

aubergines, washed and dried, after 30 minutes.

green peppers, after 35 minutes.

At the end of the 45 minutes, turn off the heat, mix in the tomatoes if you are using them and let the pan stand, covered, for 10 minutes. Roughly chop three of the eggs and mix them into the rice. Arrange the biriani on a warmed serving dish. Slice the remaining egg and lay it on top with the mustard and cress and fresh coriander.

Serve the biriani with a vegetable curry that has plenty of sauce, or hand a curry sauce separately.

Rice

Rice is nice ... so long as it's brown, that is. Brown rice is a marvellous accompaniment to any meal and it is so much better in texture and flavour than any of the polished white kinds. It does, however, take longer to cook, but providing you remember this and start preparing it soon enough it will be no trouble at all.

You can simply boil it in lightly salted water and then afterwards toss it with butter and herbs, or fry it, perhaps with onions and spices. You can steam it in a tightly covered saucepan with flavourings and just enough stock or water to be absorbed and plump the rice; or you can make a pilaf by cooking it in the oven. Rice can be a relatively plain accompaniment, or it can be the base of the main dish.

Depending on appetites, on how many other ingredients you are going to add to the rice and also on the type and quantity of the other dishes in the meal you will need 8 to 10 oz (225–275 g) uncooked brown rice for 4 people. If you find the recipes below too much or too little for your particular requirements, alter all the rest of the ingredients in proportion.

To boil brown rice, bring a large saucepan of salted water to the boil and throw in your rice by the handful. Bring the water to the boil again and stir the rice with a fork to make sure all the grains are free. Turn the heat down low, cover the pan and cook the rice for 45 minutes. Drain it in a colander and then immediately pour some cold water over it. This stops the cooking process and keeps just the right texture. If you intend to serve it quite plainly and not buttered (or margarined!) heat it up again by pouring some very hot (but not boiling) water through it, and then leave it to stand and dry slightly in a warm place such as the warming drawer of the oven, above a hot stove or on the side of an Aga cooker. If you like to half prepare dishes in advance, to be ready when you come in from a day out, for example, or if you are preparing a dinner-party for which many of the dishes need to be cooked at the last minute, plainly boiled rice is ideal. Keep it in a dish covered with foil or in a covered container.

To butter boiled brown rice, put 1½ oz (40 g) butter into a large saucepan (this will be enough for 8 to 10 oz (225–275 g) rice) and melt it on a low heat. Stir in the rice and let it get well-coated. Cover the pan and leave it on the heat for about 3 minutes for the rice to heat through. Flavour buttered rice by mixing in some chopped herbs, spring onions or watercress; caraway, dill or fennel seeds; or some grated cheese (about 1 tablespoon (15 ml) Parmesan or 2 tablespoons (30 ml) Cheddar) before covering. If you don't eat butter use a vegetable margarine. Olive oil (4 tablespoons (60 ml)) can be used as well but with this you will need some other flavourings, otherwise the dish could be a little bland.

You can also soften or brown an onion in the butter or oil first, as in the following recipe.

Brown rice with sage and parsley

10 oz (275 g) brown rice
1½ oz (40 g) butter *or* vegetable margarine, *or* 4 tablespoons (60 ml) olive oil
1 medium onion, finely chopped
2 tablespoons (30 ml) chopped parsley
12 chopped sage leaves

Cook the rice in salted water for 45 minutes. Drain it and refresh it with cold water. Melt the butter in a saucepan on a low heat. Stir in the onion and cook it until it is soft. Mix in the rice and herbs, cover them and leave the pan on the heat for 3 minutes.

❧   ❧   ❧

Plain boiled rice may also be fried in 1 oz (25 g) butter or

margarine or 4 tablespoons (60 ml) olive oil. Use a heavy frying
pan on a moderate heat and fork the rice about all the time it is
cooking. You can soften an onion and/or a garlic clove or cook
some sliced mushrooms in the pan before adding the rice; or
gently cook some caraway or dill seeds for a few minutes. Again,
fork in herbs with the rice, or spices such as paprika and turmeric,
or tamari or Worcestershire sauce or Yorkshire Relish. Here are a
few examples of differently flavoured fried rice.

Brown rice and spring onions

10 oz (275 g) brown rice
16 large spring onions, preferably those with bulbous ends
4 tablespoons (60 ml) olive oil
1 large clove garlic, finely chopped
1 tablespoon (15 ml) tamari sauce

Cook the rice in salted water for 45 minutes. Drain it and refresh
it with cold water. Cut the green parts of the onions into $1\frac{1}{2}$ in
(4.5 cm) lengths and cut each bulbous end in half lengthways.
Heat the oil in a frying pan on a low heat. Put in the onions and
garlic and cook them until the onions are soft. Raise the heat to
moderate and fork in the rice. Mix in the tamari sauce. Continue
cooking for three minutes, moving the rice about all the time.

Brown rice with paprika and Worcestershire sauce

10 oz (275 g) brown rice
8 large or 12 small spring onions, or 1 medium onion
4 tablespoons (60 ml) olive oil
1 teaspoon (5 ml) paprika
1 tablespoon (15 ml) Worcestershire sauce or Yorkshire Relish
2 tablespoons (30 ml) chopped parsley

Cook the rice in salted water for 45 minutes. Drain it and refresh
it with cold water. Chop the spring onions or thinly slice the
medium onion. Heat the oil in a frying pan on a moderate heat.
Put in the onions. Move spring onions around on the heat for
$\frac{1}{2}$ minute, but let the sliced medium onion cook until it softens.
Fork in the rice and paprika and keep moving the rice around for

2 minutes. Mix in the Worcester sauce and parsley and take the pan from the heat at once.

Rice flavoured with turmeric goes well with Chinese and Indian dishes and with many of the pulses.

Turmeric fried rice with mushrooms

10 oz (275 g) brown rice
4 tablespoons (60 ml) olive oil *or* 1 oz (25 g) butter
1 large onion, thinly sliced
1 large clove garlic, finely chopped
4 oz (125 g) mushrooms, thinly sliced
2 teaspoons (10 ml) ground turmeric

Cook the rice in salted water for 45 minutes. Drain it and refresh it with cold water. Heat the oil in a frying pan on a low heat. Put in the onion and garlic and cook them until the onion is soft. Mix in the mushrooms and carry on cooking until the onion is golden. Raise the heat to moderate and fork in the rice and turmeric. Keep forking everything around on the heat until the rice is quite dry, heated through and well-coloured (about 2 minutes).

This next dish is excellent with any kind of curry.

Brown rice with lemon and turmeric

10 oz (275 g) brown rice
1 lemon
3 tablespoons (45 ml) olive oil
1 large onion, thinly sliced
1 clove garlic, finely chopped
2 teaspoons (10 ml) ground turmeric

Cook the rice in salted water for 45 minutes. Drain it and refresh it with cold water. Cut the lemon in half cross-ways. Cut away the skin and pith and chop the segments finely. Heat the oil in a frying pan on a low heat. Put in the onion and garlic and cook them until the onion is golden. Raise the heat to moderate and fork in the rice and then the turmeric. Move the rice about on the heat for 2 minutes. Mix in the lemon and take the pan from the heat. Serve as soon as you can to keep the lemon as fresh as possible.

Egg-fried rice is a Chinese speciality and it isn't as difficult to make as you might imagine. It looks, when you first add the eggs, as if it may turn out to be sticky, but keep moving the rice about with a fork and gradually the grains will separate and become coated with fluffy, cooked beaten egg. The addition of tamari sauce gives a good savoury flavour and a slightly deeper brown colour.

Chinese egg-fried rice

8 oz (225 g) brown rice
4 tablespoons (60 ml) olive oil
1 medium onion, thinly sliced
2 eggs
1 tablespoon (15 ml) tamari sauce

Cook the rice in salted water for 45 minutes. Drain it and refresh it with cold water. Heat the oil in a frying pan on a low heat. Put in the onion and cook it until it is golden. While it is cooking, beat the eggs with the tamari sauce. Raise the heat under the pan to moderate and fork in the rice. Pour in the eggs and keep forking everything around until the rice is quite dry and coated with firm, fluffy egg.

Plainly boiled rice can be coated with a simple French dressing and served cold with salads and other cold meals. Fork in some diced cooked or raw vegetables or perhaps some fruit, and some chopped herbs or dried seeds for additional colour and flavour. Here are a few combinations to try:

skinned and chopped tomatoes, raw mushrooms, black olives and thyme;
green peppers and cooked sweetcorn with Tabasco sauce in the dressing;

chopped apples and celery with a few sultanas, with cider
vinegar dressing;

chopped dill cucumbers and dill seeds;

chopped French beans, green olives and chopped savory;

chopped orange segments and watercress with a granular mustard
in the dressing;

redcurrants, chives and tarragon vinegar;

chopped firm peaches with a curry-flavoured dressing and chives;

raw mushrooms, mustard and cress, and a lemon dressing;

cooked fresh green peas and diced baby carrots with mint;

pickled onions and pickled walnuts with lots of parsley;

diced cooked beetroot with caraway seeds and pickled gherkins
in a red wine dressing.

꒰   ꒰   ꒰

Steamed rice is richer-textured and glossy in appearance. It is
stirred into a little melted butter or heated oil and then a
measured amount of water or stock is poured in and brought to
the boil. The pan is covered and the rice cooked gently so it
gradually absorbs all the liquid. After cooking, the heat is turned
off and the rice left undisturbed for 10 minutes so that it gently
steams in its own moisture to complete the process. Whereas
with boiled rice a little too much or too little doesn't matter you
need exactly the right proportions for steaming, so it is important
to weigh out the rice and measure the liquid before you start.

The quantities are:
8 oz (225 g) rice to 1 pint (575 ml) stock or water *or*
10 oz (275 g) rice to 1¼ pints (725 ml) stock or water

To flavour steamed rice, soften a chopped onion in the oil or
butter first; add spices or caraway or dill seeds when you add
the rice; or fork in herbs or grated cheese, some diced apple or
sliced orange just after you turn off the heat.

Here is a fresh, tomato rice that is ideal with egg dishes and
many of the pulses.

Tomato rice

8 oz (225 g) brown rice
4 tablespoons (60 ml) olive oil
1 large onion, thinly sliced
1 large clove garlic, finely chopped
2 teaspoons (10 ml) paprika
2 teaspoons (10 ml) caraway seeds
1 pint (575 ml) stock
1 lb (450 g) firm tomatoes

Heat the oil in a heavy saucepan on a low heat. Stir in the onion and garlic and cook them until the onion is soft. Stir in the paprika, caraway seeds and rice and cook them for 2 minutes, stirring. Pour in the stock and bring it to the boil. Cover, and simmer on the lowest heat possible, without disturbing, for 45 minutes. While the rice is cooking, scald, skin and chop the tomatoes. Turn off the heat, quickly fork in the tomatoes, cover again and let the rice stand for 10 minutes, still on the warm plate of the stove.

Almonds, currants and cumin make a lovely, biscuit-coloured, exotic-seeming brown rice that is perfect with any curry.

Brown rice with almonds and currants

8 oz (225 g) brown rice
1 oz (25 g) butter or vegetable margarine
2 medium onions, thinly sliced
2 teaspoons (10 ml) ground cumin
1 pint (575 ml) stock
2 oz (50 g) almonds
1 oz (25 g) currants

Melt the butter in a saucepan on a low heat. Stir in the onions and cumin and cook them until the onions are just beginning to turn golden. Add the rice and cook it for 1 minute, stirring. Pour in the stock and bring it to the boil. Cover the pan tightly and keep it on the lowest heat possible for 45 minutes. Blanch and sliver the almonds. When the rice is cooked, turn off the heat, quickly fork in the slivered almonds and the currants, cover again and let the dish rest for 10 minutes.

In complete contrast, try light flavoured leeks and a savoury mustard with rice.

Steamed brown rice with leeks

12 oz (350 ml) leeks
4 tablespoons (60 ml) olive oil
10 oz (275 g) brown rice
1¼ pints (725 ml) water
pinch sea salt
2 teaspoons (10 ml) Dijon or a mild Urchfont mustard
2 tablespoons (30 ml) chopped parsley

Wash and thinly slice the leeks. Heat the oil in a heavy saucepan on a low heat. Stir in the leeks, cover them and let them sweat for 5 minutes. Stir in the rice and cook it for 1 minute, stirring. Pour in the water and bring it to the boil. Season with the salt and stir in the mustard. Turn the heat down low, cover the rice tightly, and steam it, undisturbed, for 45 minutes. Turn off the heat, quickly fork in the parsley, cover again and let the dish stand for 10 minutes.

In the following recipe more stock is used than usual because the carrots absorb a little as well. The rice is light and fluffy and all the carrots' flavour is retained.

Steamed brown rice with carrots

8 oz (225 g) brown rice
2 tablespoons (30 ml) olive oil
½ lb (225 g) carrots, diced (old carrots are best for this dish)
1 medium onion, finely chopped
1¼ pints (725 ml) water
pinch sea salt
3 tablespoons (45 ml) chopped parsley
2 teaspoons (10 ml) tamari sauce
juice ½ lemon

Heat the oil in a heavy saucepan on a low heat. Stir in the carrots and onions. Cover them and let them sweat for 10 minutes. Stir in the rice and keep stirring for 2 minutes. Pour in the water, bring it to the boil and season with the salt. Stir the rice around to separate it, cover the pan and keep it on the lowest heat possible for 45 minutes. Turn off the heat and quickly fork in the parsley, tamari sauce and lemon juice. Cover again and let the dish stand for 10 minutes.

Steamed rice with vegetables and a miso sauce can make a complete meal. The only accompaniment it needs is a light contrasting salad. This is a satisfying winter dish in which all the flavour of the vegetables is brought out.

Brown rice and mixed vegetables

10 oz (275 g) brown rice
4 tablespoons (60 ml) olive oil
8 oz (225 g) carrots, finely chopped
8 oz (225 g) white turnips, finely chopped
1 large onion, finely chopped
4 large sticks celery, finely chopped
1½ pints (850 ml) stock
fine sea salt and freshly ground black pepper to taste
¼ medium sized Savoy cabbage, shredded
for serving:
¾ pint miso, onion and parsley sauce (*see* under sauces)

Heat the oil in a large, heavy saucepan on a low heat. Stir in the carrots, onion, turnips and celery. Cover the pan and let them sweat for 10 minutes. Stir in the rice and cook it for 1 minute, stirring. Pour in the stock and bring it to the boil. Season, and mix in the cabbage. Cover the pan and keep it on the lowest heat possible for 45 minutes. Turn off the heat and let the rice stand for 10 minutes.
To serve:
divide the rice between 4 serving plates, spread it out and make

a well in the centre. Hand the sauce separately, so everyone can spoon in as much or as little as they need.

Pilafs are essentially the same as steamed rice, except they are put into the oven as soon as the liquid has come to the boil. When they are cooked they are taken out of the oven and left to stand for 10 minutes, still covered. The same flavourers can be used as for steamed rice, and the cooking time is the same. Before you start, preheat the oven to Reg 4/350°F/180°C.

This pilaf is lightly spiced and dotted with plump raisins and crunchy, toasted almonds. All you need with it is a green salad. Less liquid than usual is needed here as the mushrooms keep it nice and moist.

Mushroom, almond and raisin pilaf

4 oz (125 g) button mushrooms
1 oz (25 g) butter *or* 4 tablespoons (60 ml) olive oil
1 medium onion, finely chopped
1 clove garlic, finely chopped
8 oz (225 g) brown rice
2 teaspoons (10 ml) ground coriander
¾ pint (425 ml) stock
sea salt and freshly ground black pepper
2 oz (25 g) raisins
6 oz (175 g) almonds

Preheat the oven to Reg 4/350°F/180°C. Thinly slice the mushrooms. Melt the butter or heat the oil in a shallow, flameproof casserole on a low heat. Stir in the onion and garlic and cook them until the onion is soft. Stir in the rice, mushrooms and coriander and cook for 2 minutes, stirring. Pour in the stock, bring it to the boil, and season lightly. Cover the casserole and put it into the oven for 30 minutes. Add the raisins, fork them in, cover the casserole again and return it to the oven for 15 minutes. While the rice is cooking, blanch and split the almonds and toast them under a high grill until they are brown. Take the rice from the oven, fork in the almonds, cover and let the dish stand in a warm place for 10 minutes.

Fresh peas go beautifully with rice and if you cook them in a pilaf they gently absorb the flavours of any spices that you use. This is another complete meal. A delicate, tarragon flavoured lettuce salad would be a good accompaniment.

Green pea and almond pilaf

2 lb (900 g) green peas, weighed before shelling
8 oz (225 g) almonds
4 tablespoons (60 ml) olive oil
1 large onion, thinly sliced
1 large clove garlic, finely chopped
1 teaspoon (5 ml) ground turmeric
1 teaspoon (5 ml) ground cumin
8 oz (225 g) brown rice
1 pint (575 ml) stock

Preheat the oven to Reg 4/350°F/180°C. Shell the peas and reserve 4 of the best pods. Blanch and split the almonds. Heat the oil in a shallow casserole on a moderate heat. Put in the almonds and cook them until they are golden, stirring them around all the time. Remove them and lower the heat. Stir in the onion and garlic and cook them until the onion is soft. Add the turmeric and cumin and carry on cooking until the onions are brown. Stir in the rice and peas and cook them for 2 minutes, stirring. Pour in the stock and add the pea pods and almonds. Bring the stock to the boil, cover the casserole and put it into the oven for 45 minutes. Remove the dish from the oven and let it stand for 10 minutes before removing the pods and serving.

Peas and tarragon are the perfect summer combination and with sweet cream cheese and rice they make a delicate flavoured, creamy complete meal. Don't shy away from the vinegar – it gives flavour and freshness, but no sharpness.

Green pea, tarragon and cream cheese pilaf

2 lb (900 g) green peas, weighed before shelling
4 tablespoons (60 ml) olive oil
1 large onion, thinly sliced
1 large clove garlic, thinly sliced
8 oz (225 g) brown rice
2 tablespoons (30 ml) chopped tarragon
1 pint (575 ml) stock
2 tablespoons (30 ml) tarragon vinegar
8 oz (225 g) Somerset soft cheese (or any other sweet cream cheese)

Preheat the oven to Reg 4/350°F/180°C. Shell the peas and
reserve 4 of the best pods. Heat the oil in a shallow, flameproof
casserole on a low heat. Stir in the onion and garlic and cook
them until the onion is soft. Stir in the rice and peas and stir them
about for 2 minutes. Mix in the chopped tarragon and pour in
the stock and tarragon vinegar. Add the pea pods, cover the
casserole and put it into the oven for 45 minutes. Remove the
pea pods, mix in all the cheese and serve immediately.

Pasta

I remember about ten years ago having to search high and low for wholemeal spaghetti, but now it is quite readily available and you can also buy wholemeal lasagne, macaroni and pasta rings. If you don't eat eggs, which are usually used to bind the wheat-flour pastas, there is now a buckwheat spaghetti that has a more delicate flavour and cooks very conveniently in ten minutes. This is the ideal pasta to take with you if you are camping. Even if you don't knead your own pasta, every storecupboard is the better for a stock of the bought kinds; they are marvellous for spur-of-the-moment meals or those that have to be quickly prepared.

But if you have about three-quarters of an hour to spare and can plan a day ahead, how about having a go at making your own? It will look a little rough and ready and you won't be able to form it into long, delicate strings, but the flavour and texture are far better and it *seems* much more wholesome than the bought sort. (It also gives the cook a certain amount of satisfaction to produce even a pasta meal without resorting to what might be called 'convenience foods'.)

You can make pasta in the morning and serve it the same evening, but it is best if you can leave it for twenty-four hours or even longer to give it a chance to dry and harden. If you cook it too fresh, you may find it turns out a little slimy. Once made, fresh pasta will keep for a week in a dry place – any longer and it may go mouldy as it contains no preservative.

Here is the basic mixture:

Home-made pasta

for 4 people for 1 meal:

10 oz (275 g) wholemeal flour
1½ teaspoons (7.5 ml) fine sea salt
2 eggs
4 tablespoons (60 ml) water

for 6 people or to have some left over for a soup the next day:
1 lb (450 g) wholemeal flour
2 teaspoons (10 ml) fine sea salt
3 eggs
6 tablespoons (90 ml) water

Put all the flour onto a large, smooth, easily-scrubbable work surface and make a well in the centre. Sprinkle the salt over the top and then break in all the eggs and add the water. Gradually bring the flour from the edges to cover the eggs and mix the middle as you go. (If you have ever mixed concrete and tried frantically to stop the water from running over the edge of the sand and cement whilst bringing in the edges, this process will be quite familiar!) Gradually mix everything to a stiff dough. Knead it well for 10 minutes. It will be far heavier in texture than bread dough and you will have to work quite hard. Divide the dough into 2 pieces.

Flour your work surface and a long rolling pin with a little extra flour and roll out the first ball of dough until it is paper thin, stretching a little with the rolling pin as well as actually rolling. It's quite surprising how manageable the dough can be. It gets thinner and thinner and doesn't fall annoyingly apart as pastry can do. Set the first piece of dough aside (you can even hang it over the back of a chair) while you roll out the next piece.

You can cut the finished sheets into all kinds of shapes, but the two easiest, quickest and most convenient are lasagne and the long flat strips called tagliatelle. For lasagne cut large flat pieces about 2 in by 5 in (6 cm by 15 cm). For tagliatelle roll each sheet up loosely and cut your roll into slices about ¼ in (0.75 cm) wide then unroll them as soon as you can. Have ready some clean, dry tea cloths and lay all your pieces of pasta on these without letting them overlap. Leave the pasta for as long as you can before cooking (for at least 5 hours). After about twelve hours it can be rolled up in layers of absorbent kitchen paper and stored.

Cooking lasagne

Bring a large pan of salted water to the boil. Put in the pieces of lasagne and bring the water to the boil again. Lower the heat, cover and cook for 20 minutes. Drain the lasagne in a colander and stop the cooking process by pouring cold water over it. Lasagne is then layered in a dish with a tasty filling and the cooking finished off in the oven.

Cooking tagliatelle

Gradually bend it round in a large saucepan of boiling salted water. Bring the water back to the boil and lower the heat. Cover and simmer for 20 minutes. Drain it in a colander and pour cold water through it. Melt 1½ oz (40 g) butter or heat 4 tablespoons (60 ml) olive oil in a saucepan. Gently fold in the tagliatelle with 1 tablespoon (15 ml) grated Parmesan cheese. Cover the pan and pick it up and shake it. Set it back on the heat for 1 minute for the tagliatelle to heat through. If you do not want to butter the pasta, reheat it by pouring hot (but not boiling) water through it.

Cooking bought wholemeal pasta

For four people use 10 oz (275 g). Lower it into a large pan of boiling salted water and simmer, covered for 20 minutes. Drain and refresh as for home-made pastas.

Cooking buckwheat spaghetti

For four people use 10 oz (275 g). Lower it into a large pan of boiling salted water and simmer, covered, for 10 minutes. Drain and refresh it. Reheat it with hot water or by tossing with butter or oil.

Any of the following recipes for tagliatelle can be made with bought wholemeal spaghetti or pasta shapes or with buckwheat spaghetti. The amounts are for four people. The first three are accompanying dishes to be served alongside light main courses.

Glaze the pasta lightly with oil, flavour it with garlic and cheese and mix in aubergines that have cooked to a soft, melty texture.

Tagliatelle, aubergines and Parmesan cheese

2 small to medium-sized aubergines or 1 really large one
2 teaspoons (10 ml) fine sea salt
home-made pasta made with 10 oz (275 g) wholemeal flour or 10 oz (275 g) bought pasta
4 tablespoons (60 ml) olive oil
1 clove garlic, finely chopped
2 tablespoons (30 ml) grated Parmesan cheese

Cut the aubergines into ½ in (1.5 cm) dice and put them into a colander. Sprinkle them with the salt and leave them to drain for 30 minutes. Rinse them with cold water and dry them with kitchen paper. Cook the pasta, drain it and refresh it with cold water. Heat the oil in a saucepan on a low heat. Mix in the aubergines and garlic. Cover them and cook them gently for 10 minutes. With a fork, carefully fold in the tagliatelle. Cover and toss the pan and set it on a low heat for 1 minute. Fold in the cheese and take the pan from the heat straight away.

Tomatoes and basil make a light, pungent pasta sauce.

Tagliatelle with tomatoes and basil

home-made tagliatelle made with 10 oz (275 g) flour or 10 oz (275 g) bought pasta
4 tablespoons (60 ml) olive oil
1 clove garlic, finely chopped
12 oz (350 g) tomatoes, scalded, skinned and chopped
2 tablespoons (30 ml) chopped basil
2 tablespoons (30 ml) grated Parmesan cheese

Cook the pasta, drain it and refresh it. Put the saucepan back on the stove on a low heat and put in the oil, garlic, prepared tomatoes and basil. Cover and simmer them together for 10 minutes. Fold in the pasta, cover, and keep on the heat for 1 minute. Fold in the cheese and take the pan from the heat.

This accompanying dish goes well with egg dishes.

Tagliatelle with mushrooms and olives

home-made tagliatelle made with 10 oz (275 g) flour or 10 oz (275 g)
   bought pasta
3 tablespoons (45 ml) olive oil
4 oz (125 g) button mushrooms, thinly sliced
1 clove garlic, finely chopped
12 green olives, stoned and quartered lengthways
1 tablespoon (15 ml) grated Parmesan cheese (optional but it adds
   an extra touch)

Cook, drain and refresh the pasta. Heat the oil in a saucepan on a low heat. Stir in the mushrooms and garlic, cover them and cook them for 5 minutes. Gently fold in the pasta and olives. Cover the pan and give it a shake. Set it on a low heat for 1 minute. Fold in the cheese just before serving.

The remaining recipes in this section all make complete main courses. This mushroom dish is similar to the one above but much more substantial. Two pounds of mushrooms sounds a lot but you definitely need this quantity.

Mushrooms and pasta for a main course

home-made pasta made with 10 oz (275 g) flour or 10 oz (275 g)
   wholemeal or buckwheat spaghetti
1 oz (25 g) butter
1 tablespoon (25 g) grated Parmesan cheese
2 lb (900 g) button mushrooms
20 green olives
6 tablespoons (90 ml) olive oil
1 large onion, thinly sliced
1 clove garlic, finely chopped
4 tablespoons (60 ml) chopped parsley

for serving:
more grated Parmesan cheese

Cook the pasta, drain and refresh it and toss it with the butter
and tablespoon (15 ml) grated Parmesan cheese. Thinly slice the
mushrooms. Stone and chop the olives. Heat the oil in a large
saucepan on a low heat. Stir in the mushrooms, onion and garlic.
Cover and simmer them for 10 minutes. Mix in the olives and
parsley, cover again and simmer for 5 minutes more. Arrange the
cooked, hot pasta on a serving dish, smother it with the mushrooms and thickly strew the top with Parmesan cheese.

Use less mushrooms and mix them with eggs for a soft, creamy
flavoured main dish.

Pasta with eggs and mushrooms

home-made pasta made with 10 oz (275 g) flour *or* 10 oz (275 g)
    bought pasta
8 eggs
1 lb (450 g) mushrooms
1½ oz (40 g) butter
1 large clove garlic, finely chopped
4 tablespoons (60 ml) double cream
4 tablespoons (60 ml) chopped parsley
2 tablespoons (30 ml) grated Parmesan cheese

Cook, drain and refresh the pasta. Hard boil and chop the eggs.
Finely chop the mushrooms. Melt the butter in a saucepan on a
low heat. Stir in the mushrooms and garlic, cover them and cook
gently for 5 minutes. Stir in the eggs, cream, parsley and cheese
and gently fold in the pasta. Let the pasta heat through, uncovered, for 1 minute. Serve as soon as you can, with a salad or
a green vegetable such as spinach.

Mix the pasta with a smooth, white, cheese sauce sharpened very
slightly with lemon-rind and bitter-sweet peppers. Sprinkling the
nuts on top instead of mixing them in keeps their fresh, crunchy
quality so the dish has no trace of heaviness.

Pasta with cream cheese, peppers and walnuts

home-made pasta made with 10 oz (275 g) flour or 10 oz (275 g)
  bought wholemeal or buckwheat spaghetti
1 oz (25 g) butter
2 medium-sized green peppers, de-seeded and diced
1 large clove garlic, finely chopped
8 oz (225 g) Somerset soft cheese (or any other sweet cream cheese)
grated rind 1 lemon
6 oz (175 g) chopped walnuts

Cook, drain and refresh the pasta. Melt the butter in a saucepan
on a low heat. Stir in the peppers and garlic, cover them and
cook them gently for 5 minutes. Stir in the cheese and work it
into the butter with a wooden spoon. Mix in the lemon rind.
Fold in the pasta and let it heat through. Turn the cheese-coated
pasta into a warm serving dish and scatter the chopped nuts over
the top.

Spinach, curd cheese and lemon provide a light, refreshing contrast to wheaty, buttery home-made pasta and are also good with
the bought kinds. Cook the pasta first, toss it with butter and
Parmesan cheese, put it in a dish and cover it with this topping.

Spinach and curd cheese topping for pasta

2 lb (900 g) spinach
2 teaspoons (10 ml) chopped rosemary
1½ oz (40 g) butter
1 large onion, finely chopped
1 clove garlic, finely chopped
12 oz (350 g) curd cheese
grated rind and juice 1 lemon

Break the stems from the spinach. Put the leaves into a saucepan
with the rosemary and no more water than clings to them after
washing. Cover them and set them on a low heat for 10 minutes,
stirring occasionally. Drain the spinach and press down hard to
extract as much moisture as possible. Turn it out onto a board
and chop it finely. Melt the butter in a large frying pan on a low

heat. Mix in the onion and garlic and cook them until they are just turning golden. Mix in the spinach, cheese and lemon rind and juice and let them all heat through. Serve as soon as you can so the cheese stays soft.

Brown Chinese lentils make an authentic-tasting Bolognese sauce. Spoon it over home-made tagliatelle or over any kind of bought pasta, or layer it with lasagne, top with a thick cheese sauce and brown the dish under the grill or in a hot oven.

Brown lentil Bolognese sauce

8 oz (225 g) brown lentils
1 pint (575 ml) water
2 bayleaves
sea salt and freshly ground black pepper
8 oz (225 g) carrots
2 large sticks celery
2 medium onions
4 oz (125 g) mushrooms
4 tablespoons (60 ml) olive oil
1 large clove garlic, finely chopped
1 tablespoon (15 ml) tomato purée
¾ pint (425 ml) stock
¼ pint (150 ml) dry cider (or use 1 pint (575 ml) stock)
1 medium-sized cooking apple, grated
sea salt and freshly ground black pepper
3 tablespoons (45 ml) chopped parsley
for serving:
grated Parmesan cheese (optional)

Put the lentils into a saucepan with the water and bayleaves and season them well. Cover them, bring them to the boil and simmer them for 45 minutes. Drain them if necessary. Finely chop the carrots, celery, onions, and mushrooms. Heat the oil in a large saucepan on a low heat. Stir in the onion and garlic and cook them until the onion is soft. Stir in the carrots and celery and continue cooking until the onions are brown. Add the tomato purée and then the stock and cider (or just stock). Bring them to the boil, add the mushrooms, grated apple and parsley and season lightly. Cover and simmer for 45 minutes. Pile the sauce on top of cooked pasta and strew with Parmesan cheese.

To make a brown lentil lasagne, cook a 10 oz quantity of home-made or bought lasagne.

Make a cheese sauce with the following ingredients:

1 oz (25 g) butter
2 tablespoons (30 ml) wholemeal flour
½ pint (275 ml) milk
2 oz (50 g) grated farmhouse Cheddar cheese

Put one-third of the cooked lasagne into the bottom of a deep oven-proof dish. Cover this with one-third of the brown lentil sauce and then make two more similar layers. Pour the cheese sauce over the top and brown it under a hot grill.

For a change, you can make various fillings for lasagne with different types of cheese. This is a very simple lasagne that relies on the speciality cheese to provide all the necessary flavour.

Gloucester and chive lasagne

home-made pasta made with 10 oz (275 g) flour *or* 10 oz (275 g)
  bought wholemeal lasagne
1½ lb (675 g) ripe tomatoes (use frying ones)
10 oz (275 g) Double Gloucester Cheese with Chives (Cotswold)
1 oz (25 g) butter
2 tablespoons (30 ml) wholemeal flour
½ pint (275 g) milk
2 teaspoons (10 ml) made English mustard
sea salt and freshly ground black pepper
cheese sauce (see above)

Cook, drain and refresh the lasagne. Preheat the oven to Reg 6/400°F/200°C. Scald and skin the tomatoes and slice them into rings. Grate the cheese.

Melt the butter for the sauce in a saucepan on a moderate heat. Stir in the flour and let it bubble. Stir in the milk and bring it to the boil. Simmer the sauce, stirring, for 2 minutes.

Remove the pan from the heat and beat in the mustard and 2 tablespoons (30 ml) of the grated cheese. Lay one third of the cooked lasagne in the bottom of a large, deep oven-proof dish (a large pie dish is ideal). Arrange one-third of the tomatoes and then one-third of the cheese on top. Lay on the next third of the lasagne and the tomatoes and then all the remaining cheese, then lasagne, then tomatoes. Pour all the cheese sauce over the top and put the dish into the oven for 30 minutes for the cheese to melt and the top to brown.

Aubergines make a succulent filling. Use real Italian Mozzarella if you can get it. It will melt into the top layer and go deliciously creamy.

Aubergine lasagne

home-made lasagne made with 10 oz (275 g) flour *or* 10 oz (275 g)
    bought wholemeal lasagne
4 medium-sized aubergines
1 tablespoon (15 ml) sea salt
4 tablespoons (60 ml) olive oil
2 medium onions, finely chopped
1 large clove garlic, finely chopped
¼ pint (150 ml) dry white wine
2 tablespoons (30 ml) tomato purée
8 oz (225 g) Mozzarella cheese

Cook, drain and refresh the lasagne. Cut the aubergines into slices about ¼ in (0.75 cm) thick. Put them into a colander and sprinkle them with the salt. Leave them to drain for 30 minutes. Preheat the oven to Reg 6/400°F/200°C. Rinse the aubergines with cold water, dry them with kitchen paper and finely chop them. Heat the oil in a frying pan on a moderate heat. Put in the aubergines and cook them, stirring them about frequently, for 4 minutes so they are soft and cooked through. Remove them and set them aside. Lower the heat, put in the onions and garlic and cook them until they are brown. Mix in the aubergines. Raise the heat to moderate again, pour in the wine and mix in the tomato purée. Boil until the liquid is reduced completely then remove the pan from the heat.

Slice the cheese as thinly as possible. Put one-third of the lasagne in the bottom of a deep oven-proof dish and top it with one-third of the aubergines. Carry on with two more similar layers and top the final aubergines with slices of cheese. Bake the lasagne for 30 minutes so the cheese melts and browns.

Courgettes and Cheddar cheese contrast well – the lighter-tasting vegetable and the stronger-flavoured cheese.

Courgette lasagne

home-made lasagne made with 10 oz (275 g) flour or 10 oz (275 g)
    bought wholemeal lasagne
1 lb (450 g) courgettes
4 tablespoons (60 ml) olive oil
2 medium onions, thinly sliced
1 large clove garlic, finely chopped
4 tablespoons (60 ml) chopped parsley
8 oz (225 g) grated farmhouse Cheddar cheese

Cook, drain and refresh the lasagne. Preheat the oven to Reg 6/400°F/200°C. Wipe and thinly slice the courgettes. Heat the oil in a frying pan on a low heat. Mix in the onions and garlic and cook them until the onions are soft. Stir in the courgettes and carry on cooking until the onions are golden. Remove the pan from the heat.

Grate the cheese. Put one-third of the lasagne in the bottom of a deep ovenproof dish. Add one-third of the courgettes, one third of the parsley and one third of the cheese. Carry on with two more similar layers, finishing with cheese. Bake the lasagne for 30 minutes.

Pottages

Pottages are a cross between a soup and a stew. They originated in medieval times when any available ingredients were boiled in broth all together in one pot. They were often thickened with peas or barley and flavoured with wild herbs, and they were eaten out of bowls with a spoon. Nowadays you can make them with potatoes and all kinds of pulses and serve them as a main meal. The bowl and spoon way of eating is still the best and, as conventional soup bowls are usually too small, I serve them in pudding basins like father bear's porridge. To complete the meal, provide a substantial salad either as a first course or alongside your pottage, and have a crusty loaf or some wholemeal rolls standing by.

The first two pottages contain cheese and are thickened and made creamy with potatoes.

Celeriac, potato and Sage Derby pottage

1 lb (450 g) potatoes
1 lb (450 g) celeriac
2 medium onions
1½ oz (40 g) butter
2 pints (1.150 l) stock
1 bayleaf
sea salt and freshly ground black pepper
8 oz (225 g) Sage Derby cheese

Peel the potatoes and celeriac and chop them both into ¼ in (0.75 cm) dice. Finely chop the onions. Melt the butter in a saucepan on a low heat. Stir in the potatoes, celeriac and onions, cover them and let them sweat for 10 minutes. Pour in the stock and bring it to the boil. Add the bayleaf and seasonings, cover and simmer for 20 minutes. Discard the bayleaf. Take out half the soup, with a good proportion of the vegetables. Rub it through the fine blade of a mouli or work it in a blender until it is smooth. Mix it back into the rest of the soup and reheat it. Chop the cheese into $\frac{1}{4}$ in (0.75 cm) dice and mix them into the pottage just before serving so they heat through but don't melt.

Sweetcorn, egg and cheese pottage

4 corn cobs
1$\frac{1}{2}$ lb (675 g) potatoes
1 oz (25 g) butter
1 large onion, finely chopped
2 teaspoons (10 ml) made English mustard
1$\frac{1}{2}$ pints (850 ml) stock
2 tablespoons (30 ml) chopped parsley
2 tablespoons (30 ml) chopped thyme
2 hard-boiled eggs
6 oz (175 g) Edam cheese

Cut the corn from the cobs. Boil the potatoes in their skins, drain them, peel and mash them while they are still warm. Melt the butter in a large saucepan on a low heat. Stir in the onion and corn, cover them and cook them gently for 10 minutes. Take the pan from the heat and work in the potatoes and mustard. Gradually stir in the stock. Set the pan back on the heat and bring the soup to the boil, stirring. Add the parsley and thyme and simmer for 10 minutes, uncovered. Chop the eggs and finely dice the cheese. Stir them into the soup and heat them through without letting the cheese melt.

Chestnuts always make delicious soups. Use them to make a thick pottage with green cabbage and cider.

Chestnut pottage

1 lb (450 g) chestnuts
4 large sticks celery
$\frac{1}{2}$ small green cabbage
4 tablespoons (60 ml) olive oil

2 medium onions, finely chopped
1 large or 2 small cloves garlic, finely chopped
2 pints (1.150 l) stock
sea salt and freshly ground pepper
1 bayleaf
1 tablespoon (15 ml) mixed chopped thyme and marjoram
¼ pint (150 ml) dry cider (*or*, if not available, juice ½ lemon)

Nick the tops from the chestnuts, put them into a saucepan of cold water, bring them to the boil and simmer them for 10 minutes. Peel them as soon as they are cool enough to handle, keeping them immersed until you get to each one. Chop them finely. Finely chop the celery and cabbage. Heat the oil in a saucepan on a low heat. Stir in the celery, onion and garlic and cook them until they are golden. Stir in the chestnuts. Pour in the stock and bring it to the boil. Season and add the bayleaf and chopped herbs. Cover and simmer for 20 minutes. Pour in the cider or lemon juice and reheat. Remove the bayleaf before serving.

Gently simmer peanuts with tomatoes to soften them and put them through a blender to make a thick, orange pottage. They won't blend completely smoothly but this gives a more interesting texture.

Tomato and peanut pottage

1 lb (450 g) ripe tomatoes
1 oz (25 g) butter
1 medium onion, finely chopped
1 clove garlic, finely chopped
4 oz (125 g) shelled peanuts (not salted)
1½ pints (850 ml) stock
bouquet of basil *or*, if not available, a bouquet garni
2 tablespoons (30 ml) chopped basil *or* parsley

Scald, skin and roughly chop the tomatoes. Melt the butter in a saucepan on a low heat. Stir in the onion and garlic, cover them and cook for 5 minutes. Stir in the tomatoes and peanuts. Cover again and keep them on the low heat for 10 minutes. Pour in the stock and bring it to the boil. Add the basil bouquet or bouquet garni, cover again and simmer for 10 minutes. Remove the bouquet and cool the soup slightly. Work it in a blender until it is almost smooth. Return the soup to the saucepan and reheat it. Serve it scattered with the chopped basil or parsley.

All kinds of lentils are just right for pottages. Brown lentils make a rich, dark brown one with the earthy flavour of turnips.

Brown lentil and turnip pottage

8 oz (225 g) brown Chinese lentils
1½ oz (25 g) butter or vegetable margarine
2 large onions, finely chopped
2½ pints (1.500 l) stock
sea salt and freshly ground black pepper
1 lb (450 g) white turnips
2 teaspoons (10 ml) Dijon mustard
4 tablespoons (60 ml) chopped parsley

Melt the butter in a saucepan on a low heat. Stir in the lentils and onions. Cover them and cook them gently for 5 minutes. Pour in the stock, bring it to the boil and season. Cover and simmer for 45 minutes. Scrub the turnips and chop them into ½ in (1.5 cm) dice. Add them to the soup with the mustard and parsley. Simmer for a further 30 minutes.

You can make this red lentil pottage at any time of the year, with a whole selection of seasonal vegetables. It is thick, tasty and nourishing, and so good you can't stop eating it!

Red lentil and vegetable pottage

4 tablespoons (60 ml) olive oil
1 large onion, finely chopped
1 clove garlic, finely chopped
12 oz (350 g) red lentils
2½ pints (1.150 l) stock
sea salt and freshly ground black pepper
2 bayleaves

four or five chopped seasonal vegetables, such as:
1 large carrot
2 sticks celery and a few leaves
1 small leek
¼ small cabbage
1 green pepper
½ lb (225 g) fresh peas, weighed before shelling
few runner or French beans
few chopped Brussels sprouts
1 medium white turnip
for serving:
4 tablespoons (60 ml) chopped parsley

Heat the oil in a large saucepan on a low heat. Put in the onion and garlic and cook them until the onion is soft. Stir in the lentils and cook them for 1 minute. Pour in the stock and bring it to the boil. Add the bayleaves and seasonings. Cover the pan and simmer for 30 minutes. Add the prepared vegetables and carry on cooking for another 15 minutes. This short time makes sure all the vegetables retain their original flavours and freshness. Serve scattered with the parsley.

Simmer green lentils for slightly longer than usual so they soften and start to break up and flavour them with savoury mustard and cress.

Green lentil and mustard pottage

10 oz (275 g) green Egyptian lentils
4 tablespoons (60 ml) olive oil
2 medium onions, finely chopped
2 teaspoons (10 ml) mustard powder
2½ pints (1.500 l) stock
sea salt and freshly ground black pepper
2 bayleaves
1 tablespoon (15 ml) Dijon mustard
¼ pint (150 ml) dry white wine
2 boxes mustard and cress

Heat the oil in a saucepan on a low heat. Stir in the onions and cook them until they are soft. Stir in the lentils and mustard powder and cook them for 1 minute. Stir in the stock and bring it to the boil. Season and add the bayleaves. Cover and simmer for 1¼ hours. Mix the Dijon mustard and wine together. Stir them into the pottage and reheat it. Cut in the mustard and cress just before serving.

Pea and leek pottage was popular in medieval England during Lent. The secret is to add the leeks only at the last minute so they keep their flavour and texture.

Pea and leek pottage

8 oz (225 g) green split peas
2 pints (1.150 l) stock
2 bayleaves
sea salt and freshly ground black pepper
1 lb (450 g) leeks, white and green parts
10 chopped sage leaves

Put the peas into a saucepan with the stock, bayleaves and seasonings. Cover them, bring them to the boil and simmer for 1 hour. Meanwhile, wash and thinly slice the leeks. After the hour is up, remove the bayleaves from the saucepan and add the leeks and sage. Simmer for 7 minutes more. It needs nothing else.

Yellow split peas always go well with curry spices.

Curried yellow pea pottage

2 medium onions
8 oz (225 g) carrots
2 large sticks celery
4 tablespoons (60 ml) olive oil
1 large clove garlic, finely chopped
8 oz (225 g) yellow split peas
1 tablespoon (15 ml) hot Madras curry powder
2 pints (1.150 l) stock
8 cloves
8 allspice berries
8 black peppercorns

1 bayleaf
grated rind and juice 1 lemon

Finely chop the onions, carrots and celery. Heat the oil in a saucepan on a low heat. Stir in the onions and garlic and cook them until the onions are brown. Stir in the carrots, celery, split peas and curry powder and cook them gently for 1 minute. Pour in the stock and bring it to the boil. Crush the spices together with a small pestle and mortar and add these with the bayleaf. Cover and simmer for 1 hour. Remove the bayleaf and stir in the lemon rind and juice just before serving.

N.B. For convenience you could easily omit the crushed spices. Add lots of freshly ground black pepper instead.

Many of the dried beans make rich, thick pottages of different colours and flavours. They are best if you blend or sieve half of them to get a good, thick basic texture and keep the rest whole to make the final result more interesting.

Red bean pottage is thick, spicy and a warming red – just right for winter.

Red bean and tomato pottage

8 oz (225 g) red kidney beans
1 pint (575 ml) water
2 medium onions, finely chopped
1 tablespoon (15 ml) paprika
¼ teaspoon (half a 2.5 ml spoon) cayenne pepper
2 pints (1.150 l) stock
2 tablespoons (30 ml) tomato purée
1 lb (450 g) ripe tomatoes
1 clove garlic, crushed with a pinch sea salt
2 tablespoons (30 ml) chopped fresh coriander (*or*, if not available, parsley or chervil)
garnish with any of the following:
4 oz (100 g) grated farmhouse Cheddar cheese
1 carton natural yoghurt
croutons of brown bread

Pre-simmer and soak the beans in the water as given in the pulses section (p. 185). Bring them to the boil and simmer them for 1 hour. Drain them and reserve the liquid. Heat the oil in a saucepan on a low heat. Stir in the onions, paprika and cayenne and cook them until the onions are soft. Pour in the stock and bring it to the boil. Mix in the tomato purée. Add the beans and their liquid, cover and simmer for 45 minutes. Scald, skin and roughly chop the tomatoes and add them to the pan with the garlic. Simmer for a further 30 minutes. Cool the soup slightly and either rub half through the fine blade of a mouli or work it in a blender until it is smooth. Return it to the saucepan with the rest. Stir in the coriander (or parsley or chervil) and reheat. Pour it into large bowls and float the chosen garnish on top – the best one is the cheese.

Brown beans and dark mild ale make a thick, rich brown pottage.

Brown bean and beer pottage

10 oz (275 g) brown beans
1 pint (575 ml) water
2 medium onions
4 oz (125 g) carrots
2 large sticks celery
4 tablespoons (60 ml) olive oil
1 teaspoon (5 ml) ground cinnamon
2 pints (1.150 l) dark mild ale (draught) (or bottled brown ale)
2 tablespoons (30 ml) tomato purée
2 bayleaves
4 tablespoons (60 ml) chopped parsley

Soak and cook the beans as given in the pulses section (p. 185). Drain them and discard the liquid as it is too bitter to use for the soup. Finely chop the onions, carrots and celery. Heat the oil in a saucepan on a low heat. Stir in the vegetables, cover them and let them sweat for 7 minutes. Stir in the beans and cinnamon, cover again and cook for a further 2 minutes. Pour in the mild ale and bring it to the boil. Stir in the tomato purée and put in the bayleaves. cover and simmer for 20 minutes. Remove the bayleaves. Take out half the pottage and either rub it through

the fine blade of a mouli or work it in a blender until it is smooth.
Stir it back into the saucepan, add the parsley and reheat.

In complete contrast, haricot beans make a creamy white soup
made even creamier with double cream. Complete the meal with
tasty farmhouse Cheddar cheese.

Haricot bean and cheese pottage

8 oz (225 g) haricot beans
2 pints (1.125 l) water
1 oz (25 g) butter
2 large onions, finely chopped
1 large clove garlic, finely chopped
2 pints (1.125 l) stock
1 bayleaf
sea salt and freshly ground black pepper
1 6 fl oz (175 ml) carton double cream
6 oz (175 g) grated farmhouse Cheddar cheese
4 tablespoons (60 ml) chopped parsley

Cook the beans as given in the pulses section (p. 185). Drain
them if necessary and reserve any liquid. Melt the butter in a
saucepan on a low heat. Stir in the onions and garlic and cook
them until the onions are soft. Stir in the beans and pour in the
stock with any bean liquid. Bring it to the boil, add the bayleaf
and seasoning and simmer, uncovered for 20 minutes. Discard
the bayleaf and cool the soup slightly. Remove half and either
rub it through the fine blade of a mouli or work it in a blender
until it is smooth. Stir it back into the pan and reheat the pottage
to simmering point. Stir in the cream, cheese and parsley and
reheat gently without boiling.

There are many different recipes for minestrone. All you really
need is some pasta, a few vegetables and some good stock and
you can make countless variations, using whatever is in season
at any time of the year. Use carrots, turnips, mushrooms, cabbage,
leeks, French and runner beans, green peas, celery or cauliflower

or anything else that you can simmer. Put in enough to really pack the pottage full.

The kidney beans in this one make it really substantial. Use broken wholemeal spaghetti, or pasta rings, or broken lasagne. If you make your own pasta then make a little extra the day before and save it for minestrone.

Minestrone

4 oz (125 g) red kidney beans
2½ pints (1.425 l) stock
1 large onion, finely chopped
a selection of chopped seasonal vegetables to pack the pan
6 oz (175 g) broken wholemeal pasta
1 clove garlic, crushed with a pinch sea salt
freshly ground black pepper
2 tablespoons (30 ml) tomato purée
4 tablespoons (60 ml) chopped parsley
6 oz (175 g) grated farmhouse Cheddar cheese

Cook the beans as given in the pulses section (p. 185). Put the stock into a saucepan and bring it to the boil. Add the onion, all the fresh vegetables, pasta, garlic, pepper and tomato purée. Cover and simmer for 20 minutes. Mix in the parsley. Serve with the cheese floating on top.

Pies

No, not four-and-twenty blackbirds but cheese and eggs and vegetables. You can make deep pies in pie dishes, big flat round ones in pie plates and flan rings, open quiches and individual pasties. Have them for hot meals, cold meals or snacks, or take them on picnics.

Many wholefood cooks I have spoken to use wholemeal flour for most purposes but tend to be a little wary of it when it comes to pastry. Don't be; if you mix with light fingers you will find it as easy as white flour. For an ordinary shortcrust pastry, use twice the weight of flour as fat (butter or vegetable margarine are the best), a pinch of salt and, if it is to be a savoury pie, some freshly ground black pepper. Mix it quickly and lightly with cold fingers and bind everything together with slightly more cold water than you would use with white flour. This makes it easier to roll and handle. Leave the pastry standing in a cool place for 15 to 30 minutes before rolling it out. Brush it with milk or beaten egg and bake the pie in an oven preheated to Reg 6/400°F/200°C for 30 minutes.

Once you have used wholemeal flour for pastry several times you will probably find that you far prefer the flavour and texture. Even in appearance brown pies seem more wholesome. They won't be smooth-surfaced or too neat, but tasty and homely and full of goodness. But if when cooking for a special occasion you would like a slightly more polished appearance use the 81% or 85% flours. They contain all the germ of the wheat so much of the flavour and goodness are there, but the bran has been removed for a finer texture.

For a very crumbly, light pie-crust that rises slightly, try using wholemeal self-raising flour and make the pastry a little richer by using 4 oz (125 g) fat to 6 oz (175 g) flour. Make it up as usual. You may find it a little more difficult to handle, but if the flavour is going to be good, who minds a little patchwork?

You can even use wholemeal flour for flaky pastry, which needs as much butter or margarine as flour. It will be as light as a mixture using white flour, just as easy to handle and much more flavoursome, and will cook to a deep, rich brown.

Wholemeal flaky pastry

6 oz (175 g) wholemeal flour
6 oz (175 g) softened butter
pinch fine sea salt
squeeze lemon juice
ice-cold water to mix

Put the flour into a bowl with the salt and rub in 1 oz (25 g) of the butter. Squeeze in the lemon juice and mix in enough ice-cold water to make a manageable dough. Dust it with a little more flour and lay it on a floured board. Roll it out to a rectangle and put blobs of half the butter you have left, evenly over two-thirds of it. Fold over the remaining third and fold it over again. Roll it out in the opposite direction and fold in thirds again. Repeat this rolling and folding twice, wrap the pastry in greaseproof paper and put it into the refrigerator for 30 minutes. Roll out the pastry again and dot two-thirds of it with the remaining butter. Roll and fold as before and chill it for a further 30 minutes. You can now use it straight away or keep it in the refrigerator for several days. When you cook it, brush it with beaten egg and bake your pie for 40–45 minutes in an oven preheated to Reg 7/425°F/220°C. This kind of pastry makes cabbage, celery and cheese into a really special meal.

Cabbage, celery and sage Derby pie

flaky pastry made with 6 oz (175 g) flour
1 medium-sized green winter cabbage
1 oz (25 g) butter
1 large onion, thinly sliced

4 large sticks celery, thinly sliced
¼ pint (150 ml) dry cider
8 oz (225 g) sage Derby cheese

Preheat the oven to Reg 7/425°F/220°C. Finely shred the cabbage. Melt the butter in a saucepan on a low heat. Stir in the onion and celery, cover them and let them sweat for 10 minutes. Stir in the cabbage. Pour in the cider and bring it to the boil. Put half the cabbage mixture into a large pie dish. Thinly slice all the cheese and lay it on top. Put in the remaining cabbage mixture, cover with the pastry and bake for 45 minutes or until the top is puffy and golden.

Licky Pie is a traditional Cornish dish; top the filling of this leek and mushroom pie with clotted cream before putting on the lid.

Leek, mushroom and white wine pie

shortcrust pastry made with 8oz (225 g) flour to line a pie plate or
    flan ring 9–10 inches (24 cm) in diameter
1 lb (450 g) leeks (both white and green parts)
½ lb (225 g) flat mushrooms
1 oz (25 g) butter
4 tablespoons (60 ml) dry white wine
2 teaspoons (10 ml) English Vineyard mustard
4 eggs, beaten
4 oz (100 g) Devonshire or Cornish clotted cream

Preheat the oven to Reg 6/400°F/200°C. Make the pastry and set it aside to chill. Wash the leeks and cut them into ¼ in (0.75 cm) slices. Thinly slice the mushrooms. Put the butter, wine and mustard into a saucepan and set them on a low heat. When the butter has melted, raise the heat to moderate and let the mixture bubble. Stir in the leeks and mushrooms, cover and cook them for 5 minutes. Take the pan from the heat and let everything cool. Set aside one-third of the pastry for the top. Roll out the rest and line the flan ring or pie plate. Mix the eggs into the leeks and pour everything into the pastry. Put small blobs of the cream evenly over the top. Cover the pie with the remaining pastry, seal the edges and brush with milk or beaten egg. Bake the pie for 30 minutes and serve it hot.

The same mustard and mushrooms are used again for this pie, but with hard-boiled eggs it has a completely different flavour and texture.

Mushroom and egg pie

shortcrust pastry made with 6 oz (175 g) flour to line a pie plate or
  flan ring 8 inches (20 cm) in diameter
8 oz (225 g) mushrooms
6 hard-boiled eggs
1 oz (25 g) butter
1 tablespoon (15 ml) English Vineyard mustard
4 tablespoons (60 ml) chopped parsley
beaten egg or milk for glaze

Preheat the oven to Reg 6/400°F/200°C. Make the pastry and set it aside to chill. Finely chop the mushrooms and eggs. Melt the butter in a frying pan on a moderate heat. Mix in the mushrooms and cook them for 2 minutes, stirring them around frequently. Remove the pan from the heat and mix in the eggs, mustard and parsley. Set aside one-third of the pastry for the top of the pie. Roll out the rest and line the flan-ring or pie plate. Put in the filling and cover it with the remaining pastry. Brush with the beaten egg or milk and bake it for 30 minutes. Serve it hot or cold.

Curd cheese and beaten eggs make good light fillings for pies and quiches. They rise amazingly high when they are being cooked and hold their shape when served straight from the oven. Although they drop slightly as they cool they taste just as good. With this green pepper pie all the juices soak deliciously into the pastry leaving it moist with a slight crispy edge.

Green pepper pie

shortcrust pastry made with 6 oz (175 g) flour to line a pie plate or
  flan ring 8 inches (20 cm) in diameter

2 medium-sized green peppers
4 oz (125 g) curd cheese
4 eggs, beaten
2 tablespoons (30 ml) chopped parsley
1 tablespoon (15 ml) chopped thyme
1 oz (25 g) butter
1 medium onion, thinly sliced
1 large clove garlic, finely chopped

Preheat the oven to Reg 6/400°F/200°C. Make the pastry and set it aside to chill. Char the peppers under a high grill and skin them. Core and de-seed them and chop the flesh. Put the cheese into a bowl and gradually beat in the eggs. Mix in the peppers, parsley and thyme. Melt the butter in a small frying pan on a low heat. Stir in the onion and garlic and cook them until they are golden. Mix them into the cheese, eggs and peppers. Use two-thirds of the pastry to line the flan ring or pie plate. Pour in the filling and use the remaining pastry to cover the top. Seal the edges of the pie and brush the top with beaten egg or milk. Bake it for 30 minutes or until the top is golden brown.

Alternative: You can also bake the pie as a flan with no cover. Bake it at the same temperature until the top is golden (30-40 minutes).

The curd cheese filling for this quiche is flavoured and made moist with tomatoes.

Curd cheese and tomato quiche

shortcrust pastry made with 6 oz (175 g) flour to line a flan ring or pie plate 8 inches (20 cm) in diameter
6 oz (175 g) curd cheese
4 eggs, beaten
1 lb (450 g) firm tomatoes
10 spring onions, chopped
1 tablespoon (15 ml) chopped basil *or* 2 tablespoons (30 ml) chopped parsley

Preheat the oven to Reg 6/400°F/200°C. Make the pastry and set it aside to chill. Cream the cheese in a bowl and gradually beat in the eggs. Scald, skin, de-seed and roughly chop the tomatoes. Mix them into the eggs and cheese with the basil or parsley and onions. Line the flan ring or pie plate with the pastry. Spoon in the filling and smooth the top. Bake the quiche for 40 minutes or until the top is golden brown. Serve either hot or cold.

In the pulses section we had a savoury pumpkin pie made with red lentils. This one uses beaten eggs instead rather like a sweet pumpkin pie, but unlike the sweet kind this savoury version is best served hot.

Savoury pumpkin pie

for pastry to line flan ring 8 inches (20 cm) in diameter:
8 oz (225 g) wholemeal self-raising flour
pinch fine sea salt
5 oz (150 g) butter
cold water to mix
filling:
1½ lb (675 g) slice of pumpkin weighing around 14 oz (400 g) when skinned and chopped
2 tablespoons (30 ml) water
4 eggs, beaten
⅛ pint (75 ml) double cream
¼ pint (150 ml) milk
1 oz (25 g) butter
1 medium onion, finely chopped
4 tablespoons (60 ml) mixed chopped herbs
2 tablespoons (30 ml) tomato purée

Preheat the oven to Reg 5/375°F/190°C. Make the pastry and set it aside to chill. Cut the pith and rind from the pumpkin. Chop the flesh into small, thin pieces and put them into a saucepan with the water. Set it on a low heat for 20 minutes, covered, beating it to a smooth purée towards the end. Set the pumpkin aside to cool. Beat the eggs with the cream and milk. Melt the butter in a small frying pan on a low heat. Put in the onion and cook it until it is golden. Beat it into the eggs with the herbs and tomato purée. Stir in the pumpkin. Roll out the pastry and line the flan ring. Pour in the pumpkin and egg mixture and bake the pie for 45 minutes.

If you have some small, oven-proof serving bowls use them for individual pies. Serve them either in the bowls or slide them onto a plate after baking. If you have no such bowls the amounts below can be used to make one large covered pie in a flan ring or pie plate.

Mushroom and curd cheese pies

to make four individual pies:
shortcrust pastry made with 8 oz (225 g) flour
6 oz (175 g) mushrooms
12 oz (350 g) curd cheese
grated rind and juice ½ lemon
1 tablespoon (15 ml) Worcestershire sauce or Yorkshire Relish
2 tablespoons (30 ml) chopped parsley
beaten egg *or* milk to glaze

Preheat the oven to Reg 6/400°F/200°C. Make the pastry and set it aside to chill. Finely chop the mushrooms. Mix them into the cheese with the lemon rind and juice, Worcester sauce and parsley. Divide the pastry into two-thirds and one-third, then each subsequent piece into four. Roll out the larger ones and use these to line the bowls. Put in the filling. Roll out the smaller pieces of pastry and cover the tops of the pies. Seal the edges and brush them with beaten egg or milk. Stand the bowls on a large baking sheet so you can lift them in and out of the oven easily. Bake the pies for 30 minutes.

Cheese and onion pies are always good, but Stilton makes really special pasties. If you buy a large piece of Stilton or a whole one at Christmas, this is an excellent way of using any spare. Serve the pasties hot so the cheese is soft and melty with a slightly winey flavour.

Stilton and onion pasties

shortcrust pastry made with 8 oz (225 g) flour

8 oz (225 g) Stilton cheese
½ oz (15 g) butter
2 medium onions, finely chopped
4 tablespoons (60 ml) chopped parsley

Preheat the oven to Reg 6/400°F/200°C. Make the pastry and set it aside to chill. Crumble or finely dice the Stilton, depending on its texture. Melt the butter in a frying pan on a low heat. Mix in the onions and cook them until they are just beginning to soften. Mix them with the Stilton and parsley. Divide the pastry into four and roll each piece into a round about 6 in (15 cm) in diameter. Put a quarter of the Stilton mixture on one side of each one. Fold over the other side and crimp the edges. Lay the pasties on a floured baking sheet and brush them with milk or beaten egg. Bake them for 30 minutes and serve hot with a salad and jacket-baked potatoes.

Pizzas

A large pizza is a most satisfying thing to make and to eat. It comes from the oven risen and bubbling and smelling absolutely delicious. It forms both the main dish and the filling part of the meal, and all you need to accompany it is a selection of green vegetables or a nice big salad.

The first time I ever made a pizza the base rose so much that it pushed its way up through the middle and turned itself inside out! I'm still not quite sure why it happened, but since then I have worked out the recipe below, and used it many times, and the trouble has never occurred again. It makes a base like a moist, light bread, not too thick but firm and substantial enough to carry all kinds of juicy fillings.

Basic pizza dough

8 oz (225 g) wholemeal flour
½ teaspoon (2.5 ml) fine sea salt
¾ oz (20 g) fresh yeast or ½ oz (15 g) dried
½ teaspoon (2.5 ml) soft brown sugar
6 tablespoons (90 ml) warm water
1 egg, beaten
1 tablespoon (15 ml) olive oil

Put the flour and salt into a bowl. Cream the least with the sugar. (If using dried yeast, just mix them together.) Beat the water and egg together and mix them into the least. Leave them in a warm place to froth (about 15 to 20 minutes). Make a well in the centre of the flour. Mix in the yeast mixture and oil. Turn the dough out onto a floured board and knead it. Put it back into the bowl, cover it with a cloth and leave it in a warm place to rise for 1 hour.

Preheat the oven to Reg 6/400°F/200°C. Knead the dough lightly again and half roll and half stretch it into a round about ¼ in (0.75 cm) thick. Lay it on a large, floured baking sheet and fold over and seal a ½ in (1.5 cm) width all round to make the edge thick. Lay on the topping and let the pizza prove for 10 minutes on top of the hot stove. Bake it for 30 minutes. This sort of family pizza is so big that you will probably have to serve it straight from the baking tray, so use a fairly presentable one.

Mozzarella is the cheese most frequently used to top pizzas in Italy, but it is not always available. Edam cheese makes an excellent substitute. It isn't as creamy as Mozzarella but melts in a very similar way. The recipe below is very Italian tasting, even with Edam, particularly if you use wine.

Cheese, onion and tomato pizza

basic pizza dough made with 8 oz (225 g) flour
3 tablespoons (45 ml) olive oil
2 large onions, thinly sliced
1 clove garlic, finely chopped
1 tablespoon (15 ml) chopped thyme
2 tablespoons (30 ml) dry white wine (or stock)
12 oz (350 g) tomatoes
6 oz (175 g) Edam cheese
16 black olives, stoned and halved

Make the pizza dough and preheat the oven to Reg 6/400°F/ 200°C. Heat the oil in a frying pan on a low heat. Mix in the onions and garlic and cook them until the onions are golden. Mix in the thyme. Add the wine or stock, bring it to the boil and let it reduce almost completely. Take the pan from the heat. Scald and skin the tomatoes and slice them into rounds. Cut the cheese into very thin slices. Lay the pizza base on the floured baking sheet and raise the edge. Spoon on all the onions. Lay the cheese on top and then the tomato slices. Make a pattern on top with the olives. Prove the pizza for 10 minutes and bake it for 30 minutes.

Dark mushrooms and black olives make a rich, dark, tasty pizza filling. They are kept moist during cooking by the juice from the tomato slices arranged on top.

Mushroom and olive pizza

basic pizza dough made with 8 oz (225 g) flour
8 oz (225 g) flat mushrooms
16 black olives
8 oz (225 g) firm tomatoes
4 tablespoons (60 ml) olive oil
1 medium onion, thinly sliced
1 clove garlic, finely chopped
4 tablespoons (60 ml) dry red wine (or stock)
1 tablespoon (15 ml) chopped thyme

Make the pizza dough and set it aside to rise. Preheat the oven to Reg 6/400°F/200°C. Thinly slice the mushrooms. Quarter and stone 12 of the olives. Halve and stone the remaining four and set them aside for the garnish. Scald and skin the tomatoes and cut them into rounds. Heat the oil in a frying pan on a low heat. Mix in the onion and garlic and cook them until the onion is just turning golden. Raise the heat to moderate, mix in the mushrooms and cook them for 2 minutes, stirring. Add the wine and thyme and boil until the wine is almost completely reduced. Remove the pan from the heat. Roll out the pizza dough, lay it on the floured baking sheet and raise the edges. Spoon on all the mushroom mixture and spread it evenly. Lay on the tomato slices and make a pattern on top with the olive halves. Prove the pizza for 10 minutes and bake it for 30 minutes.

Mushrooms and tomatoes make a thick, juicy pizza in which a little of the topping sinks deliciously into the dough to moisten and flavour it.

Mixed mushroom and tomato pizza

basic pizza dough made with 8oz (225 g) flour
1 lb (450 g) ripe tomatoes
½ lb (225 g) flat mushrooms

12 green olives
4 tablespoons (60 ml) olive oil
2 medium onions, thinly sliced
1 large clove garlic, finely chopped
1 tablespoon (15 ml) chopped marjoram
1 tablespoon (15 ml) tomato purée
1½ oz (40 g) grated Parmesan cheese (1 pot)

Make the pizza dough and set it aside to rise. Preheat the oven to Reg 6/400°F/200°C. Scald, skin and roughly chop the tomatoes. Thinly slice the mushrooms. Stone and quarter 8 of the olives and stone and halve the rest. Heat the oil in a frying pan on a low heat. Mix in the onions and garlic and cook them until they are golden. Raise the heat to moderate, put in the mushrooms and cook them for 2 minutes, stirring. Mix in the tomatoes, marjoram and tomato purée. Lower the heat and simmer for 10 minutes, uncovered, so you get a good, thick pulpy mixture. Remove the pan from the heat and mix in the quartered olives. Lay the rolled-out pizza dough onto a floured baking sheet and raise the edges. Spread the tomato filling evenly over the top and strew it with the Parmesan cheese. Prove the pizza for 10 minutes and bake it for 30 minutes.

This is the tastiest, most impressive pizza of all, particularly if you can find some genuine Italian Mozzarella.

Green pepper pizza

basic pizza dough made with 8 oz (225 g) flour
2 medium-sized green peppers
1 lb (450 g) ripe tomatoes
3 tablespoons (45 ml) olive oil
1 medium onion, thinly sliced
1 clove garlic, finely chopped
1 teaspoon (5 ml) paprika
2 teaspoons (10 ml) chopped thyme
12 green olives
6 oz (175 g) Mozzarella cheese

Make the pizza dough and set it to rise. Preheat the oven to

Reg 6/400°F/200°C. Core and de-seed the peppers and cut them into strips 1 in by $\frac{1}{4}$ in (3 cm by 0.75 cm). Scald and skin the tomatoes, chop half of them and slice the rest into rounds. Heat the oil in a frying pan on a low heat. Stir in the onion and garlic, cover them and cook for 5 minutes. Put in the peppers, cover again and cook for a further 10 minutes. Mix in the chopped tomatoes, paprika and thyme. Cover the pan again and keep cooking for 15 minutes, by which time you should have a good thick mixture of vegetables. (If necessary take off the lid and continue cooking until any excess moisture has evaporated.) Remove the pan from the heat. Stone the olives, chop six of them and halve the rest. Mix the chopped olives into the pepper mixture. Lay the rolled-out pizza dough on a floured baking sheet and raise the edges. Spoon in all the mixture and spread it evenly. Thinly slice the Mozzarella and completely cover the topping with it. Decorate the top with the sliced tomatoes and halved olives. Prove the pizza for 10 minutes and bake it for 30 minutes.

A touch of sauce

You can liven up any plain dish with a touch of sauce and a little thoughtful craft. Pour sauces over plain steamed or boiled vegetables to make attractive first courses or appetising accompaniments. For a quick and simple meal coat some ready-cooked beans with a flavoursome sauce and serve them with rice, pasta or potatoes; or use the sauce for the pasta or rice and have a plainer vegetable dish. Plain hard-boiled or poached eggs can be coated with some of the sauces, and you can quickly mix cubes of cheese into others. Take a look at your sauces and at the main ingredients of a meal and see how many combinations you can think up.

Elsewhere in the book you will find references to spicy tomato sauce. Here is the recipe. It contains, in fact, no actual spices, but the mixture of molasses, vinegar and herbs make it taste as though it does. Pour it over thin slices of steamed pumpkin or cooked Jerusalem artichokes to make a first course, serve it with deep-fried vegetables, or mix it into cooked white beans or red kidney beans.

Spicy tomato sauce

1 lb (450 g) ripe tomatoes
3 tablespoons (450 ml) olive oil
1 large onion, finely chopped
1 large clove garlic, finely chopped
1 tablespoon (15 ml) molasses *or* black treacle
2 tablespoons (30 ml) malt vinegar
2 tablespoons (30 ml) chopped basil *or* thyme

Scald, skin and roughly chop the tomatoes. Heat the oil in a saucepan on a low heat. Stir in the onion and garlic, cover them and cook them for 5 minutes. Stir in the tomatoes, cover again and cook for a further 5 minutes. Mash them down to make a pulpy purée and stir in the molasses, vinegar and chopped herbs. Simmer, uncovered for 2 minutes more.

This quickly prepared tomato sauce is rich and spicy and has the texture of thin cream. It is excellent with all kinds of beans.

Quick tomato and tamari sauce

2 tablespoons (30 ml) tomato purée
2 tablespoons (30 ml) tamari sauce
1 large *or* 2 small cloves garlic, crushed without salt
½ pint (275 ml) stock

Mix all the ingredients together in a saucepan. Set them on a low heat and bring them to the boil, stirring occasionally. Simmer, uncovered, for 2 minutes.

Watercress, lemon and tamari make a slightly sharp, savoury flavoured sauce.

Watercress and lemon sauce

2 tablespoons (30 ml) olive oil
1 bunch watercress, very finely chopped
1 tablespoon (15 ml) wholemeal flour
½ pint (275 ml) stock
grated rind and juice of 1 lemon
2 teaspoons (10 ml) tamari sauce
1 teaspoon (5 ml) Tabasco sauce

Heat the oil in a saucepan on a low heat. Stir in the watercress and cook it very gently for 3 minutes. Stir in the flour and let it bubble. Take the pan from the heat and stir in the stock. Bring it to the boil, stirring. Mix in the lemon rind and juice, tamari sauce and Tabasco sauce and simmer, uncovered, for 2 minutes.

Celery and white wine make a pungent, heady sauce, that is ideal with lentils or any of the rice dishes.

Celery and white wine sauce

2 large sticks celery
1 oz (25 g) butter *or* 4 tablespoons (60 ml) olive oil
1 medium onion, finely chopped
2 teaspoons (10 ml) dill seeds
1 tablespoon (15 ml) wholemeal flour
¼ pint (150 ml) dry white wine
½ pint (275 ml) stock

Finely chop the celery. Melt the butter or heat the oil in a saucepan on a low heat. Mix in the celery, onion and dill seeds and cook them until the vegetables are brown. Stir in the flour and let it bubble. Stir in the wine and stock. Bring them to the boil, stirring, and simmer uncovered for 20 minutes.

White wine and herbs combine well in a sauce that is excellent with plainly cooked vegetables and jacket-baked potatoes.

White wine and herb sauce

1 oz (25 g) butter *or* 4 tablespoons (60 ml) olive oil
3 tablespoons (45 ml) chopped mixed herbs (any kind that will go
    well with your main dish)
1 tablespoon (15 ml) wholemeal flour
¼ pint (150 ml) dry white wine
¼ pint (150 ml) stock
grated rind ½ lemon

Heat the butter or oil in a pan on a low heat. Stir in the herbs and simmer them gently for 2 minutes. Stir in the flour and let it bubble. Take the pan from the heat and stir in the wine and stock. Bring the sauce to the boil, stirring, add the lemon rind and simmer, uncovered, for 5 minutes.

A light, lemony curry sauce is good with rice, beans, lentils and the mushroom-stuffed marrow.

Curry and lemon sauce

3 tablespoons (45 ml) olive oil
1 small onion, finely chopped
1 clove garlic, finely chopped
1 small carrot, finely chopped
1 stick celery, finely chopped
1 teaspoon (5 ml) hot Madras curry powder
1 teaspoon (5 ml) ground turmeric
1 teaspoon (5 ml) ground cumin
1 tablespoon (15 ml) wholemeal flour
1 pint (575 ml) stock
1 bayleaf
4 thinly pared strips lemon rind
2 tablespoons (30 ml) chopped parsley
juice ½ lemon

Heat the oil in a saucepan on a low heat. Stir in the onion, garlic, carrot and celery and cook them until the onion is soft. Stir in the curry powder and spices and cook for a further 1 minute. Stir in the flour and let it bubble. Take the pan from the heat and stir in the stock. Bring the sauce to the boil, stirring, and add the bayleaf and lemon rind. Simmer, covered for 40 minutes. Strain the sauce through a conical strainer or sieve, pressing down hard to get as much through as possible. Return the sauce to the rinsed-out pan. Stir in the parsley and lemon juice and simmer for 2 minutes more.

Serve this next one with deep-fried vegetables or with boiled asparagus as a first course.

Parsley, lemon and egg sauce

4 oz (125 g) butter
4 tablespoons (60 ml) chopped parsley
grated rind and juice 1 lemon
1 egg

Put half the butter into a small bowl with the parsley, lemon rind and juice. Put the bowl in a saucepan of water and set it on a low heat. Leave it until the butter melts. Soft-boil the egg by putting it into boiling water for 2 minutes. Carefully peel it and cut it open and let the yolk fall into the bowl with the butter and parsley. Work it in quickly with a wooden spoon. Keep the bowl over the heat and beat until the mixture begins to thicken. Don't let the water in the saucepan boil. Gradually beat in the rest of the butter in small pieces. Finely chop the egg white and mix it into the sauce. Serve the sauce hot as soon as possible.

A sauce with a miso base is excellent for beans, for rice dishes and for coating plainly cooked vegetables.

Miso, onion and parsley sauce

2 tablespoons (30 ml) olive oil
1 medium onion, finely chopped
1 tablespoon (15 ml) miso
½ pint (275 ml) stock
3 tablespoons (45 ml) chopped parsley

Heat the oil in a saucepan on a low heat. Put in the onion and cook it until it is soft. Take the pan from the heat and blend in the miso with a wooden spoon. Gradually stir in the stock. Set the pan back on the heat and bring the sauce gently to the boil, stirring. Add the parsley and simmer for 2 minutes.

In the section on gratin dishes I mention an alternative to the milky type of bechamel sauce made with soya flour. Here is the basic recipe. You can flavour it with herbs, spices, mustards, tomato purée, tamari sauce or lemon or orange juice.

Basic soya bechamel

4 tablespoons (60 ml) olive oil
4 tablespoons (60 ml) soya flour
½ pint (275 ml) water

Heat the oil in a saucepan on a low heat. Stir in the flour and cook it gently until it becomes corn-coloured. Stir in the water, bring it to the boil, stirring, and simmer for 5 minutes, stirring all the while. By the end it should be thick and bubbly.

Pancakes

Pancakes are usually a Shrove Tuesday treat. I serve them straight from the pan to one person at a time and have on the table a jar of honey, a bowl of Barbados sugar and innumerable wedges of lemon, so everyone can sweeten them and roll them as they please. They need not, however, be a once-a-year sweet speciality, as filled with different savoury mixtures they can be served as first or main courses at any time in any season.

Although there is nothing to beat taking a pancake straight from the pan and sliding it onto a plate, it can be inconvenient and very time-consuming for the cook, and as pancakes can easily be kept and heated up later there is no need to stand over the hot stove at the last minute if you are making a main pancake meal. In fact savoury stuffed pancakes are ideal for a meal that has to be partly prepared a day in advance. Reheat them while you quickly prepare a filling and a green salad and that is all you will have to do.

The recipe below makes 16–20 pancakes. Allow 4 per person for a main course and 2 for a first course or sweet. Any left over can always be stored and served in a completely different way the next day.

Use a well-seasoned, round-sided omelet pan for cooking pancakes so they don't stick and can be lifted easily with a fish-slice or palette knife. Have a warm plate handy to slide them on to when they are done and always make sure you have extra butter or oil standing by.

Wholemeal flour doesn't make the pancakes heavy-textured. They will be just as thin and light as those made with white flour and will have a slight wheaty flavour.

Basic pancake recipe

8 oz (225 g) wholemeal flour
½ teaspoon (2.5 ml) fine sea salt
2 eggs
2 egg yolks
1 pint (575 ml) milk (skimmed milk or milk powder makes a
   lighter mixture)
2 tablespoons (30 ml) olive oil or melted butter
for frying each pancake: a small knob of butter about ½ in (1 cm)
   round or ½ tablespoon (7.5 ml) olive oil

Put the flour into a mixing bowl and sprinkle the salt over the
top. Make a well in the centre and drop in the eggs and egg yolks.
Stir vigorously, in small circles at first, breaking the egg yolks
and gradually bringing in flour from the edges. Pour in a little of
the milk and keep stirring and beating until you have a thick
batter made with half the milk. Beat in the oil or butter and then
the rest of the milk. Beat vigorously, turning the bowl with your
other hand until there are bubbles floating on top of the batter.
Leave it to stand in a cool place for 30 minutes. Heat your butter
or oil for the first pancake in an omelet pan on a moderate to
high heat. Spoon in 2 tablespoons (30 ml) of the batter and
quickly tip it around so it spreads out thinly and aquires a lacy
edge. When the underside is patterned a golden brown and the
top is set flip the pancake over quickly with your fish-slice or
palette knife (or 'toss it if you can'!) and brown the other side.
The edges should be just slightly crisp. Slide the pancake onto
a plate and keep it warm. Add the next butter or oil and continue until all the batter is used up.
N.B. As the second pancake finishes cooking you will probably
find that the heat is getting a little too fierce. If so, lower it just
a little while you start to make the next one. Then raise it again
if you find the heat drops too much. After a while you will get
the feel of the heat and the effect it has on the pan and by raising
and lowering you will be able to keep the heat constant. As you
finish the pancakes, pile them up in a stack and keep them in a
warm place.

Keeping several hours: Keep the pancakes in a pile on a heat-proof plate and cover them with a large heatproof serving dish. To reheat, put them in an oven preheated to Reg 6/400°F/200°C for 10 minutes.

Keeping for the next day: Pile up the pancakes with a sheet of greaseproof paper between each one. Wrap them in foil or put them into a polythene bag and put them in the bottom of the refrigerator. To reheat them if you are going to serve them plain (like my Shrove Tuesday way) lay them on a large buttered baking sheet and brush them with melted butter. Put them into an oven preheated to Reg 6/400°F/200°C for 10 minutes. If on the other hand you are going to stuff them, there is no need to heat them alone first. Fill them, lay them on a heatproof serving dish and put them into the oven at the same temperature, again for 10 minutes, so the pancakes and filling heat up together.

Folding and rolling: There are various ways of filling pancakes and folding them up so they look attractive and the stuffing stays securely inside. You can also stack them up, unfolded in a pile with the filling sandwiched in between. In this case, serve them cut into wedges like a cake.

Ideas for filling individual pancakes:

Spread the filling all over the pancake and roll it up.

Put the filling down the centre and fold over two sides.

Put a round of filling in the centre and fold in four sides.

Put the filling just off centre, fold in the two equal sides and fold it in half.

Put the filling in the centre and fold in three sides to make a triangle.

❧   ❧   ❧

Here are some ideas for pancake fillings. The amounts given will fill 16 pancakes for a main meal for 4 people. Either stuff all the pancakes with one mixture or make two or more different kinds.

In this case, either fill the pancakes before reheating or heat the pancakes and fillings separately so everyone can help themselves to the ones they like best.

As pancakes are very rich they need a slightly sharp flavour in the dressing to act as a contrast. In the following two recipes this is provided by sour cream.

Mushroom and sour cream filling

2 lb (900 g) mushrooms
1½ oz (40 g) butter
2 large onions, finely chopped
1 large clove garlic, finely chopped
juice 1 lemon
2 cartons sour cream
4 tablespoons (60 ml) chopped parsley

Finely chop the mushrooms. Melt the butter in a large frying pan on a low heat. Stir in the onions and garlic and cook them until the onions are soft. Raise the heat to moderate and mix in the mushrooms. Stir them around on the heat for 2 minutes. Pour in the lemon juice and let it bubble. Transfer the contents of the pan to a bowl and let them cool a little. Stir in the cream and parsley. This filling can be layered between a stack of pancakes or can be rolled up or folded in any of the suggested ways.

Tomato and cream cheese filling

1½ lb (675 g) firm tomatoes
12 oz (350 g) Somerset Soft Cheese (or any other sweet cream cheese)
4 tablespoons (60 ml) sour cream
2 tablespoons (30 ml) chopped basil (or chervil or parsley if none is available)

Scald, skin and chop the tomatoes. Cream the cheese and sour cream together in a bowl. Mix in the tomatoes and basil. This is best folded inside individual pancakes.

The tangy contrast in this carrot filling is supplied by the curd cheese.

Carrot and curd cheese filling

1 lb (450 g) carrots
1 large onion, finely chopped
1 clove garlic, finely chopped
1 oz (25 g) butter
¼ pint (150 ml) dry white wine
¼ pint (150 ml) water
    (or instead of this combination, use ½ pint (275 ml) stock)
12 oz (350 g) curd cheese
2 tablespoons (30 ml) chopped parsley

Thinly slice the carrots. Put them into a saucepan with the onion, garlic, butter, wine and water (or stock). Cover them and set them on a moderate heat for 20 minutes so the carrots are just tender and all the liquid is absorbed. Turn all the contents of the pan onto a board and finely chop them. Cream the cheese in a bowl and mix in the chopped carrots and onions and the parsley. You can layer this filling in a stack of pancakes or fold or roll it in individual ones.

Succulent courgettes and cottage cheese make an attractive green-flecked filling which in this case is sharpened with lemon juice.

Courgette and cottage cheese filling

1 lb (450 g) courgettes
1 oz (25 g) butter
1 large onion, finely chopped
1 clove garlic, finely chopped
juice 1 lemon
4 tablespoons (60 ml) chopped parsley
12 oz (350 g) cottage cheese

Wipe and finely chop the courgettes. Melt the butter in a frying pan on a low heat. Stir in the onion and garlic and cook them until the onion is just beginning to soften. Mix in the courgettes and cook them until they are soft and tender but not coloured. Pour in the lemon juice and let it bubble. Turn the contents of the pan into a bowl and cool them a little. Mix in the parsley and cheese. This filling is best folded up in individual pancakes.

If you use a strong, hard cheese or some grated Parmesan cheese in the filling they will provide a different kind of tangy flavour to contrast with the pancakes. Spring onions and Gruyere cheese make one of the simplest of fillings, that is none the less delicious.

Spring onion and Gruyere filling

24 medium-sized spring onions
1 oz (25 g) butter
12 oz (350 g) grated Gruyere cheese

Finely chop the onions. Melt the butter in a frying pan on a low heat. Mix in the onions and cook them until the green parts are just beginning to wilt (only about 1 minute). Take the pan from the heat and let the onions cool. Mix them into the grated cheese. Layer this filling between a stack of pancakes or roll it or fold it in individual ones.

Here are some other recipes from the other chapters that you could use for filling pancakes.

Mushrooms and Spring onions with Curd Cheese (double ingredients)

Aubergine Cheese Dip (double ingredients)

The curried mushroom filling for marrow

Cottage Cheese and Tomato Bake

Cottage Cheese and Watercress Bake

Cottage Cheese, Pepper and Tomato Bake

Cottage Cheese and Beetroot Bake (With all the bakes, mix them together, stuff the pancake and then heat up. Don't cook the cheese first.)

Creamy mushroom and Egg Scramble

Leek and Mustard Scramble

Red Pepper and Tomato Scramble

The fillings from both the roulades with ingredients doubled

Boiled Eggs and Leeks

Any of the sharper flavoured bean dishes without thick, heavy sauces. Those made with tomatoes are excellent. In each case make the 8 oz (225 g) quantity of beans.

Brown lentils with mushrooms and onions. Use 8 oz (225 g) lentils

Brown Bean Curry

Red Kidney Bean Curry

Green Mung Bean Curry

Curried Courgettes (double ingredients)

Spinach and Curd Cheese Topping for Pasta

Brown Lentil Bolognese

A mixture of tomatoes and grated Double Gloucester and Chive cheese as for Gloucester and Chive Lasagne.

Use the aubergine filling as for aubergine lasagne and fold it up inside individual pancakes with a small sliver of Mozzarella cheese or sprinkled with grated Parmesan cheese

The filling for courgette lasagne using the same amount of courgettes and 12 oz (350 g) Cheddar cheese.

The filling for the Mushroom and Egg Pie using 12 oz (350 g) mushrooms and 8 eggs

The filling for mushroom and curd cheese pies

The filling for Stilton and Onion Pasties

The filling for Mixed Mushroom and Tomato Pizza folded inside individual pancakes with a thin slice of Edam cheese, or a sprinkling of grated Parmesan cheese.

Breads

There is nothing like the warming, homely, yeasty smell of freshly baked bread. It pervades the whole house from about five minutes after the loaf has been put into the oven until long after it has been taken out and placed on a rack to cool. I love baked potatoes and enjoy brown rice and pasta, but for me a good, basic wholemeal bread will always take first place. With a salad, a soup, a pâté or just a hunk of cheese it makes the perfect simple meal. An absolute must in every home is a crock or bin containing the plain and simple treasure of well-baked bread. If you haven't the time for yeasted bread, you can always make soda bread, scones or a savoury cake within an hour.

If you regularly bake your own bread, then you will probably have your own favourite recipe that always works and your favourite kind of flour. You will know the exact amount of liquid that you need down to the last tablespoon and can tell by instinct when you have kneaded the dough enough and it is ready to put to rise.

If not, here is a plain, basic recipe that always works for me. For an everyday loaf use 100% wholemeal flour (stone-ground and organically grown if you can get it) or granary bread meal. You can also try half wheat and half rye flour, or use half barley flour for a sweet, almost pungent flavour. A mixture of three-quarters wheat flour and a quarter oatmeal, either fine or coarse, will give a soft, crumbly texture.

I usually set the yeast to work with a teaspoon of honey, but you can also use soft brown sugar, malt extract or molasses. This last, even if you only use a teaspoonful, colours the bread a little darker than usual and flavours it very slightly.

Everyday loaf

1½ oz (40 g) fresh yeast or ¾ oz (20 g) dried
1 teaspoon (5 ml) honey
½ pint (275 ml) warm water
1 lb (450 g) 100% wholemeal flour or granary bread meal
2 teaspoons (10 ml) salt
extra flour for kneading, flouring hands, etc.

Crumble the yeast into a bowl and work it with the honey (or just mix the dried yeast and honey together). Mix in 4 fl oz (125 ml) of the water. Put the bowl in a warm place (next to a radiator or fire, above a hot stove or Aga cooker, or even in a warm, sunny window) for the mixture to froth. It will take about 10 to 15 minutes.

Put the flour into a bowl and toss in the salt with your fingers. Make a well in the centre and pour in the frothed yeast and the remaining 6 fl oz (150 ml) water. Mix everything to a dough with a long, rounded knife. Turn it out onto a floured board and knead it with well-floured hands until it is smooth and elastic. Put the dough back into the bowl and make a cross-cut in the top. Cover it with a clean teacloth and set it in a warm place for 1 hour to rise. It should about double in size.

Preheat the oven to Reg 6/400°F/200°C. Have ready a floured baking sheet *or* 1 greased 2 lb (900 g) loaf tin *or* 2 greased 1lb (450 g) loaf tins. Knead the dough again and either keep it together or cut it into two. Shape it as you wish. It's great fun to experiment with different shapes of loaves. You can make them large or small, round or long, or make the dough into small, round rolls. Make sure long shapes are thin and high when you lay them on the baking sheet, or they will spread out and become too flat as they rise. You can cut patterns on the top of plain-shaped loaves with a sharp knife; as the bread rises they will expand slightly and become more pronounced. Make a cottage loaf by dividing the dough into approximately one-third and two-thirds. Make each into a slightly flattened ball, put one on top of the other and make a hole right down through the centre with a rounded knife, your finger or the handle of a wooden spoon.

To make a plait, divide your dough into three even pieces and roll them into long sausage shapes. Join them at one end, plait them several times and then join them at the other end.

If you are using bread tins, form the bread into a rough shape first, put it into the tin and knock it down into the corners with the back of your fist. Once the bread is shaped and ready, stand the tray or tin(s) above the hot oven. Cover the bread with the cloth and let it stand for 30 minutes to rise again. This is known as 'proving'. Bake the large loaves for 50 minutes, the smaller ones for 40 minutes and the rolls for 20 minutes.

When the bread comes out of the oven, put your ear to it. If it is still singing loudly it isn't ready, you should hear just a slight hissing. Tap the bottom and if it sounds hollow, it's done. Put the bread on a wire rack to cool. Plainer breads are best if you can keep them on the cooling rack for at least 12 hours after they come out of the oven. That way, they develop a crispy crust and light inside. The rolls are nicest eaten as soon as they are cool.

Bran bread

Bran provides essential roughage and can easily be added to any bread recipe so long as you remember to use a little more liquid or cut down the flour. Here are the proportions for a basic bran loaf. Use the same kinds of flour as for the plain one and bake it in exactly the same way.

1 lb (450 g) flour
3 oz (75 g) bran
2 teaspoons (10 ml) sea salt
1½ oz (40 g) fresh yeast or ¾ oz (20 g) dried
1 teaspoon (5 ml) honey
12 fl oz (325 ml) warm water

Flavoured breads

Flavoured breads are excellent with all kinds of vegetable dishes and sometimes can even be served as meals in themselves. They are not at all hard to make. Use the same proportions of flour and yeast (and bran if you like) as for the everyday loaf and add any of these to your flour:

4 tablespoons (60 ml) chopped herbs
2 teaspoons (10 ml) paprika *or* mustard powder
2 teaspoons (10 ml) dill *or* caraway seeds
2 oz (50 g) grated strong cheese
1 very small grated onion
1 medium onion, sliced or chopped and browned first in ½ oz (15 g) butter *or* 2 tablespoons (30 ml) oil
1 tablespoon (15 ml) tomato purée added to the final water

The following two onion breads are made with a richer mixture that makes them really light. They are best eaten quite soon after they are cool as, like all things slightly more exotic, they are less practical than the basic breads and go stale rather more quickly.

Stilton and onion loaf

1 oz (25 g) fresh yeast *or* ½ oz (15 g) dried
1 teaspoon (5 ml) honey
1 egg, beaten
3 fl oz (75 ml) warm water
6 oz (175 g) wholemeal flour
2 oz (50 g) bran
½ teaspoon (2.5 ml) fine sea salt
1 oz (25 g) vegetable margarine (non-vegetarians use lard)
1 small or ½ medium onion
2 oz (50 g) Stilton cheese

Cream the yeast with the honey, mix in the beaten egg and water and put them in a warm place to froth. This will take about 20 minutes. Put the flour, bran and salt into a mixing bowl and rub in the margarine or lard. Grate in the onion and Stilton and toss everything together with your fingers. Make a well in the centre and pour in the yeast mixture. Mix everything to a dough with a long, rounded knife. Turn it out onto a floured board and knead it well. (N.B. The onion and cheese will make it fairly moist and sticky.) Return the dough to the bowl, make a cross-cut in the top, cover it with a clean teacloth and put it in a warm place for 1 hour to rise.

Preheat the oven to Reg 6/400°F/200°C. Knead the dough again and put it into a greased 1 lb (450 g) loaf tin. Cover the loaf with the cloth and stand it above the stove to prove for 15 minutes, or until it has risen about ½ in (1 cm) above the top of the tin. Bake the loaf for 40 minutes so it rises high and has a nutty brown top. Turn it out onto a wire rack to cool.

This next one is made with rye flour and milder flavoured spring onions. It turns out golden brown, flecked with green and is fairly moist, light and fluffy in texture.

Rye and spring onion bread

8 oz (225 g) rye flour
1 oz (25 g) vegetable margarine, butter *or* lard
½ teaspoon (2.5 ml) fine sea salt
1 oz (25 g) fresh yeast *or* ½ oz (15 g) dried
1 teaspoon (5 ml) honey
1 egg, beaten
6 medium-sized spring onions, chopped
3 tablespoons (45 ml) chopped parsley
4 fl oz (100 ml) warm water

Put the flour and salt into a mixing bowl and rub in the fat. Cream the yeast with the honey, mix in the beaten egg and leave them in a warm place to froth. Toss the onions and parsley into the flour with your fingers. Make a well in the centre and mix in the yeast and egg mixture and the water with a long, rounded knife. The mixture will be quite wet so knead it in the bowl with your hand, bringing it from the sides to the middle and turning the bowl with your other hand all the time. Cover the bowl with a clean teacloth and put it into a warm place for 1 hour.

Preheat the oven to Reg 6/400°F/200°C. Knead the dough again with your hand and then pile it into a greased 1 lb (450 g) loaf tin. Cover it with the cloth and put it above the oven to prove for 10 minutes or until the dough has risen about ½ in

(1 cm) above the top of the tin. Bake it for 40 minutes and turn it out onto a wire rack to cool.

As well as flavouring bread, vegetables can make up the actual substance of the dough. Mashed potato makes a superb bread. It doesn't flavour it strongly but definitely adds to the final effect. The texture is light and airy and the loaf has a thin but very crisp crust that develops as it cools. The herbs in this recipe make it a savoury loaf, but leave them out and it is an all-purpose bread just as delicious with something sweet like honey as it is with cheese.

Potato bread

1 medium-sized potato weighing 4–6 oz (125–175 g)
8 oz (225 g) wholemeal flour
½ teaspoon (2.5 ml) fine sea salt
1½ oz (40 g) butter *or* vegetable margarine
1 tablespoon (15 ml) chopped parsley
1 tablespoon (15 ml) chopped savory
½ oz (15 g) fresh or dried yeast
1 teaspoon (5 ml) honey
1 tablespoon (15 ml) skimmed milk powder
¼ pint (150 ml) lukewarm water
1 egg, beaten

Boil the potato in its skin and peel it while it is still warm. Mash it and rub it through a sieve. Put the flour and salt into a bowl and rub in the butter. Toss in the chopped herbs with your fingers and rub in the potato. Cream the yeast with the honey. Mix the skimmed milk powder and warm water together and add them to the yeast. Set them aside in a warm place to froth. This will only take about 5 minutes. Make a well in the centre of the flour and potato and pour in the yeast mixture and the egg. Mix everything to a stiff dough and knead it with your hand in the bowl, taking the mixture from the sides to the middle and turning the bowl all the time with the other hand. Do this for about 5 minutes. Cover the dough with a clean teacloth and set it in a warm place for 1 hour to rise.

Preheat the oven to Reg 7/425°F/220°C. Once the dough has risen it will be more manageable so turn it out onto a floured board this time to knead it. Knock it down into a greased 1 lb (450 g) loaf tin, cover it with a cloth and put it above the stove to prove for 20 minutes, or until it has risen about ½ in (1 cm) above the top of the tin. Bake the loaf for 30 minutes. Turn it out onto a wire rack and cool it completely before cutting. N.B. When it comes out of the oven it won't be as crusty as other breads and the 'tapping the bottom' test isn't valid. It will sound hollow but feel rather soft.

This pumpkin bread is a meal in itself. Serve it hot, straight from the oven, with a salad or cheese or a golden pumpkin soup. It is golden brown with a crisp, thin crust and you can taste wheat, herbs and pumpkin all together. It is best baked in a round cake tin.

Pumpkin and herb bread

8 oz (225 g) chopped pumpkin
1 tablespoon (15 ml) water
1 oz (25 g) butter
¾ oz (20 g) fresh yeast *or* ½ oz (15 g) dried
1 teaspoon (5 ml) honey
1 egg, beaten
6 oz (175 g) wholemeal flour
2 oz (50 g) bran (or you can use all flour)
2 teaspoons (10 ml) fine sea salt
2 tablespoons (30 ml) chopped mixed herbs

Put the pumpkin into a saucepan with the water. Cover it and set it on a low heat for 20 minutes, beating occasionally with a wooden spoon to make a thick purée. Take the pan from the heat and beat in the butter. While the pumpkin is cooking, cream the yeast with the honey and mix in the egg, and set them in a warm place to froth. Put the flour, bran, salt and herbs into a mixing bowl and make a well in the centre. Pour in the yeast mixture and the pumpkin purée and mix everything together well. The dough will be fairly wet, so knead it with your hand in the bowl, taking the sides to the middle and turning the bowl all the while with the other hand. Cover the dough with a clean teacloth and put it in a warm place for 1 hour to rise.

Preheat the oven to Reg 6/400°F/200°C and grease a cake tin 6 in (15 cm) in diameter. Knead the dough in the bowl again, put it into the prepared tin and smooth over the top. Cover it with the cloth again and set it above the stove to prove for 15 minutes or until the dough has risen to about ½ in (1 cm) above the top of the tin. Bake the loaf for 45 minutes. Turn it out of the tin, cut it in half crossways and thickly butter the top and bottom. Press the two halves together again and serve it hot.

Here is another light, flavoured bread that looks most attractive baked in a round tin. It has a really pungent, tomato-y smell when it comes out of the oven and is browny-orange in colour with a thin, crispy crust. It tastes strongly of thyme and tomatoes with just a hint of onion.

Tomato and onion bread

8 oz (225 g) wholemeal flour
1 teaspoon (5 ml) fine sea salt
1 tablespoon (15 ml) chopped thyme
1 very small onion
1 oz (25 g) butter
½ oz (15 g) fresh or dried yeast
1 teaspoon (5 ml) honey
1 tablespoon (15 ml) skimmed milk powder
3 fl oz (90 ml) warm water
1 egg, beaten
3 tablespoons (45 ml) tomato purée

Put the flour, salt and thyme into a bowl and rub in the butter. Grate in the onion. Cream the yeast with the honey. Mix the skimmed milk powder and water together and mix them into the yeast. Put them in a warm place to froth. Make a well in the centre of the flour and pour in the yeast mixture, the egg and the tomato purée. Mix everything to a dough with a long, rounded knife. Turn it out onto a floured board and knead it. Return it to the bowl and make a cross-cut in the top. Cover with a teacloth and leave it in a warm place for 1 hour to rise.

Preheat the oven to Reg 6/400°F/200°C and grease a high-sided cake tin 6 in (15 cm) in diameter. Knead the dough again and knock it down into the prepared tin. Cover it with the cloth and put it above the stove to prove for 20 minutes or until it has risen about ½ in (1 cm) above the top of the tin. Bake the loaf for 30 minutes. Serve it hot or let it cool completely on a wire rack.

Serving suggestions:

For a meal in itself, cut the loaf horizontally into three while it is still hot. Butter each cut surface and press the pieces together again with sliced tomatoes in between. Return it to the oven on a heatproof plate for 2 minutes to heat through.

Serve the loaf cold with a tomato salad containing lots of chopped basil.

Mix some basil into saltless butter, cut the cold loaf into three, spread it thickly and sandwich it together again.

Let it cool completely, cut it into three, spread it thickly with cream, curd or cottage cheese and take it on a picnic.

❧   ❧   ❧

Whenever I haven't time to wait for yeasted bread to rise, I make a scone-type bread which can easily be prepared and baked in 45 minutes, or even less if the recipe is a simple one. You can use all flour (the same types as for the ordinary bread) or a mixture of flour and bran to give a crumbly almost crisp texture.

Sour milk is an important ingredient in scones and soda breads and you will probably find it useful to always keep a bottle handy in the refrigerator. If you haven't any, use fresh milk with ½ teaspoon (2.5 ml) cream of tartar dissolved in every ¼ pint (150 ml).

Here is the basic recipe using bran. If you would rather have all flour use 8 oz (225 g) and keep all the other ingredients the same.

Basic scone mixture

6 oz (175 g) wholemeal flour

2 oz (50 g) bran
½ teaspoon (2.5 ml) fine sea salt
½ teaspoon (2.5 ml) bicarbonate of soda
1 oz (25 g) butter *or* lard
¼ pint (150 ml) sour milk *or* fresh milk with ½ teaspoon (2.5 ml)
   cream of tartar

Preheat the oven to Reg 6/400°F/200°C. Put the flour, bran,
salt and soda into a mixing bowl and rub in the fat. Make a well
in the centre and pour in the sour milk. Mix everything to a
dough, turn it out and knead it on a floured board. (There is no
need to rise or prove this mixture.)
Either:
shape it into a high round, make a cross-cut in the top and set
   it on a floured baking sheet;
or press it into a lightly-greased 8 in (20 cm) skillet or cake tin
   and score the top into 12 triangles;
or roll it out so it is about ¾ in (2 cm) thick and cut it into round
   or triangular scones.
Bake the large scones for 30 minutes and the small ones for 20.
Eat them hot or cold.

As with the basic bread recipe, you can flavour the scones with
herbs, spices, cheese or grated or browned onions. You can also
use natural yoghurt or buttermilk instead of sour milk.

   Here, as an example, is a recipe for scones made with a granary
bread meal and flavoured with browned onion. They rise high
and light as they bake, and the onions give them a golden colour
and a slightly sweet flavour that contrasts with the nutty pieces of
malted wheat. Have them hot or cold – they are just as good
either way.

Granary and onion scones

1 large onion
1½ oz (40 g) butter
8 oz (225 g) granary bread meal
1 teaspoon (5 ml) fine sea salt
½ teaspoon (2.5 ml) bicarbonate of soda
1 tablespoon (15 ml) chopped thyme

¼ pint (150 ml) sour milk *or* fresh milk and ½ teaspoon (2.5 ml)
cream of tartar

Preheat the oven to Reg 6/400°F/200°C. Thinly slice the onion
and brown it slowly in ½ oz (15 g) of the butter. Put the granary
meal, salt, bicarbonate of soda and thyme into a mixing bowl
and rub in the remaining butter. Mix in the browned onion.
Make a well in the centre and pour in the sour milk. Mix everything to a dough. Turn it out onto a floured board and knead it
lightly. Divide the dough into 8 pieces and shape them into
rounds ¾ in (2 cm) thick. Lay them on a floured baking sheet
and bake them for 25 minutes.

For a change, roll out scone dough about ¼ in (0.75 cm) thick,
spread it with tomato purée, chopped herbs, peanut butter or
tahini, roll it up and bake it for 30 minutes.

The following three scones are excellent hot or cold, so you
can serve them with salads or take them on picnics. The filling
softens and moistens the dough in the middle while the outside
crisps nicely.

Mushroom scone roll

4 oz (25 g) mushrooms
1½ oz (40 g) butter
1 small onion, finely chopped
6 oz (175 g) wholemeal flour
2 oz (50 g) bran
½ teaspoon (2.5 ml) fine sea salt
½ teaspoon (2.5 ml) bicarbonate of soda
1 tablespoon (15 ml) chopped thyme
¼ pint (150 ml) sour milk *or* fresh milk with ½ teaspoon (2.5 ml)
cream of tartar

Preheat the oven to Reg 6/400°F/200°C. Finely chop the mushrooms. Melt ½ oz (15 g) of the butter in a small frying pan on
a low heat. Put in the onion and cook it until it is soft. Raise the
heat to moderate, mix in the mushrooms and cook them for
1 minute. Take the pan from the heat and let the contents cool.

Make up the scone mixture according to the basic recipe, tossing in the thyme before adding the sour milk. Knead the dough and roll it out into a rectangle ¼ in (0.75 cm) thick. Spread the mushrooms and onions over the surface, leaving a small gap all the way round. Roll the dough up and lay it on a floured baking sheet. Bake it for 35 minutes.

Watercress roll

6 oz (175 g) wholemeal flour
2 oz (50 g) bran
½ teaspoon (2.5 ml) fine sea salt
½ teaspoon (2.5 ml) bicarbonate of soda
1 oz (25 g) butter *or* lard
1 carton natural yoghurt
1 tablespoon (15 ml) Worcester sauce
½ bunch watercress, finely chopped

Preheat the oven to Reg 6/400°F/200°C. Mix the Worcester sauce into the yoghurt and make up the scone mixture in the usual way, using this liquid instead of milk. Knead the dough and roll it out to a rectangle ¼ in (0.75 cm) thick. Scatter the watercress over the top and roll it up. Lay it on a floured baking sheet and bake it for 30 minutes.

Mustard and cress roll

6 oz (175 g) wholemeal flour
2 oz (50 g) bran
2 teaspoons (10 ml) mustard powder
½ teaspoon (2.5 ml) fine sea salt
½ teaspoon (2.5 ml) bicarbonate of soda
1½ oz (40 g) butter *or* lard
¼ pint (150 ml) sour milk *or* fresh milk with ½ teaspoon (2.5 ml) cream of tartar
1 teaspoon (5 ml) made English mustard
1 small onion, finely chopped
1 teaspoon (5 ml) mustard seed
1 box mustard and cress

Preheat the oven to Reg 6/400°F/200°C. Make up the scone

dough according to the basic recipe, mixing the mustard powder into the flour and rubbing in 1 oz (25 g) of the butter. Roll it out to a rectangle ¼ in (0.75 cm) thick and spread it with the made mustard. Soften the onion with the mustard seed in the remaining butter and arrange them evenly over the dough. Scatter over the mustard and cress. Roll up the dough and set it on a floured baking sheet. Bake it for 30 minutes.

The mustard doesn't make this scone roll hot, just very savoury, and when it is cold the mustard and cress makes it taste rather like a Chinese crispy pancake roll!

By doubling all the basic ingredients you can make these filled scones into a main meal. With a substantial vegetable filling you need nothing else apart from a salad. Serve this one hot.

Kale and dill scone

8 oz (225 g) curly kale
1 medium onion, thinly sliced
12 oz (350 g) wholemeal flour
4 oz (100 g) bran
1 teaspoon (5 ml) fine sea salt
1 teaspoon (5 ml) bicarbonate of soda
2 teaspoons (10 ml) dill seeds
2 oz (50 g) butter *or* lard
½ pint (275 ml) sour milk *or* fresh milk with 1 teaspoon (5 ml) cream of tartar
2 tablespoons (30 ml) tomato purée

Preheat the oven to Reg 6/400°F/200°C. Remove the stalks from the kale and tear the leaves into pieces about 1 in (3 cm) square. Put it into a saucepan with the onion and about 1 in (3 cm) water. Set it on a moderate heat and cook it for 15 minutes, stirring occasionally. Drain it well and press out as much moisture as possible. Make up the scone mixture according to the basic recipe, adding the dill seeds with the salt and soda. Divide it into two and roll each one into an oblong about ¼ in (0.75 cm) thick. Spread each one with 1 tablespoon (15 ml) tomato purée. Divide the kale between them and arrange it evenly on top leaving a gap of about 1 in (3 cm) all round. Roll them up and lay them on a large, flat floured baking sheet. Bake them for 40 minutes, and serve half a one, hot, to each person with a salad.

Cooked mashed potato with plenty of butter or margarine and no milk makes a different kind of scone. These can be eaten hot or cold at any time, and the next day you can split and toast them and serve them like muffins. If you use a griddle, they will be softer-textured.

Potato scones

12 oz (350 g) potatoes (raw)
3 oz (75 g) butter *or* vegetable margarine
freshly ground black pepper
¼ teaspoon (half a 2.5 ml spoon) fine sea salt
6 oz (175 g) wholemeal self-raising flour
2 tablespoons (30 ml) chopped chives, Welsh onions *or* spring onions
1 tablespoon (15 ml) chopped parsley

Either preheat the oven to Reg 6/400°F/200°C and flour a baking tray, *or* lightly grease a griddle. Boil the potatoes in their skins until they are tender. Drain them and peel them while they are still warm. Rub them through a sieve into a mixing bowl. Beat in the butter, seasonings, chopped chives or onions and parsley. Gradually work in the flour and knead the dough in the bowl until it is smooth. Turn it onto a floured board and roll it out to about ½ in (1.5 cm) thick. Stamp it out into rounds with a small pastry cutter or cut it into shapes. There should be about 15. Leave the scones in a warm place for 10 minutes. Either bake them for 20 minutes or cook them on a griddle on a low heat for 10 minutes on each side.

If you don't use milk, you can make good quick scones with self-raising flour. They have a light crumbly texture, delicious on the first day, but they don't keep very well. Here is the basic recipe.

Self-raising scones without milk

8 oz (225 g) wholemeal self-raising flour
¼ teaspoon (half a 2.5 ml spoon) fine sea salt
2 oz (50 g) vegetable margarine
8 tablespoons (120 ml) cold water to mix

Preheat the oven to Reg 6/400°F/200°C. Put the flour and salt into a bowl and rub in the margarine. Mix everything to a smooth dough with the water. Turn it out onto a floured board and knead it lightly. Divide the dough into 8 pieces and make them into rounds or rectangles. Lay them on a floured baking sheet and flatten them to about ¾ in (2 cm) thick. Bake them for 30 minutes.

You can add chopped herbs or spices to any scone mixture. For just a hint of rosemary flavour, melt the fat with the rosemary in a covered saucepan and leave it on the lowest heat possible for 5 minutes. Then strain the fat into the flour. Onion scones can be made by grating in a little raw onion or by softening a small, sliced onion in an extra ½ oz (15 g) margarine and adding them to the flour.

These two savoury cakes made only with a little fat and mixed with water are easy to make and are excellent accompaniments to salads, pottage-type soups or cheese. They are moist and tasty and if you serve them hot have a slightly crispy edge. When cold, they are ideal for packed lunches and picnics. I have found that the best fat for them is lard, but you can easily use butter or a vegetable margarine.

The paprika in this onion cake is just evident in the flavour and it helps to give a lovely golden brown colour.

Onion cake

6 oz (175 g) wholemeal flour
2 oz (50 g) bran
¼ teaspoon (2.5 ml) fine sea salt
1 tablespoon (15 ml) paprika

1 teaspoon (5 ml) dill seed
2 oz (50 g) butter *or* vegetable margarine
1 large onion, thinly sliced
¼ pint (150 ml) water

Grease a skillet or cake tin 7–8 in (17–20 cm) in diameter. Preheat the oven to Reg 6/400°F/200°C. Put the flour, bran, salt, paprika and dill into a bowl and rub in 1½ oz (40 g) of the fat. Melt the rest of the fat in a frying pan on a low heat, put in the onion and cook it until it is golden. Mix it into the flour. Make a well in the centre and pour in the water. Mix everything to a stiff dough and press it into the prepared tin. Bake for 45 minutes.

This one with leeks has the same moist texture and the mustard gives a savoury flavour without making the cake hot.

Licky cake

4 oz (125 g) wholemeal flour
2 oz (50 g) coarse oatmeal
2 oz (50 g) bran
½ teaspoon (2.5 ml) fine sea salt
2 teaspoons (10 ml) mustard powder
2 tablespoons (30 ml) chopped parsley
2 oz (50 g) butter *or* vegetable margarine
8 oz (225 g) leeks
1 oz (25 g) grated farmhouse Cheddar cheese (optional)
¼ pint (150 ml) water

Grease a skillet or cake tin 7–8 in (17–20 cm) in diameter. Preheat the oven to Reg 6/400°F/200°C. Put the flour, oatmeal, bran, salt, mustard powder and parsley into a bowl and rub in 1½ oz (40 g) of the butter or margarine. Thinly slice the leeks and soften them in the remaining fat. Mix them into the flour and add the cheese if you are using it. Make a well in the centre, pour in the water and mix everything to a dough. Press it into the prepared skillet or cake tin and bake it for 45 minutes.

Puddings

Whole-food eating doesn't have to stop when the main course is cleared away – it can be carried right through to the end of the meal. Some people prefer cheese to finish with and some prefer something sweet.

If cheese is on the menu, have wholemeal biscuits or oatcakes to accompany it. You can buy them in whole-food shops or better still have a go at making your own. Serve a selection of three cheeses of varying textures and flavours so you can be sure everyone's taste is catered for. If celery is in season, stand some cleaned sticks in a jar of water for crunching with the cheese, or have a selection of fresh fruit arranged in a bowl.

When, however, cheese has been the basic ingredient of the main dish, you will not really want to serve it a second time, so I think that sweets are a more necessary part of a varied and healthy vegetarian diet than they are, perhaps, of one that includes meat and fish. Remember that 'sweet' does not have to mean sickly sweet or over-rich. It is just a term for the finishing touches to the meal.

Sweets can be complicated or absolutely plain, and the plainest of all, but no less delicious if it is presented right, is the fresh fruit bowl which can vary excitingly in contents with the seasons. In the autumn, fill it with apples and pears and sweet dessert plums. Round about November grapes, both green and white, are at their cheapest; and soon after come the Christmas satsumas and tangerines and the Spanish oranges. Citrus fruits and bananas can be bought throughout the year, but home grown fruits begin to get scarce at Easter. If you like fairly sharp apples you will find Bramleys get very mellow at that time and can sometimes last until June or July. At the beginning of summer there are apricots and peaches and fat, yellow dessert gooseberries; and in July you can have a large bowl brim-full of strawberries or raspberries, or large, juicy cherries joined together in ear-rings.

If you are serving a selection of the larger fruits, make sure everyone has a plate, a sharp knife and a paper napkin. I like my strawberries absolutely plain, but if you wish to add a sweeter touch have a large bowl of Barbados sugar on the table so people can put a small pile on their plate in which to dip each seperate strawberry. If raspberries are the chosen fruit, they are best served in small bowls as they are so tiny. Serve brown sugar and whipped fresh or sour cream separately.

Look in markets and specialist greengrocers for foreign exotica such as fresh figs and dates, and when you can't find them, serve the dried ones instead. Figs, dates, bananas and apricots are the best for eating without pre-soaking. They are delicious served alongside the fresh fruits so you get a good combination of concentrated sweetness and refreshing sharpness.

Nuts always go well with fruit. Put them on the table, still in their shells, with enough nut-crackers to go round (one between two should be enough) or serve a smaller bowl of shelled nuts, either mixed or of one kind.

Fruit salads take the idea of fresh fruit a little further. Chop up a selection of fruit about an hour before you wish to serve it. Cut peel and pith from oranges and grapefruits but just wipe apples and pears. All the goodness lies just under the skin and they look attractive, too, with a thin line of contrasting colour round the edge of each slice. Cut grapes in half and remove the pips. You can peel the green ones first if you like, but it's a bit fiddly. Stone cherries with a cherry-stoner and halve and stone plums and greengages. You need not peel peaches and apricots but if you would rather, pour boiling water over them, leave them for half a minute and the skin should slip off easily. Top and tail gooseberries, hull strawberries (raspberries should be already hulled) and string red and white currants. Fresh pineapples make a good winter addition. Hold the stalk while you trim the end, cut away the husk and slice the juicy centre. Cut out

the centre cores and cut the slices into chunks. Peel and slice
bananas and have them at any time of the year.

There is no need to make a sugar syrup with white sugar for
a fruit salad. Just put the prepared fruit into a large bowl and
sprinkle over some Barbados sugar or spoon in some clear honey.
Chill the fruit salad for an hour and serve it in individual bowls
with whipped fresh or sour cream or natural yoghurt spooned
over the top and some chopped nuts or sunflower or sesame
seeds scattered over that. For a special occasion, sprinkle the
fruit with brandy, kirsch or a little liqueur before you chill it.

You can also make fruit salads with a selection of dried fruits.
(Don't laugh at prunes – they can be delicious!) Place the fruit
in a bowl and completely cover it with water or something a
little more special such as cider or wine, and leave it to soak for
12 hours. For flavour add a cinnamon stick or some strips of
lemon or orange peel to the liquid. When the fruit has soaked,
taste it for sweetness. You may find you won't need to add anything, but if you find it slightly sharp add brown sugar or honey
to your taste. Dried fruits are best served with something fresh
and tangy such as sour cream or yoghurt.

Fresh or dried fruit can be poached or baked or made into
compôtes and served hot or cold. Sweeten it with honey and
flavour it with cloves or cinnamon sticks and sprinkle it with
blanched and flaked almonds, pine nuts or sunflower or sesame
seeds just before serving.

Don't forget baked apples. I learned to love these when I was
at college. There was a large apple tree in the garden where I
rented a room and, being a typical broke student, I practically
lived on them one autumn term. I stuffed them with a mixture of
butter and brown sugar so they ended up swimming in a sticky
sauce. You can fill the middles with raisins and currants, chopped
dates, or a home-made mince-meat or chunky marmalade. Stick
the outside with cloves and sprinkle sesame seeds or browned
crumbs over the top before putting them in the oven. For a
savoury-sweet change, try filling them with a mixture of breadcrumbs and grated farmhouse Cheddar cheese, or pack them
completely with a soft, ripe Stilton.

Fruit can provide the basis for all kinds of other sweet dishes as well as being served plain. For example, you can rub soft fruits (strawberries, raspberries, blackberries, peaches and apricots) through a sieve to make a simple uncooked purée. You can get the same result with the harder and sharper fruits by simmering them first with a very small amount of water and then rubbing them through a sieve. Sweeten your purées with honey if necessary. You can make them into sauces for other fruits (try a purée of strawberries over a ripe honeydew melon, or rhubarb, sweetened with honey poured over slices of pineapple), and also for plain custards and junkets, milk puddings and sponge puddings. Fruit purées can be made into a mousse with eggs and whipped cream, into snows with whipped egg whites and fools with custards and cream.

If cakes and biscuits or steamed or baked puddings are your idea of a 'pud' use wholemeal flour and sweeten them with honey, Barbados sugar or dried fruits. You will find they taste far better than any made with white flour, they are healthier and also fill you up quicker so you don't consume too many calories. As with pastry, forget the idea that they will be heavy.

Talking of pastry, fruit can be put into pies and crumbles. Sweeten the fruit with honey and use the ordinary shortcrust or the flaky pastry given in the savoury pies chapter. For crumble toppings use a mixture of wholemeal flour, Barbados sugar and butter or vegetable margarine in the same quantities as you would white flour and sugar. These crumbles will not be as light as the white ones, but slightly chewy and far more delicious.

Milk, eggs, cream and yoghurt can also be made into healthy sweets. Forget the custard powder and make your own creamy yellow mixture with milk and egg yolks; or make little baked custards with eggs and cream. Buy some rennet and make a junket, flavoured only with a little grated nutmeg sprinkled on top. Mix natural yoghurt with fresh, dried or stewed fruits, flaked or chopped nuts, or just honey.

In medieval times, sugar was an expensive luxury and cooks cunningly learned to use parsnips and carrots in sweet dishes. Cooked in certain ways, these vegetables provide a really sweet, but not rich or cloying, flavour that cuts down considerably on the amount of sugar that you need.

I always put grated raw carrot into my Christmas pudding and never add any sugar. The combination of carrot and rich dried fruits and candied peel provide all the sweetness needed. This pudding is slightly lighter and can be eaten at any time of the year. Brandy butter, though, is still its best accompaniment. Serve it hot.

Boiled carrot pudding

2 oz (50 g) wholemeal breadcrumbs
2 oz (50 g) wholemeal flour
2 oz (50 g) grated raw carrot
½ teaspoon (2.5 ml) ground cinnamon
freshly grated nutmeg (about one eighth of a nut)
grated rind and juice ½ orange
4 tablespoons (60 ml) sherry or vintage cider
1 egg, separated
2 oz (50 g) raisins
2 oz (50 g) sultanas
little butter for greasing small pudding basin
brandy butter:
4 oz (125 g) saltless butter
2 oz (50 g) Barbados sugar
3 tablespoons (45 ml) brandy

Put the breadcrumbs, flour, carrot, cinnamon, nutmeg and orange rind into a mixing bowl. Mix them together and make a well in the centre. Beat the orange juice, sherry and egg yolk together and pour them into the well. Mix them in well and stir in the raisins and sultanas. Stiffly beat the egg white and fold it into the mixture with a metal spoon. Quickly transfer everything to a small, buttered pudding basin. Cover it with a layer of buttered greaseproof paper and then with foil and tie them securely. Bring a saucepan of water to the boil. Lower in the pudding and steam it for 2½ hours making sure the water is topped up all the time. To make the brandy butter, beat the butter until it is fluffy and gradually beat in the sugar. Add the brandy by the teaspoon, beating well. Pile it into a small dish and chill it before serving with the hot pudding.

This baked pudding is rich and buttery and again best served hot. Don't throw away any left-overs, though as you can easily eat it cold!

Baked carrot pudding

8 oz (225 g) carrots
4 oz (125 g) butter
4 eggs, beaten
3 tablespoons (45 ml) brandy (or orange juice)
freshly grated nutmeg
2 oz (50 g) chopped candied peel
2 tablespoons (30 ml) honey
little butter for greasing deep 7 in (18 cm) diameter cake tin

Preheat the oven to Reg 4/350°F/180°C. Scrub the carrots. Bring a saucepan of unsalted water to the boil, put in the carrots and simmer them for 30 minutes. Drain them and rub off their thin outer skins. Grate the outer red parts only so you have about 4–5 oz (125 g). Melt the butter in a saucepan on a low heat without letting it bubble or brown. Stir in the carrots and immediately take them off the heat. Beat the eggs and brandy or orange juice together and stir them into the carrots. Mix in the nutmeg and peel. Spread the honey evenly in the base of the prepared cake tin and pour the egg and carrot mixture on top. Bake the pudding for 30 minutes and turn it out onto a warm flat plate to serve.

This parsnip pudding needs no sweet ingredient in the main mixture. The honey provides just enough sweet sauce to run down the sides as you turn it out.

Parsnip pudding

2 lb (900 g) parsnips

½ teaspoon (2.5 ml) ground ginger
½ teaspoon (2.5 ml) ground cinnamon
freshly grated nutmeg
1 egg, beaten
2 oz (50 g) sultanas
2 tablespoons (30 ml) clear honey
little butter for greasing small pudding basin
unwhipped double or single cream for serving

Scrub the parsnips, cut them in half lengthways and remove the woody cores. Simmer them in unsalted water for 20 minutes. Drain them and rub them through a sieve or the fine blade of a mouli. Put them into a bowl and mix in the spices, beaten egg and sultanas. Put the honey into the bottom of a lightly greased small pudding basin. Spoon in the pudding mixture. Cover it with a sheet of buttered greaseproof paper and a piece of foil and tie it down. Lower the pudding into a saucepan of boiling water and steam it for 1½ hours, topping up the pan when necessary. To serve, turn the pudding out onto a warm, flat plate so the honey runs down the sides. Hand the cream separately.

Sweetened parsnip purées can be made into tarts. In this one, the stem ginger provides a little sweetness as well as flavour, so you don't need too much honey.

Parsnip and ginger tart

shortcrust pastry made with 4 oz (125 g) wholemeal flour to line
 a 7 in (18 cm) diameter pie plate or flan ring
for the filling:
1 lb (450 g) parsnips
3 pieces preserved stem ginger
¼ teaspoon (½ a 2.5 ml spoon) ground cinnamon
1 egg, beaten
2 tablespoons (30 ml) clear honey
freshly grated nutmeg

Preheat the oven to Reg 6/400°F/200°C. Make the pastry and set it aside to chill. Scrub the parsnips, cut them in half length-ways and remove the woody cores. Simmer them in unsalted water for 20 minutes. Drain them and rub them through a sieve or the fine blade of a mouli. Put them into a bowl. Finely chop the ginger and mix it into the parsnips with the cinnamon and nutmeg. Beat in the egg and honey. Roll out the pastry and line the flan ring or pie plate. Fill it with the parsnip mixture. Bake the pie for 30 minutes. Serve it hot, again with unwhipped cream.

Use parsnips to make a lemon meringue instead of the usual cornflour mixture. No one will ever know!

Parsnip and lemon meringue

for pastry to line an 8 in (20 cm) diameter pie plate or flan ring:
6 oz (175 g) wholemeal flour
3 oz (100 g) butter
pinch fine sea salt
water to mix
for filling:
1 lb (450 g) parsnips
grated rind 1½ lemons
juice 2 lemons
2 tablespoons (30 ml) clear honey
little freshly grated nutmeg
2 eggs, separated

Make the pastry and set it aside to chill. Preheat the oven to Reg 6/400°F/200°C. Scrub the parsnips, cut them in half lengthways and remove the woody cores. Cook them in unsalted water for 20 minutes. Drain them and rub them through a sieve or the fine blade of a mouli. Put them into a bowl and rub in the grated rind of 1 lemon, the juice of 2, the honey, nutmeg and egg yolks. Roll out the pastry and line the flan ring or pie plate. Put in the parsnip mixture and smooth the top. Bake the flan for 30 minutes. Take it out and lower the heat of the oven to Reg ½/250°F/120°C. Stiffly beat the whites with the remaining lemon rind and pile them on top of the parsnips. Return the pie to the oven until the top is nicely browned (about 20 minutes). It's best served hot.

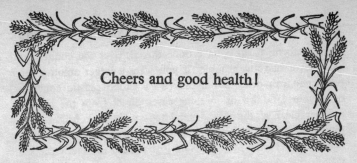

Cheers and good health!

Being a wholefood eater doesn't mean you have to give up alcohol, but if you do drink, make sure it is something good and unadulterated. It was this way of thinking that led me some time ago to join the Campaign for Real Ale. Compared to most of my fellow members I perhaps don't drink a lot, but I enjoy what I have and would hate to see it disappear.

Real ale, or traditional British beer, or whatever you wish to call it, is made with malted barley, hops and yeast. These are the basic, essential ingredients, but many brewers add sugar to some of their beers to increase the strength. Most of this is fermented out, however, so it does you little harm. There should be no substitute ingredients put into beer, such as maize or hop extract, and no chemical additives. When the fermentation period is over, real beer is racked into barrels called casks (once wood, but now mostly metal) and natural finings are added to make all the yeast particles sink to the bottom.

When the beer leaves the brewery it is a natural, working, living substance. In the pub it should stand for a few days to settle and then a soft peg (or spile) is knocked into a hole in the top of the barrel. This allows the beer to undergo a secondary fermentation and during this process carbon dioxide is given off through the spile. The beer is then ready to be served. The soft spile is replaced by a hard one which will prevent the beer deteriorating and the wholesome liquid is served straight from the barrel (by gravity) or through a hand-pump or an electric pump.

If you want to serve such a drink with your meal take a jar to your nearest real ale pub (most of the branches of CAMRA produce local guides to tell you where to find them) and ask the landlord to fill it up. I have done this all over the country and have never had any trouble. If you want a larger amount for a party you can order a polypin (a 4½ gallon plastic container) from your landlord or in some cases direct from the brewery.

Steer clear of the shiny metal taps with their bright plastic tops and shining lights. Out of these pours top pressure or keg beer. Beer served on top pressure is produced in exactly the same way as that served by gravity or through a hand-pump, but once in the pub cellar it is attached to a cylinder of carbon dioxide which is forced into it to enable it to get up to the bar at the touch of a switch. The beer cannot work naturally and the very substance that it should be giving off is forced back into it!

Keg beer is even worse. It is filtered in the brewery and then chilled and pasteurised to kill off any yeast particles that may remain. It is then forced into a cylindrical barrel called a keg under pressure of the dreaded gas. It is a dead, fizzy, tinny-tasting substance in something similar to a large aerosol can. Not the British beer that for centuries has been drunk with the traditional farmer's lunch of good bread and farmhouse cheese.

Our other traditional drink, not so popular now as it once was, is cider, and the same rules apply to this as to beer. There are all kinds of fizzy, sweet, not very flavoursome substances sold in bottles and also through keg dispensers in some pubs (where it is wrongly termed 'draught'). This, like keg beers, has been filtered, pasteurised and carbonated. Amongst cider drinkers, I count myself rather lucky, for I go down to a farm where they do nothing but make cider. The apples are pulped and then pressed between hessian mats as they have been in this country for centuries. The juice runs down into a tank and is put into 56-gallon wooden barrels. It stands out in the orchards for six months and ferments naturally. No sugar is added, and by the time I come along with my 5-gallon barrel to be refilled it is a still, dry, refreshing and definitely alcoholic cider which goes superbly well with all wholefood meals, whether vegetarian or not.

You can buy farm ciders in all apple growing counties and many of these are naturally produced. Aspall cider is one available from many health food shops. Again it is still and dry and what's more made only from organically grown apples. Bulmers are one of the few larger firms to produce a very dry uncarbonated cider. Their Number Seven is sold in half-pint bottles.

Several articles have appeared recently about additives in wine, and even without the additives, some of the cheaper ones are not very palatable and good only for cooking. Buy a really good bottle for special occasions and if it is a white wine you are looking for try one of those made in this country. You will be surprised at how good they can be.

For everyday, how about having a go at making your own wine? Don't buy the kits. Go out and pick dandelion heads, broom flowers, crab apples, blackberries or elderberries. Wait for the second frost, wrap up warm and go gathering rose hips, hawthorn berries or rowan berries. Find someone with a quince tree or pick your own apples and pears so you can get them at a reasonable price. Take advantage of seasonal things in shops such as parsnips and Seville oranges. If you want to give your wine extra strength and body, add some raisins or dates instead of the grape concentrates that come in tins. Experiment with different types of yeast – Bordeaux makes blackberries into a rich red wine and a sherry yeast will make rose-hips into a medium sherry. You will be able to make red wines and white wines, sweet, medium and dry, to go with every course of every meal and before and after as well.

What is available if you don't wish to drink alcohol? Natural fruit juices are best of all. Look at the labels carefully when you buy them and make sure they actually say 'natural'. This means they have no sugar in them and no other additives. There are several brands of 'Vitamin C Enriched Specials' on the market, but look at what else they are enriched with! There are various chemicals in all of them so it's best to leave them alone. Steer clear, also, of the special breakfast drinks that come in powder form. Most supermarkets sell very reasonably priced natural orange and grapefruit juices and in many areas now they are even brought round by the milkman, so you should have no trouble in getting supplies.

Apple juice is a lovely refreshing drink and it can be bought in many health or wholefood shops and is sometimes made in the same places as the natural cider. Buy it still and not carbonated and serve it all through the meal.

Natural grape juice is sweeter and richer than the other juices, but it is excellent chilled and served as an aperitif.

Don't forget 'Adam's Ale' and mineral and spring waters for special occasions.

It is no effort to eat whole food and drink whole drink. You will find after a while you will automatically turn away from foam-rubber sliced white bread and packets full of chemical, not because you feel you ought to but because you genuinely have no taste for them any more and wholefood has made the complete process of preparing, cooking and eating into an absolute pleasure that everyone can share.

You don't have to be a vegetarian to think in this way. As I said at the beginning, I have always eaten meat and fish and shall continue to do so; but I am truly dedicated to the whole-food idea and live, eat and drink as naturally as I can. Everyone should – you feel so much better and enjoy life so much more.

So, whatever your chosen good food and drink – Cheers! – and most important of all – Good Health!

Measurements and temperatures

Whether we like it or not, metrication is slowly but surely creeping into our lives. We no longer measure our flour by the bushel or peck and our fields in rods, poles and perches, so I expect before long our pound weights and pint measures will be laid aside for kilo scales and litre jugs. Our fast-burning fires and kitchen ranges were translated into Fahrenheit and now Celsius isn't far behind.

To help a little, here is a chart of metric weights, measures and temperatures. The amounts in most cases are not the exact equivalents, but the nearest workable measures. Don't therefore use half-and-half when going through a recipe. Stick to either the metric or imperial amounts and you won't go far wrong. After all, you can't metricate an egg or the juice of a lemon, so the new weights and measures are not that different!

Pounds and ounces (lb and oz)	Kilos and grams (k and g)
1 oz	25g
2 oz	50g
3 oz	75g
4 oz	100 or 125g
5 oz	150g
6 oz	175g
7 oz	200g
8 oz	225g
9 oz	250g
10 oz	275g
11 oz	300g
12 oz	350g
13 oz	375g
14 oz	400g
15 oz	425g
1 lb	450g
2–2¼ lb	1k

Imperial spoon measures	Metric spoons measure
1 tablespoon	15ml
2 teaspoons	10ml
1 teaspoon	5ml
½ teaspoon	2.5ml
¼ teaspoon	½ a 2.5ml spoon

Fluid ounces (fl oz)	Millilitres and litres (ml and l)
1 fl oz	25ml
2 fl oz	50ml
3 fl oz	75ml
4 fl oz	125ml
5 fl oz (¼ pint)	150ml
6 fl oz	175ml
7 fl oz	200ml
8 fl oz	225ml
9 fl oz	250ml
10 fl oz (½ pint)	275ml
11 fl oz	300ml
12 fl oz	350ml
13 fl oz	375ml
14 fl oz	400ml
15 fl oz (¾ pint)	425ml
16 fl oz	450ml
17 fl oz	475ml
18 fl oz	500ml
19 fl oz	525ml
20 fl oz (1 pint)	575ml
35 fl oz (1¾ pints)	1litre

Gas regulo mark	Degrees Fahrenheit	Degrees Centigrade (Celsius)
¼	225	110
½	250	120
1	275	140
2	300	150
3	325	160
4	350	180
5	375	190
6	400	200
7	425	220
8	450	230
9	475–500	240–260

Index

NOTES

NOTES

Carol Bowen
The Vegetarian Microwave Cookbook £3.99

How to cook with a microwave – without meat

The microwave opens up a new range of vegetarian recipes for today's cook. It will save time and produce superb results – for eating that is healthy and different.

Wholegrains, vegetables, fruits, pasta, rice and other ingredients are all normally cooked in a fraction of the time they would otherwise take. The microwave takes the chore out of preparing dried pulses – staples of many delicious and nourishing vegetarian dishes – by eliminating the need to soak them before cooking.

Carol Bowen, an expert on microwave cookery, has wide experience in testing the basic ingredients which are suitable for cooking the microwave way. *The Vegetarian Microwave Cookbook* is full of advice, tips and recipes for every meal occasion. Packed full of new ideas, it makes an indispensable guide for getting the most out of vegetarian cooking.

Madhur Jaffrey
A Taste of India £7.99

A Taste of India is Madhur Jaffrey's most ambitious book so far. More than a culinary tour of the sub-continent, it is a rich and fascinating insight into its treasures, customs and people, with over 100 mouthwatering recipes to tempt cooks from the raw beginner to the expert.

From her home town of Delhi, north to the saffron-rich Kashmir and south to the vegetarian traditions of Tamil Nadu, Madhur vividly brings to life all the colour and diversity of India's culinary heritage, spicing clear and accessible cook's instructions with a wealth of history, legend, anecdote, and her own reminiscences.

'The sketches of her travels mix straightforward information . . . with personal evocation, and a full-blooded lyricism that borders on the incantatory. The recipes she gathers on her wanderings are thrilling to read – much more so to eat' HARPERS & QUEEN

'Gorgeous . . . *A Taste of India* adds important and fascinating information to our knowledge of Indian cuisine' NEW YORK TIMES

'Whether one is interested in just reading the book as a fascinating study of the foods of India or in actually trying out some of the recipes, *A Taste of India* can be considered among the finest books ever written on Indian cooking' INDIAN EXPRESS

Antonio Carluccio
An Invitation to Italian Cooking £8.95

An Invitation to Italian Cooking is a personal guide to the splendours of Antonio Carluccio's homeland's irresistible cuisine. In every recipe, he perfectly captures the wonderful smells, sights and tastes that are vital elements in the very best Italian food.

He lends his own imaginative touch to a huge variety of tantalizing dishes – each one clearly outlined with Carluccio's characteristic brand of wit and enthusiasm. With the emphasis on simple preparation of the freshest, finest ingredients, he guides us through succulent and authentic antipasti and pasta to sumptuous creations of his own like Fagotelli di Granchio (Crab Parcels) and an exquisite array of desserts.

'Antonio Carluccio's first book is the distillation of his great love of food and his enthusiasm for the dishes of north-west Italy' VOGUE

Theodora Fitzgibbon
A Taste of the West Country £3.95

'What a tasty dish! Dozens of them, and all with regional connections . . . Somerset braised lamb, clotted cream and syllabub, Dorset jugged steak, Devon pork pie and cider – the recipes for these and many more are presented, facing a period photograph, some more than 100 years old, of West Country places and people are described in accompanying texts. The blend makes it a recipe book that gives that little something extra . . .'
EXETER EXPRESS AND ECHO

Colin Spencer
Colin Spencer's Fish Cook Book £6.95

Since childhood, *Guardian* cookery writer Colin Spencer has been a devoted admirer of fish, the most versatile of foods. Now, in this complete and highly individual guide he has collected over 200 of his best-loved recipes, gleaned from his travels around the world. Starting with expert tips on how to choose and prepare your fish and which cooking methods are best suited, he goes on to describe more than 90 varieties, including all the traditional favourites plus some rare ones which you can ask your fishmonger to get. The book is illustrated by the author's own line drawings and Roger Phillips' superb colour photographs.

Katie Stewart
The Times Cookery Books £5.99

Carefully chosen from the recipes published in *The Times* over the last few years, and including many new ones, this collection of recipes by Katie Stewart is practical, varied and imaginative.

Selected to suit both everyday needs and special occasions, these recipes provide a rich source of new ideas for anyone who enjoys cooking.

Rita G. Springer
Caribbean Cookbook £4.99

Rita Springer, a leading expert on every aspect of Caribbean food, presents a whole spectrum of mouthwatering recipes, reflecting the influence of European, American and Chinese food as well as the traditional recipes of the islands.

Includes a chapter on Caribbean kitchen equipment, a helpful glossary, and details of how to obtain the more unusual ingredients from British suppliers.

'Exciting cooking' SUN

All Pan books are available at your local bookshop or newsagent, or can be ordered direct from the publisher. Indicate the number of copies required and fill in the form below.

Send to: **CS Department, Pan Books Ltd., P.O. Box 40, Basingstoke, Hants.   RG21 2YT.**

or phone: 0256 469551 (Ansaphone), quoting title, author and Credit Card number.

Please enclose a remittance* to the value of the cover price plus: 60p for the first book plus 30p per copy for each additional book ordered to a maximum charge of £2.40 to cover postage and packing.

*Payment may be made in sterling by UK personal cheque, postal order, sterling draft or international money order, made payable to Pan Books Ltd.

Alternatively by Barclaycard/Access:

Card No.

Signature:

Applicable only in the UK and Republic of Ireland.

While every effort is made to keep prices low, it is sometimes necessary to increase prices at short notice. Pan Books reserve the right to show on covers and charge new retail prices which may differ from those advertised in the text or elsewhere.

NAME AND ADDRESS IN BLOCK LETTERS PLEASE:

Name—

Address—

3/87